I Shouldn't
Be Telling
You This

Also by Kate White

I Shouldn't Be Telling You This

• • • • • • • • • • • • • • • • •

HOW TO ASK FOR THE MONEY, SNAG THE PROMOTION, AND CREATE THE CAREER YOU DESERVE

KATE WHITE

HARPER
BUSINESS

An Imprint of HarperCollins*Publishers*
www.harpercollins.com

HarperCollins books may be purchased for educational, business, or sales promotional use. For information, please write: Special Markets Department, Harper-Collins Publishers, 10 East 53rd Street, New York, NY 10022.

A hardcover edition of this book was published in 2012 by HarperBusiness, an imprint of HarperCollins Publishers.

FIRST HARPERBUISINESS PAPERBACK EDITION PUBLISHED 2013

Designed by Michael Correy

Library of Congress Cataloging-in-Publication Data has been applied for.

ISBN 978-0-06-212210-0

13 14 15 16 17   DIX/RRD   10 9 8 7 6 5 4 3 2 1

Additional Praise for

I Shouldn't Be Telling You This

"*I Shouldn't Be Telling You This* is packed with practical lessons Kate White has learned over a long tenure as a leader."

—*Fast Company*

"White's advice is smart and pithy—and maybe I shouldn't be telling you this, but guys can get plenty from this book, too."

—*Reader's Digest*

"Whether you are a just-hatched college grad or a sacred elder in need of an occupational overhaul, Kate White can help. The editor in chief of *Cosmo* for fourteen years, White combines the story of her own career path with interviews and research to impart sensible lessons about getting ahead in the world while still having a personal life." —*USA Today*

"Kate's fierce courage and determination make this book a witty, fun, and refreshingly blunt read for career women—teachers and CEOs alike!" —Mika Brzezinski, cohost of *Morning Joe* on MSNBC and author of *Knowing Your Value*

"This is *not* your mother's plodding, nose-to-the-grindstone, put-on-a-power-suit career guide. Kate White gives us her witty and wise secret sauce to fast-tracking your career, thinking big, having fun, and getting the money you deserve—all while pursuing your passion." —Claire Shipman, ABC News correspondent and coauthor of *Womenomics*

"White offers straight-shooting career advice to women at all stages of their professional lives. . . . Her advice is useful and delightfully no-nonsense. A smart, savvy guide for working women looking to climb the professional ladder and maintain positions of power."

—*Kirkus Reviews*

"Packs a powerful punch: Ms. White covers every possible topic that the up-and-coming female executive will need to tuck into her Prada portfolio." —*New York Journal of Books*

"It will come as no surprise that White, the editor in chief of *Cosmopolitan* magazine, would write a career guide that's lively, funny, and rife with quick-read tips." —*Publishers Weekly*

To my mom, Anne White,
who always encouraged me to go big
for the career I dreamed about

{ Contents }

{ Acknowledgments }

'm so very grateful to everyone at HarperCollins and Harper-Business who supported and guided me with *I Shouldn't Be Telling You This*. In particular I want to thank the awesome Kathy Schneider, who sensed my secret wish to write this book and then told me to go for it; Hollis Heimbouch and Colleen Lawrie for their incredibly valuable direction and editing; Rachel Elinsky for her unrelenting and imaginative efforts on the PR front; Robin Bilardello for kick-ass art direction; and Emily Walters for her generous patience with such a micromanager.

I also want to thank my absolutely terrific agent, Sandy Dijkstra, and her entire team, including Elise Capron, Elizabeth James, and Andrea Cavallaro.

Last, thanks to all the smart, gutsy, successful women who taught me so much along the way.

{ Introduction }

We haven't met (unless you're a friend of mine who was nice enough to buy this book!), but I know something about you. The very fact that you've started reading a book about the secrets of success says that you're clearly interested in and even committed to the idea of getting ahead in a career you love, supersizing that success, and then being able to relish the rewards that come along with it.

This book will offer you plenty of ways to do all that. It includes smart, gutsy advice from some of the incredible women I've met professionally over the years and also plenty of strategies from my own delicious career in the magazine business and as the author of a dozen books, both fiction and nonfiction. Why am I so eager to share my favorite secrets? Because I'm at a point in my career where it costs me nothing to do so—and I'm grateful for all the advice that's been offered to *me*. I hope you'll find the book not only useful but also very fresh and candid. From years spent writing cover lines for *Cosmopolitan*, I've learned to be pretty frank!

This isn't my first career book, by the way. In the late 1990s I wrote a best-selling book called *Why Good Girls Don't Get Ahead ... but Gutsy Girls Do* that many women have told me made a major impact on how they approached their work and their careers. I've always been intrigued by how people move ahead and achieve what they long for, and I love sharing what I've learned with younger women. This book is based on many of the things I've discovered since I wrote *Gutsy Girls*, particularly from being the editor in chief of *Cosmopolitan* magazine for fourteen years. From the moment I arrived at *Cosmo* I realized that overseeing such a big, iconic brand meant that I would have to simultaneously do the job and teach myself everything I could.

There's something fairly ironic about the fact that I ended up running *Cosmo*. When I was seventeen, my mother handed me a copy of *Sex and the Single Girl*, the classic 1962 best seller by Helen Gurley Brown, and encouraged me to read it. I felt briefly flustered by the idea that my mother was giving me a book of sex tips (at that age you're still not convinced your parents have ever *had* sex), but it was soon clear that she had another motive: she wanted me to use Helen Gurley Brown as a role model.

My fabulous mother knew, you see, that I yearned to be a writer and maybe a magazine editor one day, and I think she assumed that Helen's career could be a kind of blueprint for me. After writing her best seller, Helen, as many women know, went on to brilliantly reinvent *Cosmopolitan* magazine, starting in 1965. Of course, I don't think my mom ever expected that I'd take her advice quite so literally and one day become the editor in chief of *Cosmo* myself.

It would be nice if I could tell you that from reading the book I absorbed a bunch of helpful strategies, and then, following college, strode boldly into Manhattan and shot up the ladder of success. *Not*.

Though the book helped fuel my passion to head to New York City one day, it unfortunately offered no specific tips for breaking into the magazine business. When I left college, in fact, I felt pretty clueless. The Internet didn't exist yet, so it was tough to research a career field, and internships hadn't come into vogue either, so there was no easy way to scout out opportunities. I also had a lot of good-girl tendencies then, which meant I wasn't going to burst onto the scene, bidding for attention. Therefore, like a lot of other young women in the 1970s, I just kind of stumbled into Manhattan, hoping for the best.

Though my arrival wasn't very glamorous, it did grab a little attention. The night I left upstate New York for good, my brother Jim accompanied me to the train station, and much to my annoyance, asked an older man on the platform to watch out for me. The guy ended up sticking to me like a Velcro hair roller for the entire ride, even sitting in the seat next to me. I noticed after a while that people had begun to gawk at us, though I had no idea why. It wasn't until I made my way back from the restroom that I understood the reason. Coming down the aisle, I saw for the first time that the man had an emblem on the lapel of his blazer. It said GREEN HAVEN CORRECTIONAL FACILITY. Good God, I thought in horror. People clearly assume that I'm a convicted criminal being transported to a downstate prison.

Things thankfully improved a tiny bit from there. I had won *Glamour* magazine's Top 10 College Women contest and appeared on the cover during my senior year, and Ruth Whitney, the legendary editor in chief of *Glamour*, had promised to help me find a job at the magazine. But because I felt too timid and self-conscious to say I wanted to be a writer, I ended up accepting a job on the business side—in the merchandising department. It involved running the slide carousels for breakfast presentations and doing the dishes afterward. I was utterly miserable.

But at least I was smart enough to see I'd made a dumb move and needed to correct it. I started volunteering to write for a section of the magazine that featured short items on relationships, health, and self-improvement. Over time Ruth seemed to note my enthusiasm for writing. When Ringling Bros. and Barnum & Bailey Circus asked the magazine if it wanted to send someone to be a guest clown for a day and write an article about it, I was chosen. Oy. That idea held no appeal for me, but I decided that if donning a red rubber nose and performing in Madison Square Garden would help jumpstart my career, I would have to throw myself into it. After I handed in my story, Ruth summoned me into her office and told me that she not only really liked my piece and was paying me extra for it but she was also making me a writer in the articles department. That was one case where fortune favored not the bold but the buffoon!

From there I moved up fairly steadily—though I encountered my fair share of bumps in the road. After *Glamour* I became a senior editor, and later the executive editor, at the Sunday newspaper supplement *Family Weekly* (which eventually became *USA Weekend* magazine) and then the executive editor in charge of articles at *Mademoiselle*. After being promoted to the number two position at *Mademoiselle*, I went on to run four different magazines: *Child*, *Working Woman*, *McCall's*, and *Redbook*. On a Sunday afternoon during my fourth year at *Redbook*, my boss at the Hearst Corporation called me at my family's weekend home and asked me to come to her office, where she announced that she wanted me to take over *Cosmopolitan*, the most successful young woman's magazine in the world.

All my jobs have been great in their own ways, but *Cosmo* turned out to be the most thrilling and rewarding. Despite the occasional migraine-producing moment—such as getting a call from a record company executive saying Lady Gaga was having a minor meltdown and would have to cancel the cover shoot three days from then (see "18 People Principles: Because Now You Really, Really Need Them," for how I salvaged the situation without having to give away my firstborn son)—I could see from the start that it was going to be a fantastic job, full of variety, surprises, and rewards. A few years after my arrival, *Cosmo* became the number one–selling magazine on the newsstand in the United States—circulation on my watch grew by 700,000. Readers regularly write in to *Cosmo* to say how much the magazine empowers them and encourages them to go after everything they want in life: from loving, supportive relationships to great sex to fabulous careers. Eventually my job evolved to include overseeing the *Cosmo* website, *Cosmo* books and e-books, television projects, various brand extensions, and all the digital projects and apps. And hey, I shouldn't neglect to mention what turned out to be one of the most fun parts of the job: writing cover lines such as "Mattress Moves So Hot His Thighs Will Burst into Flames."

As a friend of mine once pointed out, an interesting phenomenon occurs when you take a backward glance at a more or less successful career: some of the wackier choices and decisions seem to make better sense in hindsight—as if your subconscious had always been guiding you to a certain destination. Even the whopping goofs—and I've made many—can seem part of a destined learning curve.

I'm not sure my subconscious brain had a master plan, but looking back at my entire career, particularly the *Cosmo* years, I do see in much sharper relief the strategies that helped me come out on top. And in this book, I'm going to share these strategies with you. They're organized into three separate sections:

Success: how to get it. The first years of a career can be especially tricky. You're excited and game—in fact, you may want success so much you can practically taste it—but first you have to convince someone to let you come on board. Once you get started, you quickly discover that your workplace isn't necessarily like a teaching hospital: no one feels obligated to show you the ropes. You have to figure so much out on your own, and you don't have any momentum going to help ease you along during dicey periods. You may not even be a hundred percent sure that you've picked the right field to try to excel in. In this section I'll explain how to determine what you really want to do, nail a job interview, navigate the early days of a job, dazzle your boss, develop a golden gut, ask for what you want, generate buzz about your achievements, and score your first major career breakthroughs.

By the way, this section isn't just for those who are in a first job. It's also good to read if you're switching jobs, getting back into your career after a mommy sabbatical, feeling stuck, or have woken up one morning and realized it's time to brilliantly reinvent yourself. And the tips on stuff like asking for what you want, trusting your gut, and generating buzz are beneficial for whatever stage you're at in your career.

Success: how to go big with it. Okay, now you're off and running in your career. There's a nice momentum that begins to happen at this stage. Success begets success to some degree, and certain doors open simply because of what you've already accomplished. But there are also plenty of challenges. Office politics become more complicated. You're expected to generate big ideas and make them work. And it can be tricky to balance your demanding workload with prepping for the future. It's at this stage that I see some women lose their way. They seem to either rest on their laurels or become unsure about what steps they need to be taking to reach the next level. In this section I'll explain how to supersize your success by generating wow ideas, being an inspiring boss, breaking the rules (yes, you need to!), and managing your career at the same time you're managing your job.

Success: how to savor it. Success isn't worth much if it doesn't bring you pleasure and make your life better. Helen Gurley Brown once said that she loved to go home at the end of a challenging workday and sniff the panties she'd been wearing. Um, sorry— that may not be an image you want to hold in your head for very long, but on one level I found it kind of inspiring. It means that she loved kicking off her stilettos at night and relishing the day she'd just spent at her demanding, yet fantastic job.

But it can be tough at times to enjoy success, especially if you're trying to juggle motherhood with work. In many businesses you're expected to be on call 24/7, responding to e-mails late into the evening and even on your days off. There's a crazy one-upmanship thing happening lately about how many hours people clock working. Recently I caught an episode of a TV reality show about interns working in a fashion-related field. During that particular episode, the female boss was using a very snooty tone to chew out an intern. She wanted to know why the girl hadn't come to her and asked a critical question. "You can't use the excuse that I'm not around," the boss said. "I'm the first one in every morning, and usually the one who turns off the lights at night." All I could think when I heard the comment was "What the hell fun is *that*?" I was tempted to call that woman and suggest she try leaving a little earlier some nights—and maybe even give her panties a nice sniff when she got home.

I've tried to savor my career, and I've never let myself be a slave to it. I have a solid marriage and two good kids, and in the past twelve years, I've also authored eight mysteries and thrillers. In this section you'll find strategies on how to find more minutes in the day, balance your family with your work, create more moments of pleasure just for yourself, survive insane days, fulfill a back-pocket dream, and even reinvent yourself if you so desire. But no more about panties, I swear!

I hope this book turns out to be a valuable resource for you. I hope it helps you not only gain the success you want but also enjoy the amazing perks that come along with it. I'd love to hear what you think about the book and which strategies have benefited you the most. Let me know, will you? Just e-mail me at Kate@katewhite.com.

Part I

{ Success: How to Get It }

When I think back on my career—the highs, the lows, the big wins, and the sometimes cringe-worthy blunders— I realize that some of the most challenging times were in the very early years when I had just started my career. It wasn't as if I was trying to save the euro or learn how to perform brain surgery, but I still felt very confused and uncertain. As an editorial assistant at *Glamour*, I was thrilled to have been given an entrée into the world of magazine journalism, yet I soon realized that getting my foot in the door was no guarantee that I'd be a success. I looked at the women above me in awe. They seemed to not only perform their jobs very well but also really relish them. I thought, "I want some of *that*," but I had no freaking clue how to get there.

If you're right out of school or starting a brand-new career, I'm sure you're able to relate. I think most women experience that new-girl-on-the-block anxiety. You're excited to be in the game and longing to make it, but you feel baffled at moments, not at all sure of how to pull off that first project, deal with your new boss effectively, or score your first big win. You'd be more than willing to accept guidance, but your boss and other senior people in your area may be too crazy busy to explain things in more than a cursory manner. At *Cosmo* I once had a disgruntled intern's mother write me and say that no one had ever shown her poor daughter where the ladies' room was. I laughed out loud when I read that. I wished the girl was still at *Cosmo* so I could have told her, "Sweetheart, we're not your mommy here." The bottom line is that when you start a new job, they may not even show you the way to the loo, let alone how to master your assignments or deal with the psycho chick who works in the cube at the end of the hall. You have to figure out all sorts of details like that on your own.

And it's not just basic stuff you need to concentrate on. At the same time that you're learning the lay of the land and how to handle your assigned responsibilities, you must begin plotting the moves that will make you stand out from the pack and charge ahead in your career. According to a recent Pew Research Center Report, two thirds of eighteen- to thirty-four-year-old women say being successful in a high-paying career is "one of the most important things" or "very important" in their lives (59 percent of guys feel the same way), which means you have a ton of competition. You'll never make your mark if you concentrate solely on the assignments you're given.

I hope I haven't made your heart start to pound in fear. Sure, new jobs are challenging, but they're exciting, too—they're where you first get a taste of success and can begin to run with it.

And though, as I said before, no one in your workplace may pull up a chair, plop down beside you, and explain the ropes, *I* intend to do that—right now. This section of the book is all about scoring your first successes. You'll find strategies for figuring out what your calling in life is, nailing a job interview, knocking your new boss's socks off, trusting your gut, handling coworkers successfully, asking for what you want, generating buzz, separating yourself from the pack, and finally, propelling yourself to the next big level of your career.

{ Rule #1: Go Big or Go Home }

once heard someone famous say that what separates successful people from the unsuccessful ones is their willingness to work really, really hard. Sure, hard work is part of the equation, and so are well-honed skills. And in certain cases, success is even somewhat about the people you know. But I think those factors get you only so far. From what I've seen again and again, success is most often the result of doing the bold *extra* something that no one else has thought of or dared to try.

I call it the go-big-or-go-home strategy. And before I even talk about the ins and outs of gaining your first career successes, I need to stress the importance of going big. It's a strategy you need to use now and during every other stage of your career.

You've heard the phrase "go big or go home," right? My first encounter with it was about five or six years ago. A young staffer used it when she was talking about her plans for Saturday night. What she meant was that if she wasn't willing to give the whole night an extra push—with her outfit, her hair, her makeup, her attitude—she should bag the entire thing.

I secretly co-opted that phrase for everything I did in the next years at *Cosmo*. The magazine is geared toward fun, fearless females, and from the moment I arrived I tried to factor that into my approach. But I liked having a specific mantra to work with. With every photo, article, and cover line I began to ask myself: did I go big or go home with it? If the answer was that I went home, I gave myself a swift kick in the butt and rethought what I was doing.

Soon I began using that mantra in other parts of my life. And as I thought about it, I realized that most of my successes—and the successes of women I knew—always involved *going big*. Doing a job well is not enough. The key is to do *more* than what's expected, power it up, go balls to the wall.

Going big doesn't always have to involve some huge undertaking. You can go big in key little ways, too. Here's a sampling of how I've used the strategy in my own career.

- When I was up for my first big job—as editor in chief of *Child* magazine—the headhunter mentioned that the magazine was looking for someone who was "mediagenic." So right before my first interview, I had my hair professionally blown out and styled. And I swear that my long, flowing, "mediagenic" locks helped me land the job.

- When I shot a cover of Pierce Brosnan, his partner, Keely Shaye Smith, and their newborn for *Redbook*, they asked the photographer to take a few pictures of the baby breast-feeding for them to keep personally. But when I saw *those* photos, I decided, with the couple's permission, to run one as the cover image. That photo literally became news around the world.

- When one of my top staffers at a magazine resigned to take another job, I didn't just graciously (or grumpily) accept her resignation. I wrote a memo called "Ten Reasons You Shouldn't Leave" and left it on her chair. She decided to turn down the offer and stay.

You'll see the "going big" theme running through everything I talk about in this section, as well as the rest of the book. You may be just beginning in a particular job or field, but in order to score your first major successes, you're going to have to go big—with your job search, the interviewing process, your early career moves, everything.

In this world of the supersized, going big is, in fact, probably more important now than ever. Everything seems to be bolder and even more badass. When *Cosmo* interviewed Pink after the birth of her daughter, she told us she was going to get back into the game full throttle. "I want my album to be really great, and I want to do an amazing tour. I'm going to up the ante, even if it means covering myself in Velcro, lighting myself on fire, and shooting myself out of a cannon. I'll do that, no prob."

I'm not suggesting you shoot yourself out of a cannon, but you need to push the envelope these days.

You have to be strategic, though, and assess your surroundings first. If you're in a new job, how much (from what you can tell) will your new work culture welcome the big idea, the bold new strategy? How much will your *boss* welcome it? What *kind* of big ideas is your boss likely to be receptive to? Good bosses will respond positively and love you for it.

A small warning: when you go big, whether it's early in your career or later, there will be people wishing you had gone home instead. Perhaps you're pulling off a feat someone else wishes *she'd* thought of or you're infringing on her turf—at least in her own mind. Or maybe one of your accomplishments has necessitated a change in someone else's daily work MO and that person now has to take care of business each morning rather than spending an hour nibbling on his blueberry muffin. You may end up with a few haters.

Regardless, you can't get caught up in worrying about whether everyone you work with likes you. Ultimately you want the respect of your coworkers, but you don't need them to be your buddies. No one says this better than Mika Brzezinski, the cohost of MSNBC's *Morning Joe*, whom I asked to write a work column for *Cosmo*. "Look, it took me twenty-five years in television news and writing two books to realize that it doesn't matter if everyone adores me," she says. "Being liked is what women strive for. But when you make that mistake, it diverts your attention from more important tasks at hand."

So go big, love the thrill of it and the prizes it brings, but know that when you make a big move, it creates a big breeze, and that can sometimes ruffle feathers.

{ What Are You *Really* Lusting For? }

One day at *Cosmo* my art director, John, was driving to a photo shoot in a van with a bunch of twenty-something models. All of a sudden one of the male models noticed that the van was headed out of Manhattan, and when he asked for an explanation, he learned for the first time that the shoot was in the suburbs and the group wouldn't be returning to the city until at least nine that evening. "Wait," he told John. "I've got plans with a girl tonight. I can't get back that late."

"Sorry," John told him. "Your booker should have explained the situation. There's nothing I can do now."

Ten minutes later, just as the van was approaching the entrance to the highway out of the city, the model clutched his abdomen and began to moan. "Can you pull over?" he muttered to the driver. "I feel sick." Once the van stopped, the model stepped outside, leaned over for a moment as if he was about to hurl the contents of his stomach, and then, yup, stood up and took off down the street like a bat out of hell, never again to be seen by the *Cosmo* crew.

I burst out laughing when I heard the story the next day. "Well," I said to John, "at least the guy knows what his priorities are."

One thing almost all the successful women I know have in common: they're doing something they really love and that matters to them. Your chances of being a success are much greater when you follow a course that you're totally passionate about. Because passion energizes you, creates clarity about your choices, and makes you fearless. And it provides plenty of pleasure. Of course, it also has to be something that pays the bills—unless you've got a nice trust fund.

I was passionate about writing and editing from the time I was little. At about seven I started writing plays and stories, and also producing little newspapers and minimagazines. By the time I was in high school, I was fantasizing about moving to New York one day and becoming a magazine writer or editor or author.

But just because you might not have figured it all out before you're twenty-one doesn't mean you're at a huge disadvantage. It often takes people a while to discover their true passion, and that's fine. You don't want to get stuck toiling for years at something that barely stirs your libido. It will be tough to ever feel satisfied or grab the success that could be yours elsewhere. Plus, the longer you stay on a career path you're not excited about, the harder it will be to shift gears into an entirely new area. Why not start thinking now about where you really *should* be? If a bad economy makes it difficult to act on your idea, you will at least be poised to move when things improve.

Fortunately, there are a few tricks for figuring it out. Even if you're pretty sure of the answer already, these are good to have up your sleeve. That's because over time, you may feel an urge or need to try something brand new but may not be sure of the possibilities. Or you may have a general sense of what you want but haven't nailed down the specifics. These strategies should help.

Be a glutton for unusual, even weird experiences.
From interviewing women for one of my previous career books, I made a fascinating discovery—though it didn't occur to me until the book was actually published. Most of the women, I realized, had found a career they loved not by contemplating what would turn them on but by *bumping into it* someplace out in the world.

If you haven't found your calling yet, the best thing to do is get your butt off your chair, fill your life with a wide array of unusual experiences, and allow yourself to bump into what will exhilarate you.

This advice may seem a bit contrary to what you've heard elsewhere. When you're about to finish school (or are further along in your career but feeling restless), well-meaning family members and friends will often suggest that you "think about what you want" or grab a legal pad and list the pros and cons of a variety of fields. Or someone may direct you to a book such as *What Color Is Your Parachute?*, which suggests that you fill out pages of a workbook to determine your calling. That may do the trick for some people, but as I said, it's not how many of the successful women I know figured it out. And the "bump-into-it" way is a hell of a lot more fun.

One of my former fashion editors described this serendipitous approach beautifully. I asked her one day how she had decided to become a fashion editor. My assumption was that she'd probably always loved clothes as a girl and had gone to some kind of fashion school. Her answer took me totally by surprise. She said that she'd actually been an art major in college and had graduated with no clue as to what she wanted to do. She and her boyfriend had decided to head to Africa, just for the adventure of it. They were traveling around Egypt by bus, and at one of the stops they came across a fashion shoot for a European magazine. As my fashion editor stared at the stylist who was dressing the models, she had a eureka moment. That, she realized, was what she wanted to do. "Sometimes," she said, "you have to be on the bus to Cairo to know what you want." I love that story.

You don't have to take her advice literally by heading to Cairo, but you should hop on the bus metaphorically. Have lunch with people you've just met or haven't seen in years. Wander down streets you've never been on before. Take one-night classes in surprising subjects that you might not automatically think to delve into. Go on an Earthwatch expedition (I did several trips of that nature during my twenties, restoring an old stone site on the South Pacific island of Rarotonga and tagging penguins in Patagonia, and they opened my eyes to all sorts of things). Visit people you know at their jobs and note how you respond to the vibe. Check out the websites of newspapers in cities you don't live in. Go to art galleries, especially ones with the type of art you rarely look at. Visit friends in towns you've never traveled to. Stop at bookstores and breeze through books you wouldn't normally bother with—or browse through books and DVDs online. Check out www.uroulette.com, which takes you to an evolving, random list of websites (the Baltimore Symphony Orchestra website might appear right next to one called All About Pumpkins), and you can then click on any one that catches your fancy. Read old letters people wrote you and/or journals you kept; be on the lookout for a passion you once had but abandoned. And actually *go* to Cairo—or Paris or San Francisco or Santa Fe.

You can also volunteer or freelance in certain fields to gain a feel for them and measure your response. Though I loved the idea of being a writer, other fields sometimes beckoned me and I wanted to be sure I'd made the right choice. During my mid-twenties I was the volunteer coordinator at night in a couple of different political campaigns and also worked as a model on my lunch hours and days off (when people in my office would see me in ads, I'd tell them it was my doppelgänger). During my late twenties, I volunteered at a tiny TV station and eventually anchored a newscast one night a week. These were all fascinating ways to test the waters.

When you're exploring, look for moments when you feel your curiosity stir. Is there something about a certain experience that makes you inordinately satisfied or excited? Do you long to repeat it? Dr. Ellen Marmur, a fantastic dermatologist I met through *Cosmo*'s Practice Safe Sun campaign, left college unsure of what she wanted to do—maybe go into business, maybe study to be a rabbi, she just didn't know. On the fence about what her next move should be, she signed up to help lead a camping trip that involved canoeing through the wilderness. One day one of the campers fell and broke her leg. The group was miles from nowhere, but, rather than feel frightened, Marmur moved into super-control mode. "I knew," she said, "that the camper would have to be carried out on a makeshift stretcher and that somehow I needed to create a splint for the broken bone. I picked up one of the canoe paddles and snapped it in two over my knee. And there was something so incredibly satisfying about the crack it made. It was a defining moment for me. I began to sense then that what I really wanted to do was be a doctor, taking charge, helping people."

By the way, your passion doesn't have to be utterly precise. Perhaps, for starters, you just feel an urge to work with kids or *organize* things, or create a website. Start with an instinct, tease it into different directions (by researching, talking to people, etc.), and see which area not only fits well but also could pay off. Kate Spade and I worked at the same magazine and later, after she'd started her business, I asked her how she'd developed the idea. Her answer surprised me. I remember her saying that her initial inclination had been to simply be an entrepreneur, maybe even open a restaurant. Her then boyfriend, now husband, Andy, had said, "You know, you really like handbags—you have so many." And things began to evolve from there.

Don't believe everything you think. Even if you have a sense of what you want, you need to challenge yourself about it. Is it definitely what *you* want or simply what other people—such as your parents—want for you? Or could it be what you've always told yourself you wanted but isn't the case anymore (or perhaps never was). Are you thinking boldly enough? Is there something bigger waiting for you that you've been afraid to envision for yourself?

One Sunday afternoon in August 1998, my boss phoned me at my family's weekend home, a little farmhouse in Pennsylvania. My knees immediately went wobbly because she *never* called me at home. She asked if I would drive into the city right then so she could talk to me about a special situation. I was the editor in chief of *Redbook* then, but I guessed that was about to change. Because hey, when your boss calls you on a weekend and asks you to cross a state line, you can bet that *something* big is afoot.

Leaving my family behind to wrap things up in Pennsylvania, I drove into New York and headed for my boss's office. I was so nervous I was practically hyperventilating. Once I arrived, she asked me to sit down and then delivered this wallop of a line: "Kate, we'd like you to be the next editor of *Cosmopolitan*." Bonnie Fuller, the editor in chief who had replaced Helen Gurley Brown for just eighteen issues, was defecting to *Glamour.*

It's not an exaggeration when I say I was speechless. Not only had there been no inkling that Bonnie was bolting, but I'd also never once imagined myself connected to *Cosmo*. I said yes, of course. *Cosmopolitan* was the Hearst Corporation's most successful magazine, and being asked to run it was a major honor.

I was unable to reach my husband by phone, and when he burst into the house later that afternoon, he was dying to know what the deal was. As soon as I gave him the news, a big, mischievous grin spread across his face. "Wait," he said, "you mean I'm going to bed tonight with the editor of *Cosmo*?" In his mind it was as though I'd managed to learn the entire Kama Sutra between the time I was given the job and when I arrived home.

But though he seemed happy as a pig in you-know-what, I was secretly miserable. Sure, it was an incredible job and I hadn't even had to do a thirty-page proposal to land it, as you so often have to do with editor in chief jobs, but I just couldn't see myself heading up *Cosmo*. I hadn't read it much in my twenties and I had barely glanced at it in years. I couldn't imagine how I was going to relate to the content. Plus, because it was such a huge cash cow for the company, I sensed that the pressure would be unbearable. I was 100 percent certain, in fact, that if the job had come up on the open market, I would not have even thrown my hat in the ring.

For the first few months I sucked it up and tried my best. I had terrible insomnia and often went to work having slept for only an hour or two. Tons of Bonnie's new staff followed her to *Glamour*, so in addition to trying to get the magazine out the door every day, I had to focus on plugging the holes in the dike. I left the office at five thirty every day because my kids were young and I didn't want to shortchange them, but after they went to bed I worked for hours more each night.

And then something funny began to happen: the newsstand sales numbers started coming in for my first issues, and it turned out I was selling tons of copies. *Cosmo* readers were gutsy and fun to talk to. The content was irreverent and over the top and wonderful to create. I soon realized that I actually loved what I was doing now. In many ways it was the job I'd been waiting for all my life.

Maybe I should have just smiled and accepted how fascinating fate is, but over the next year I was bugged by how blind I'd been. I kept wondering how a bunch of people in suits had known so clearly what I should be doing professionally and I had been so *dead wrong*.

And then one day while I was reading the edit of one of our self-help articles, a line really grabbed my attention. It said, "Don't believe everything you think." The point was this: we don't always see clearly what's right for us, no matter how smart and self-aware we are.

Why *can't* we see? It's sometimes because we've been led astray from our natural instincts. Though I have a risk-taking gene, twelve years of Catholic education and some second-guessing had tamped down those instincts. The idea of running *Cosmo* at first scared the pants off me. It was only when I was thrust into it that I saw that the job really suited me.

Of course, parents can play a big role in shaping the way you view your future. When researching my thriller *The Sixes*, I interviewed Dr. Jill Murray, a terrific psychotherapist from Los Angeles. Dr. Murray had paid her own way through undergraduate school since her parents didn't believe she needed college the way her three brothers did. One day when she was an adult, her mother mentioned to her that she'd had an intriguing dream that one of her children, one with big hands, would become a doctor. Murray and her mother spent time that day trying to analyze the dream but were puzzled because none of her brothers had big hands. Years later, when Murray was about to go to the podium to receive her doctoral degree, she suddenly remembered her mother's dream and looked down at her hands. *She* was one with the big hands. At the time of the dream she had been so locked into her parents' sense of her that she had never considered herself to be the doctor candidate.

So how do you make certain you're not thinking all wrong

about your destiny? You need to always challenge your thinking, *especially* anything you're especially adamant about. (Be wary of thoughts like, "I would never be a. . . .") Ask yourself why you're so sure and what the alternative would be like. Don't be afraid to ask, "What if . . . ?"

Encourage friends to challenge your thinking, too. We published research in *Cosmo* showing that our friends are often better judges than we are of whether our romantic relationships will last. I think they can also sometimes see our career identity more clearly than we do. Take a friend out for a drink and ask, "What do you see me doing?" or "If I were going to change careers, what do you think I should choose next?" or "Is there something you think I'm good at that I might not see?"

Consider, too, how you *feel*. "So many young women treat life as a constant status update," says Jane Buckingham, CEO of the consumer research and trend-spotting company Trendera, whom I hired my first day at *Cosmo*. "They're thinking about how their lives look instead of how their lives feel."

Determine the viability. It's fabulous when you can follow a career path you love, but is the one that's emerging for you going to pay off financially? Do you have the right instincts and skills for it—or could you get them? Is there a need—and potentially a continued need—for what you have in mind?

"You have to consider what the world wants from you," says Alexa Hirschfeld, cofounder of Paperless Post, "not what you want from the world."

Be open to tall dark strangers. If you're going to find what you're truly lusting for, you have to be open to the sexy stranger who comes out of nowhere. Maybe you majored in economics and totally saw yourself in that field, but one night you attend a political rally and you feel totally charged by the experience. Be open. Ask questions. There's nothing wrong with being seduced if you love what you see.

What if you still don't know what you want? Then "follow the river" for a while. That's a great phrase I heard from the comedian Amy Schumer. I met Schumer when she was first performing in New York. Since then I've watched her become a finalist on *Last Comic Standing*, appear on shows such as *Ellen*, *Conan*, and *Curb Your Enthusiasm*, and get her own TV show. "I always knew I wanted to entertain people *somehow*," she says. "When I was little, I had all these characters I created, but I never had a big endgame or pictured how that goal of entertaining would take shape. I really followed the river. As opportunities appeared, I went after them and saw where they took me. For a while that even meant acting in theater until I started doing stand-up."

So jump in—and see if the river takes you someplace magical.

{ Ballsy Strategies for Finding a Job }

Wouldn't it be nice if once you decided for sure what you wanted to do professionally, you could just go out and *do* it? But life doesn't work that way. You've got to go out and "find" a job first. That can seem like the most daunting challenge in the world—whether you're just starting out or ready to take your career up a level or two. Don't freak. There are ways to make the process less of a mind-numbing challenge.

The Search

Let me start with a little story. After I'd been at *Glamour* magazine for about five years, working during the last years as a feature writer, I realized I was overdue to make a change. The next logical step in my career was for me to be an associate editor—or, if I was lucky, a senior editor—but I sensed that it was not going to happen at *Glamour*. Not only were there no openings on the horizon, but I had trapped myself into a top-ten-college-winner-turned-sometimes-boisterous-and-mischievous-staff-writer persona (I'd once been called into the managing editor's office and told there was "too much frivolity" in my area). Finally, after a certain amount of dragging of feet, I took a Monday off from work, determined to spend the entire day job hunting. Early in the morning I sat down at my home desk with a new ringed notebook. On each page I listed a particular magazine that I'd been keeping my eye on and any contacts I had there. Then I started making calls.

One of the magazines I'd listed was *Family Weekly*, a Sunday newspaper supplement (similar to *Parade*) that reached almost 30 million people. It wasn't a very classy publication, but I thought that it might be easier to snag a senior editor job at a place that clearly wasn't on everyone's radar. The offices happened to be on the same floor as a magazine I sometimes wrote freelance pieces for, so I called my editor there and asked if she knew anyone I could talk to.

It turned out that her boss was newly married to the editor in chief of *Family Weekly* (they'd actually met on the floor!), and she had her boss call me a short time later. The boss was more than happy to help because, it turned out, *Family Weekly* needed a senior editor. The very next day I met with the editor, Art Cooper (who later went on to fabulously reinvent *GQ*). The interview couldn't have gone better. On Wednesday, Art called and offered me the job, and the next day I resigned from *Glamour*. I'd snagged not only the title I wanted but also a chance to reinvent myself as a mature career girl.

I can't tell you how amused my two cubby mates were about my news. When I'd taken the Monday off, I'd confided my plan to them. "Jeez," one of them said to me, "this all happened because of a *notebook*?"

Well, it wasn't so much the notebook that did it; it was the fact that out of desperation, I'd created a system to work with. And that's what you need for a job search.

Terri Wein, cofounder of Weil & Wein, a fantastic company that specializes in executive coaching and career optimization, suggests that rather than relying on a notebook, you should work with two spreadsheets on your computer; you use one to list all the companies you're aware of in the field or fields you're interested in and the other to list every single contact you have.

If you've already worked in some capacity or done any internships, your contacts are everybody you've met in your work plus all your personal contacts. If you haven't been employed yet, you still have plenty of contacts. "Take out your college yearbook," says Wein. "Who sat next to you in class? Who do you know that's gone into the field you're interested in? You don't have to know them well to put them on the list." You'd also include any contacts your parents have, friends of your parents, people you met on family vacations, even kids you knew in summer camp.

Then join LinkedIn, the professional networking site. Wein says LinkedIn is an enormous asset for anyone doing a job search. Connect with all of your contacts who are on LinkedIn and discover which of them—and *their* connections—are in an area you want to work in.

"Now you need to reach out and reintroduce yourself," says Wein. "Most people don't have the time to meet in person so ask for a ten-minute phone conversation. Be specific. Tell them you're looking and would appreciate any help they can give. Could they introduce you to a key person in their own organization?" You can also request they make an introduction to one of their LinkedIn connections.

During this time, you also need to work your spreadsheet of companies. Perhaps you're interested in the health care field, though at this point you're still exploring and haven't yet decided which *area* of health care. So divide your spreadsheet into sections covering different areas—hospitals could be one, medical devices another, health-information services or health-focused websites yet another.

Every day you should also be checking job boards to track positions as they open up. In addition to the job boards on company websites, use public job boards such as Monster, Indeed, LinkedIn, and any specialty sites. There's also your alumni website, etc. When a job pops up that seems promising, you should turn to LinkedIn again.

"Let's say you are interested in the health field and there's a job at WebMD that sounds really appealing to you," says Wein. "It's not only a job in health care that you're looking for but the Internet, which also appeals to you. Use LinkedIn to find out if anyone in your entire network—or those in *their* networks—knows anyone at WebMD. If you find someone who does, ask him to help you get your résumé on the top of the pile. Ask that person to make an e-mail introduction and to send your résumé to the appropriate manager."

Using contacts is really the best way to expedite a job search. If you simply send in your résumé via the company website, you'll be mixed in with possibly hundreds of candidates. If you must resort to this, at least leave a phone message with HR saying that you've forwarded your résumé and you'd love to interview for the job. That may lead to the person on the other end at least sorting yours out from the pack.

During your job search, you must also be networking as much as possible, attending events, talk, lectures, and conferences where you'll meet people you can add to your contact list. Wein says it's important to have a very brief "elevator pitch" to use when you meet someone who might be able to help you. Start with a two-line summary of your background, and then say what you're looking for, being as specific as possible. It could go something like this: "I just graduated with a degree in economics, and I worked at a hospital for my past two summers. I'd love a job at a health-related website. I know you once worked for WebMD, and I'd really welcome a personal introduction."

Don't be shy about asking for help from everyone and enlisting anyone you can in your efforts. That's how a former assistant of mine ended up landing an interview with me and ultimately the job. One of the top people in HR at my company had called a house inspector to report that his house had been hit by lightning. When the secretary picked up the phone, she realized from the caller ID that the person was phoning from a big magazine company. After she'd taken the message, she told my colleague, "My son's girlfriend is looking for a job in magazines—do you have any advice?" He agreed to meet with her and sent her résumé on to me.

Your Résumé

There are plenty of books and articles available on how to write a résumé, and you should turn to them for a full set of guidelines. But don't get so caught up in a formula that your résumé sounds wooden, unconnected to a human being. I love résumés that seem to have personality to them, that showcase something really interesting or even unusual that the person has done. I saw a résumé lately of a varsity athlete who had written a thesis on Oscar Wilde, which couldn't help but grab my attention. (I'm in a creative field, of course, and the rules are different here.)

Though it's nice when a résumé shows a diversity of experience, you don't want it to seem all over the map. When I'm looking at résumés for people applying for positions at magazines, I want to see that the choices they've made have been pointing them in that direction. This means playing up everything related to creating content and possibly eliminating activities that lead to a hodge-podge feel. If you are looking at several fields, you will need a résumé for each because you might want to add or drop certain activities (but, of course, never lie!).

Wein says that the biggest mistake women make with their résumés is playing down their achievements. "A man who has only had four years of high school French will think nothing of putting 'fluent in French' on his résumé," she says, "whereas a woman who's actually studied in France will make her language skills seem simply adequate. You need to be factual, but you don't have to be modest."

Depending on your field, you may also want to create a website to showcase your résumé and work so far. For instance, if you want to be a journalist, you'd feature "clips" of articles you wrote for your campus magazine.

Your Cover Letter

I really dig a great cover letter. In fact, it's a cover letter or e-mail, far more than a résumé, that makes me decide if I want to meet a job candidate.

Here are the three things that, for me at least, make a letter impossible to ignore.

First, I love to see *passion*. Let me know that you'd love to work for me, and describe some of the things you admire most about both me and my company. In other words, seduce me.

I can't tell you how many cover letters I've received over the years that make it sound as if I'm just another girl in a bar, er, I mean another name on a long list. You need to customize each letter so the person knows you're writing to him and him alone. Don't feel guilty if over time you end up showering a whole bunch of people with the same amount of admiration. No one will sue you for doing so.

Second, I love a candidate who seems real. Relax and let your personality come through. Here's a sentence that hooked me—from a cover letter I received a few years ago. It was for an internship, but it could just as easily have been in a cover letter for an entry-level job.

"My favorite afternoons," the letter writer told me, "are spent in mismatched pajamas, coffee in hand, flipping through the glossy pages of *Cosmo*."

She had me at mismatched pajamas. It sounded so authentic, and I could even picture her in my mind. I definitely wanted to meet her. Of course, you wouldn't want to start talking about your jammies in a letter to a law firm or the State Department, but you should still find appropriate ways for the real you to shine through.

Last, you need to let me know what you're going to do for me. Take a look at this excerpt from a letter I received recently, and tell me what's wrong with it:

"Since graduating I've taken some time off to travel and write. I want to work for a company I'm excited about and step outside my comfort zone for a change. I've looked at all my options, and I feel that *Cosmo* is *the* place I desire to work."

What's wrong with this letter is that it screams "ME, ME, ME." But prospective employers don't give a rat's ass about your need to be excited or step outside of your comfort zone or fulfill your desires. We want to know what you can do for *us*! What skills have you learned so far that you can bring to the company or organization? (FYI: we also don't want to read spoiled-sounding statements, such as one suggesting that you just spent three months in Aix-en-Provence with your laptop and plenty of rosé!)

Some additional advice from Terri Wein: brevity is key. She suggests that you summarize your credentials in just two lines.

A Little Trick for Aerobicizing the Process

No matter how methodical you are about your search and no matter how many leads you explore, there will be lulls in the action, possibly even times when you feel as if you're stuck in some horrible doldrums and sense that absolutely nothing is ever going to happen.

One of the best things you can do then is to work at something. No, you don't have a job yet, but you can volunteer someplace, offer to be a free intern (or the free assistant to a writer or artist), create a website or blog (not about yourself but an interesting, relevant topic). The talent manager Sue Leibman, the president of Barking Dog Entertainment, and I were once discussing how Hollywood actors keep their careers alive, and she mentioned that when her clients are in lulls, she encourages them to take whatever work that's offered. "Work begets work," she said. "It just does."

When you are out there, doing things and meeting people, it's as though this weird law of physics takes hold—and a job could easily find its way to you.

In a study with the Society for Human Resource Management (SHRM) that I initiated at *Cosmo*, 70 percent of respondents said that they felt an unpaid internship in your field carries more weight than a paying job in an area unrelated to your field. If you need to pay bills by, let's say, waitressing, you could try to find an internship to work at during your off-hours.

Special Advice for Gen Y

If you're a member of Gen Y, you probably always got plenty of attention from adults while you were growing up, but you have to be careful about assuming that you're on the same playing field as the people you interview with. Lately someone I work with was setting up an interview with a job candidate and the young woman told her, "I'm fine at two. Does that work for you?" *Wrong.* She should have first found out what worked for the interviewer.

Recite after me: "My time and needs are not as important as the interviewer's."

{ Know What They Know About You }

'm sure you're aware that some companies check out job candidates online before they even consider hiring them. But you may not realize how many companies now do this and how extensive their sleuthing is. In a survey of recruiters in the United States, 75 percent reported that their companies have formal policies in place that require hiring personnel to research applicants online. And a whopping 90 percent regularly google candidates to see what they can find out at a glance. Forty-six percent say they've uncovered digital deal-breakers, such as ethics violations, that forced them to eliminate a candidate from consideration.

And what a recruiter considers bad behavior may be tame in your eyes. In a careerbuilder.com survey, more than half of the employers who chose not to hire someone because of an online revelation did so because of provocative photos (in some instances this was simply a picture of the candidate in a bikini). Forty-four percent said their decision had been based on a reference to drinking or drugs. And get this: some even were turned off by poor online communication skills.

You must be ruthlessly diligent about the information that is available about you online. It's important to have a presence—on Facebook, LinkedIn, Twitter, and so on. After all, you don't want to seem like someone who was kidnapped by aliens five years ago and just brought back to Earth. But you need to control what goes onto the Internet, monitor it, and do your best to bury anything that is negative.

Start by making sure your privacy settings on sites such as Facebook are in place. Be sure, too, that information that appears about you online is consistent. If your LinkedIn profile is even slightly different from the résumé you send out, it's going to make a prospective employer wonder.

Before you begin a job hunt, Jane Buckingham, the CEO of Trendera and author of *The Modern Girl's Guide to Sticky Situations*, recommends that you do a Google search on yourself and see what turns up. You should also sign up for a Google alert on your name so that you are always aware of what's being posted about you.

If you find anything negative, you unfortunately can't erase it, but you can make it harder to find. One strategy is start a blog and frequently create new content. Search engines rank the most recent and frequent results first, so your blog will show up at the top and a negative story will move lower and lower. (Companies such as ReputationDefender use similar tactics.)

Speaking of blogs, they're fine to do and can enhance your online profile, but you need to make yours professional in nature. "Personal blogs can really lead to problems," Buckingham says. "Lots of personal information doesn't appeal to many employers."

Your blog should carry info related to your field: links to important articles, for instance, or insights from a talk you attended.

There are two other important points to keep in mind. First,

"It's not just about what *you* do with information about yourself," Buckingham says. "It's about what *others* do with it. Today it's all about the power of the send."

Let's say you go to a Halloween party dressed as Snooki. You have no intention of posting a picture of yourself in the costume. But a friend might take one and tag it. Watch out for anyone snapping photos. If you see a questionable shot of yourself on someone's Facebook wall, ask him or her to take it down immediately. Better yet, don't ever dress like Snooki!

Second, be sure to understand how social media sites work. When you check someone out on LinkedIn, for example, it will alert him or her to the fact that you've done that. Do you want people to know that kind of stuff? If not, make yourself anonymous under your profile view setting. When you update your LinkedIn profile, it will send an alert to anyone who is following you, which could signal to an employer that you're ready to look for a new job. So you might want to disable that feature as well.

Of course, there's also good, old-fashioned word of mouth to be conscious of. If, for instance, you develop a reputation for being difficult, bitchy, or indecisive, people will hear about it soon enough.

{ How to Nail a Job Interview }

Over the course of running five magazines, I've interviewed hundreds of job candidates. When someone dazzles me during an interview and I find myself thinking, "*Yes*, this is the one," it's almost as if a chemical reaction has taken place. Fortunately, if you're the one being interviewed, it's possible to *create* that chemical reaction.

First, though, you have to be a good fit for the job. No matter how brilliantly you come across during an interview, a smart employer won't want to bring you on board if your skills and experience level aren't right. Not long after I arrived at *Cosmo*, I made it mandatory for all editorial assistant candidates to take a writing test before they were even granted an interview—because if you can't master *Cosmo*-speak, you won't thrive at the magazine. A new job should always be a stretch, but not such a stretch that you're destined to bomb at it.

So if you're right for the job, here are the strategies that will leave an interviewer panting to hire you.

Own the First Five Minutes

After I arranged for *Cosmo* to team up with the Society for Human Resource Management (SHRM), we surveyed five hundred of its members to determine what they were looking for during a job interview. Here's a stat that really grabbed my attention: almost 35 percent said they had made the decision *not* to hire someone in about five minutes. Though it may be hard to tell if a candidate is a perfect fit in such a short amount of time, the interviewer can often quickly decide whether the person is simply all wrong in his opinion. My God, I thought, you've barely had time to step into the room, shake hands, and will your sweat glands into submission before your fate has already been decided.

Many HR managers said they gave a person more time than that, but I suspect that some of them didn't want to admit to how quickly they sized up a candidate. Plus, remember that HR managers are trained to be open-minded. When you meet with a prospective boss, he or she may react less neutrally. I know I develop a feel about a person very, very quickly—and I don't fight it.

The bottom line: the early minutes of an interview are critical. Don't make the mistake of thinking that the interviewer is giving you a chance to warm up and get your bearings. He isn't. He's judging you. He's deciding whether you're a good choice. Here's what you need to pay attention to so that you own those first minutes and make the very most of them.

Your appearance. I'll never forget my very first job interview in Manhattan. Though I was pretty sure I wanted to be in magazines, a contact arranged a meeting for me with the owner of a small advertising agency and I jumped at it, thinking that at the very least I would gain some practice at presenting myself. As the interview was drawing to a close, the arrogant, cocky owner leaned back in his chair and said, "I think this could work. But you'll have to get the stain out of your dress first." *Ouch*. I was so humiliated that I never followed up on his offer for me to take the discussion to the next level, but it taught me how closely people pay attention to your appearance.

You need to make sure your hair, makeup, nails, clothes, and shoes all look impeccable (see "Success Style: 10 Easy Steps" for more specifics). Go very, very light on cologne or skip it altogether (it's a real turn-off for some people). Do *not* flash cleavage (unless you're applying for a job at Hooters) or wear clothes that are too short or too tight. In the *Cosmo* survey, 95 percent of the HR managers said that dressing provocatively was a big problem and 67 percent said it would be an outright deal breaker.

How dressy should you be? Years ago there was a uniform you could wear for a job interview—a boring suit—and it worked in a huge variety of fields. That look makes sense today only in very conservative settings (thank God!), and you need to customize your interview outfit to the field you're applying in. For instance, if you're gunning for a job as a publicist, you may want to make a statement with a trendy accessory and great shoes to show you're in the loop with what's hot. And if you're applying for a job as a teacher, you'll want to show you can dress for the principal and parents as well as the kids—so look polished, for instance in a nice pants suit with a great scarf.

Of course, since you don't work at the place, you can't be expected to know the dress code firsthand. But you can check out the company's website, watch people going into the building, ask anyone you know who once worked there. Then take it up *at least* a notch for the interview. For instance, a top IT director told me that she'd expect any woman applying for a job in IT to be dressed in a blouse, jacket, skirt, or pants, even though she might wear jeans on the job.

Your body language. From the time I was in my twenties I've been writing, editing, and publishing articles about how people use body language to communicate, often without realizing they're doing so. It can speak volumes and is often far more accurate than what's being said verbally. You'll have the upper hand if you not only learn how to read it but use your own strategically.

Of course, when you're interviewing for a job, you've got a lot of balls to keep in the air, and you may feel the last thing you can do is concentrate on your body language. But you'll come across far more confidently if you're conscious of certain details. I learned about many of them from Janine Driver, a body language expert I've worked with frequently and the author of *You Can't Lie to Me: The Revolutionary Program to Supercharge Your Inner Lie Detector and Get to the Truth*.

Your handshake. This is one of the first ways the interviewer connects with you, and you need to do it right. Driver says to make certain the web of your hand is positioned in the web of the interviewer's and that you point your thumb to the sky. Also, tilt back your hand a little—that's what Driver calls "the pauper's handshake." It acknowledges the other person's power, she says. You're saying, "I know who's in charge here."

Your sitting position. Once you're sitting down, Driver recommends you move the chair about thirty degrees, so it's slightly off center. Being directly face-to-face often makes the other person anxious.

Your head and your eyes. Keep your head level when listening. Janine points out that lots of body language is literal and holding your head level translates as—yes, you got it—levelheadedness. Most people, she says, are comfortable with eye contact about 60 percent of the time, so don't overdo it. She recommends that you occasionally glance away while speaking, giving the other person a break, and look to your bottom left—it signals that you're having an internal dialogue or, in other words, considering what the interviewer is saying.

Your legs and feet. I can't help it—I often check out a job candidate's feet and legs, and from what Janine says, so do many prospective employers. Do not cross your legs, she advises. Keeping both feet on the ground signals that you, well, *have both feet on the ground*.

Pacifiers. These are body gestures we use to calm ourselves. Hands can be terrible offenders—they sometimes flail and fuss when we're nervous. Driver says that women rely on two pacifiers in particular. One is touching the dimple just below our necks, especially when we're asked an awkward question such as "Why is there a six-month gap in your résumé?" Driver suggests instead grabbing your chin between your thumb and forefinger (it looks thoughtful). The other bad pacifier is playing with your cuticles. Getting a manicure the day before the interview can help you resist the tendency to do that. Driver says that if you feel the urge to move out of nervousness, do some toe crunches since the interviewer won't notice those.

I have to add one more nervous habit: playing with your hair. I've had young women right out of college practically give themselves new hairstyles during interviews. If you know you do this, consider wearing your hair up or back.

Your manners. BE ON TIME. That's critical. Almost 60 percent of the managers in the *Cosmo* survey viewed lateness as a major problem/deal breaker. I once sent home an editorial assistant candidate without even conducting the interview because she was ten minutes late. Who wants an assistant who can't be on time?

Do not arrive with any kind of beverage. I feel I should say this because at *Cosmo* we once had a guy who was applying for an assistant position show up with a jumbo-size iced coffee and sip it through the interview. Before taking a chair, wait for the interviewer to sit down first or gesture for you to do so. And turn off your damn cell phone. It's so lame when someone's phone rings and they have to fumble for it in their bag.

And while we're on the subject of manners, I want to point out here that you absolutely must follow up with a thank-you note. Snail mail or e-mail? One top career expert I know says that the era of the handwritten thank-you note is dead. "By the time it arrives," she says, "they're already onto the next candidate."

But some people are funny; they like and expect the old-fashioned kind of note. In fact, when we asked in the *Cosmo* survey what managers preferred, 50 percent said e-mail and the other half said they'd want a handwritten note. If you've interviewed with someone on the older side or it's a conservative company, you might want to cover yourself both ways. Shoot off an e-mail saying "A handwritten note will follow, but I just wanted to say how much I enjoyed talking to you. The job sounds terrific."

Show Them the Love

For years I tried to analyze why I loved talking to certain job candidates whereas others, even those with great skills, left me cold. What I finally decided is that some people seem more fully engaged in the process, more excited and delighted to be there. There's even a little bounce to their step when they walk into the room, and you may sense that bounce even when they're sitting in the chair talking to you. They want the job, and they're not afraid to show their passion. It's another way of going big or going home. And you know all that stuff I just told you about things like the right shoes and a perfect handshake? They might not even matter all that much if you get *this* right.

Recently I bumped into Frank Farrell, the executive recruiter who had first called me to interview for the job as editor in chief of *Redbook*, and it gave me a chance to finally ask him a question. After I'd been offered the *Redbook* job, Frank had phoned and congratulated me, and before he signed off, he had told me never to change the way I came across during an interview. I was so caught up in the moment, I hadn't asked him to elaborate, but later I'd wondered what he'd meant exactly. This was finally my opportunity to inquire. He told me I'd just seemed very passionate about my work and the job we were discussing. "You turned beet red when you were talking about it," he said. I nearly died when he shared that info, and I'd hardly recommend you go into an interview looking as if you've strayed too close to a blowtorch. But you get the point: I'd shown the love that day, and it had worked.

Unfortunately, some job candidates tamp down their passion. Maybe they're afraid that seeming effusive will make them look goofy and unprofessional. But here's what you must remember: it's the hot tamale who wins the day, not the girl who's as cool as a cucumber. As soon as you meet the interviewer, try to be fully present. Take in the space, the ambience, the person, and if something about the situation moves you, go ahead and say so—like "I really like the open floor plan here. It must be a great environment to work in."

When you answer questions about your educational or work history, let your enthusiasm about different projects and situations come through (e.g., "It was so much more than I could have hoped for in an internship. I had the chance to actually write up the newsletter and work with a designer to put it together. I loved every minute of it."). You don't want to sound like a phony, though. Be authentic, sharing the positive feelings you experienced. And under no circumstances should you say anything negative about a previous school, company, or boss, even if the interviewer opens the door to it.

It's important, too, that your answers be intelligent, so anticipate in advance what questions you are likely to be asked (researching the job and the company will give you direction about what questions might arise) and prepare responses. When I asked one college grad in an interview a few years ago what her favorite magazine was—a question she could easily have anticipated—you know what her answer was? *Glamour.* That sure wasn't showing the love!

Some tricky questions may be shot at you—about a low GPA, for instance, or a firing, or a gap in your résumé. You should not only prepare answers but also rehearse them so you don't sound awkward responding. Your answers should be concise and nonevasive, and you should frame things as positively as possible. Instead of "I was never superhappy with my major, so I don't think I did as well as I could have," say, "As much as I enjoyed my courses, I felt really passionate about my work at the campus radio station and poured a lot of my energy into that."

And remember that showing the love means not making things disproportionately about *you.* That may sound hardhearted, but as I said before, most employers don't *care* about your personal needs. They want to know what you can do to meet *their* needs. So don't make comments that reflect any urgent desires of your own—such as "I really need to find a job in Denver" or "I'm anxious to get my foot in the door." In the SHRM survey I initiated, many managers said they didn't like hearing the phrase, "It's my dream job." Why? In part because it seems insincere but also because *it's all about you*! Instead make comments such as "The work you're doing here is very exciting. I think I could make an important contribution."

Eventually the interviewer will ask if you have any questions.

Never, ever, *ever* let the phrase "No, I think you've answered every-thing" escape from your lips. You need to have three or four smart questions ready, and it's nice to have them on a note card you take out so you really seem prepared. Good questions are those that show that you not only want the job, you are prepared to knock the ball out of the park once you have it. So ask, "What would a suc-cessful year in the job look like?" or "What did you most value in the person who left?" You've done a Google search of the field and the company, of course, and one of your questions could be about emerging trends. Interviewers love it when questions relate to them and their accomplishments ("I've heard you made some exciting changes recently. What has the outcome been?").

Ask for the Business

The first major job I ever went after was editor in chief of *Child* magazine, and I wanted it sooo badly. I made it through two inter-views and was invited to a third with the publisher and the president of the company's magazine division. I knew I must be one of the final candidates. At the end of the meeting, the publisher asked if I had any additional questions. Without even realizing what I was about to say, I told her no (I'd already asked my three questions and then some), but there was something I wanted to add. "I've loved learn-ing about the position," I said. "It sounds incredibly exciting, and I know I could take the magazine exactly where you want to go."

I got the job. Not long afterward the publisher took me to lunch, and just as we were finishing, she looked at me and smiled. "You know what we really liked about you at that final interview," she said. "We liked that you asked for the business." I hadn't heard that phrase before—I'd simply been acting instinctively that day, hungry for the job—but I later learned that it's a phrase commonly used in sales. A good salesperson closes a meeting by boldly asking for the order. And that's what you need to do at the end of an interview. Come right out and say you want it: "It's been great hearing you talk about the position. I'd love to work here, and I think I could do a terrific job for you."

A salesperson I know puts it this way: "In the case of a tie, the person who wants it the most wins." Let them know you want it. Just don't look desperate. Saying it once should be enough. And under no circumstances should you grab the interviewer around the ankles!

Another Special Note for Gen Y

Over and over again, I hear people who hire complain that Gen Y job candidates are often too familiar-acting in interviews. Maybe it's because they grew up interacting more casually with adults than previous generations. It can really rub baby boomers and members of Gen X the wrong way. And those are the people who most likely will be interviewing you for jobs.

Let me give you a few examples. During a job interview, a candidate asked one of my top editors at *Cosmo* a question about our celebrity coverage. After the editor responded, the candidate replied, "Good answer." Your role as a job candidate does not involve critiquing the person interviewing you!

And here's a real doozy. A year or so ago, a woman who came in for an exploratory interview announced upon meeting me, "You're adorable. I want to wrap you up and take you home." Ugh. The only person I wouldn't mind hearing that comment from is George Clooney.

In an attempt to be charming and not appear uptight, do not be cutesy or try to seem buddy-buddy with the interviewer. In fact, unless you are talking about work matters, avoid any personal statements or questions that include the word "you" or "your." A Gen Y job candidate asked me lately, "How's your day going so far?" and even that seemed just too nosey.

{ 9 Things You Should Never Do in a New Job }

1. Fail to clarify with your boss exactly what's expected of you. You must excel at the basic responsibilities of your job—and so you need to be certain what they are. Sure, your new boss is bound to rattle off some instructions on your first day, or she may even ask a coworker with similar responsibilities to show you the ropes. But rather than settle for that kind of hurried, possibly fragmented crash course, schedule a sit-down with your direct boss and establish what she expects you to be focusing on in the first days and weeks of the job. Take written notes and determine—this is especially important—what your deadlines are. In a new job people often expect you to have some amazing intuitive sense of when things are due, but how *can* you? If you get timetables wrong, however, it will be an early mark against you. And then be sure to request feedback about how you're doing. A few weeks after you've started, schedule another meeting with your boss. Don't say,

"Am I doing okay?" Say, "I'm really enjoying my job. Are there any suggestions you'd offer?"

2. Forget the little things. "Little things are actually huge," says Hannah Storm, the stunning cohost of ESPN's *Sports Center* and one of the best TV interviewers I've ever experienced. "Being superprepared, acting positive, being on time, getting back to people, thanking others—which plenty of people never do," she says. "We tend to think of these things as so basic, and yet they can make you stand out and kick ass in your career." She notes that it was observing all those little things in her first job as a sportscaster on a radio station in Houston that helped her start to get noticed.

3. Resist the culture. One of the most charming interns I met at *Cosmo* was a guy who worked in the fashion department and wore his shiny black hair in a giant ball on top of his head. He was like a human topiary, and when I first spotted the do, my eyes bugged out a little. But that wonderful over-the-top style was the kind of look that was totally appropriate for the fabulous *Cosmo* fashion department, a land of short shorts, sky-high heels, and faux fur vests (but not, thank God, worn at the same time). Everyone loved that intern's hairstyle. But it wouldn't have flown at a bank or a law firm. It's key to pay attention to the office culture you're settling into—and not only how people dress. What time do they generally arrive each morning? Leave for lunch? Leave for the day? How do they handle personal phone calls? How often do they chat with one another? Do they listen to music at their desks? It's not smart to go against the ecosystem—until you're the boss!

4. Shrink back. A common mistake I see people make when they start a new job is to try to recede into the woodwork while they get up to speed. Don't do that. People— your boss and your coworkers—are paying attention even if they don't seem to be. Yes, you may want to find your way without a big fat spotlight directed at you, but you also need to seem fully engaged from the start. Smile at people, pop your head into your boss's office regularly and say hello, and come to your first meeting with something really smart to say.

5. Not know how to triage. I'm sure you've heard the term "triage." It's a method medical personnel use to prioritize the injured and sick at big accidents and disasters. In the Simple Triage and Rapid Treatment (START) type of triage, people are placed into four categories: the expectant, who are beyond help; the injured who can be helped by immediate transport; the injured whose transport can be delayed; and those with minor injuries who need help less urgently. What does this have to do with work? Well, when you are first in a new job, your boss may throw a lot of stuff at you right from the start. Some people, especially those new to the workforce, end up concentrating on the task that's tossed at them at a given moment or the first thing they see on their desk in the morning. The result: they don't finish a more important project on time. So you need to prioritize, using your own brand of triage. Determine the importance of and the deadline for everything you're working on, and then figure out how much time you think every task will take. Each day, give your main attention to the tasks that must be "transported" immediately because of how urgent they are. Other tasks can be back-burnered temporarily, but you still need to give them deadlines on your calendar. Some tasks might not even be necessary (just like those poor people who are beyond help), but don't ignore any of them until you have a sense of what would happen if you don't do them.

By the way, if at some point your boss gives you way more than you can handle, you need to subtly make him triage *for* you. When he hands you a new assignment, say something like "That sounds really interesting. I'm working on A, B, and C right now. Which should I set aside in order to focus on this project?"

6. Get too cozy with coworkers. When you're new in a job, it's great to discover that there are nice coworkers on site, people who are happy to share important info and may even become friends over time. Act cordial and gracious, because your coworkers are passing judgment on you right now. But remember that in the early weeks, you won't have any idea whom you can trust. Do not gossip with new coworkers, admit to any insecurities or concerns, complain to them, or solicit too much in the way of guidance (they will peg you as clueless), especially if they are at your level or below. Doing any of those things could later bite you in the butt.

7. Turn up your nose at grunt work. When Essie Weingarten, founder and creative director of Essie Cosmetics, Ltd., was working as a salesgirl at Henri Bendel early in her career, a man came in just before closing one night to buy gifts. Because the person who did the gift wrapping had already left for the day, Weingarten volunteered to wrap the purchases herself. As she was finishing, Geraldine Stutz, the legendary president of Bendel, happened to walk by. "She noticed what I was doing," says Weingarten, "and from that moment on she had her eye on me and supported my career."

Don't turn your nose up at grunt work—whether it's getting coffee, opening mail, or trying to unjam the printer. When I look back at all the editorial assistants who were promoted at the magazines I ran, they were never the girls who rolled their eyes or seemed put out by those kinds of jobs.

8. Neglect to let your boss know you like the work. Bosses like happy campers. Smile, look invested, and when you hand in certain projects, say you enjoyed working on them. Do so even if you're not sure yet whether the job is the perfect fit for you. If you suspect you've made the wrong choice, tell yourself you will focus on the work without ruminating on it for at least two months. If you start questioning your situation too much now, it will color your experience.

9. Take on only the work you've been told to do. More about that in the next chapter.

{ Now Knock Their Socks Off }

As I mentioned earlier, it's essential in a new job to clarify with your boss what he or she expects of you. That will help guarantee, at least temporarily, that you know what to do and that your boss will be satisfied with your performance. In the long run, however, you must go beyond leaving your boss feeling content. To become a success, you need to knock your boss's socks off. And you can't do that by simply being proficient at your responsibilities. One of the key mistakes I see young women make in the early stages of their careers is doing exactly what they've been told to do—*and no more.*

"It's not enough to do what's expected of you, to hit the numbers," says MetricStream CEO Shellye Archambeau. "You have to excel beyond what others are doing and find ways to differentiate yourself, and show your value." In other words, you have to go big or go home.

"You must get out of the 'check the box' mentality on assignments," says ESPN's Hannah Storm. "When you're first starting out, one of the surest ways to make sure you're noticed is to do something that's not in one of those boxes."

Easier said than done, though, right? How do you know what to go big with? Here are some surefire tactics.

Do things a hell of a lot better than they imagined was possible. It goes without saying that you should aim to handle your work fabulously. But not everyone does. Figure out what you need to know (through feedback, keeping your eyes and ears open, research) to tackle your projects spectacularly. This is the first step to dazzling your boss, and you shouldn't try to jump over it.

Kick it up *at least* one notch. Look at a basic responsibility you've been given and expand it, even if no one has instructed you to. Here's the perfect example from Lori Andrews, a professor of law at IIT Chicago-Kent College of Law and a leading adviser on genetics and reproductive fertility to Congress, the World Health Organization, and the Centers for Disease Control.

"I always pick very smart people as my research assistants, but recently there was one who was just hitting it out of the park compared to the others," says Andrews. "She saw the whole picture and what needed to be done and then just took things a step further. For instance, I had asked her to proofread a chapter of my book, but she didn't just proofread it, she started to make really great suggestions. She'd say something like, 'Well, you've got this thing here, and you could end the chapter with this whole new idea that parallels it.' "

If you've been given a certain assignment in relation to a project, ask yourself what would make it even better? What extra step could you do?

Let's say, for example, that your boss asks you to pull together numbers on your department's performance in one area. Instead of just downloading the figures, study them and see if they tell you anything. If you spot a pattern, include a note when you turn them in, offering your observation (something like, "I happened to notice when I put these together that . . .") and even making a recommendation if you're pretty sure it's on the mark. Chances are more than good that your boss will be impressed by your comments, especially if they're shrewd. If it becomes clear that your boss isn't interested in hearing this kind of observation from you, you haven't overstepped your bounds in an obnoxious way. And you've also discovered that your boss may not be the type you want to stick with for very long.

Ask yourself, "What's missing?" A great way to go big is to add something new and valuable to a workplace that no one has contributed before—especially if it doesn't cost anything, tax the system, or cause unnecessary grief. That's what Hannah Storm did. "In the beginning of my sports career—on the radio in Houston—I was supposed to mainly report scores of the local teams," she says. "But I convinced my bosses at the station that it was important for our listeners to have a sense of live reporting from the big sporting events like the Super Bowl and the Final Four. So I paid my own way to those events and did phone-in calls to the station. It was a total win-win situation. I got great experience reporting from a live event, and the radio station got something interesting for listeners."

And you know what *really* pays off? If the tasks you take on or the ideas you generate not only provide special dividends for your workplace, thus setting you apart from the pack, but also allow you to begin developing your own unique specialty.

In my first year or so as a writer at *Glamour*, I worked on a lot of small items for a section in the magazine called "The How to Do Anything Better Guide." I enjoyed writing these, but I also knew I wasn't going to make much of a mark for myself with pieces like "How to Get Rid of a Pimple by Saturday Night." So I started pitching ideas for big reported pieces. But the editor in chief told me I didn't yet have the reporting skills to do that kind of article.

I could have tried to beef up my skills with *short* reported articles, but another strategy began to form in my head. As a young single woman in Manhattan, I was wrestling with so many issues, but there was rarely anything in *Glamour* on that topic. We ran service articles, not essays. So without an assignment, I went ahead and wrote a wry first-person piece about being single and dropped it on the editor in chief's desk. Two hours later she walked down to my cubby and told me she loved it. She published it in the next issue and we received lots of letters from young women saying how much they related to the piece. From then on I began writing personal essays for the magazine and eventually my own column. There was a kind of gap in the magazine and I was able to fill it, thanks to a wonderful editor in chief. But I was also beginning to develop a specialty—different from my peers—that would serve me for years.

Ask for more. Bosses love this, as long as you're already doing your main job well. One of the best approaches is to volunteer to take on a task your boss doesn't have time for or one that was previously handled by a colleague above you who was downsized. The beauty of this is that it will prove that you're capable of tackling something above your pay grade.

Fix something that that no one else has ever gotten around to fixing. One of the fascinating aspects about so many workplaces is that there is always something that doesn't function perfectly or hasn't been figured out yet. It's like a bedroom bureau with a broken leg that has been propped up with a block of wood for months, even years. And guess what? *It's yours for the taking.* You can score points by being the one who comes to the rescue.

When I was at *Glamour*, the magazine routinely rated every item and feature in the magazine for overall reader satisfaction. The findings were generally pretty straightforward, but there was one result involving "The How to Do Anything Better Guide" that editors found baffling. Though the section was one of the most popular in the magazine, the overall rating could vary as much as twenty points from one month to the next. The managing editor, who was in charge of the section, worked hard to put together a good batch of items each month. The articles staff, which included me, would pitch ideas, and she'd fill the section with twenty-five or so of what she considered the best ones—a combination of fashion, beauty, health, relationship, and lifestyle tips. She had no clue why some months readers rated the section so much higher than others.

On my own, I decided to try to figure it out. I pulled together all the ratings and analyzed the months the section had rated the highest and the months it had rated the lowest—and finally I had the answer. Though the managing editor picked decent ideas and made sure all the right categories were covered, many of the topics tended to be very specific (there was once even an item on how to deal with a diabetic pet!); it was clear that she never stepped back and considered the right overall *mix* of topics.

In analyzing the ratings, I discovered that if all the items in the section were very specific, the overall rating tended to be low. It wasn't hard to figure out why. A reader might not find anything for herself in that kind of mix. If, on the other hand, the section contained at least five items of more universal appeal—such as how to beat insomnia or ask for a raise—the ratings went through the roof. I'd figured out how to fix the broken bureau leg.

Caveat: I (stupidly) ended up getting cold feet about turning in the analysis; I was afraid the managing editor might view it as my trying to show I was smarter than she was. But in hindsight I know it would have knocked the editor in chief's socks off. All wasn't lost, though; I went on to use that type of analysis in every job I had after that.

{ How to Pull Off a Project Perfectly }

Okay, I hope I've impressed on you the importance of doing far more than what you've been told to do, of generating ideas that will knock your boss's socks off. But now it's time to talk about actually *executing* those ideas, as well as whatever else your boss puts on your plate. You need to know how to get a project off the ground, keep the momentum of it going, *and* see it through to its conclusion. Law professor Lori Andrews told me recently that many of the projects she's been asked to take on actually involve finishing what someone else has started. "You wouldn't believe how many projects just don't get completed," she says.

These strategies will help guarantee your projects never derail.

Be absolutely certain of what you are supposed to accomplish. When your boss assigns you a project, take good notes and ask questions regarding anything you're not sure about. Over the years, I've noticed that junior staffers are often reluctant to ask too many questions about a project—perhaps out of fear of looking stupid—but then they fail to do the project well. The key question to ask: "What are the results you're looking for?" Sometimes a boss can forget to spell that out. It may sound as though she wants a simple PowerPoint presentation about the business, but if she's hoping to persuade a client of something, you'll want your slides to help do that. Be clear, too, about deadlines and who needs to be looped in on the project.

In some cases giving your project a name can help motivate you. Lili Root, the terrific executive director of events marketing for Hearst, told me that she comes up with a name for every event she does even if one hasn't been provided. "A name just helps you focus," she says. "As you brainstorm ideas, you can hold them up against the name and see if they fit or not."

Make a plan. You need to figure out exactly what must be done to complete the project, and then you must break it down into what the productivity expert Julie Morgenstern calls small, "complete-able" steps. Otherwise, the project will seem overwhelming. Morgenstern (whom I've hired on occasion to teach me better time-management strategies!) says that one of the smartest things you can do is talk to someone who has done a similar project before and confirm what those steps are. Perhaps it's the person you've replaced, who has just moved up in the department. Go to him and say you heard he did a brilliant job and you'd like to pick his brain.

If no such person exists, look through files and old records to see what they might tell you. Nothing there? Get as much info as possible from those you will be interacting with. Let's say you've been given the task of organizing a luncheon for your boss. Tell the caterer or restaurant manager that this is your first time and you'd love her to provide you with a to-do list and also any information you might not think of. She can tell you, for instance, the date by which a final head count is needed.

Morgenstern says that one helpful strategy for kicking off an overwhelming-seeming project is to figure out the first three steps.

"It's as if you're focusing on just the things you can see with your car headlights," she explains. "So if you're setting up a luncheon, those first three steps will be (1) determine the goal of the event, (2) decide on a theme, and (3) pick the venue."

It's extremely important to factor in deadlines. Figure out how long each step will take and then work backward rather than forward. Let's stick with the idea of arranging a luncheon. If the date for the event is October 25 and the restaurant has told you it needs the head count by October 18, you will need to have "RSVP by October 16" on the invitation to allow time for stragglers. The invitation will need to go out around two to three weeks in advance (the length of time you give people to respond depends on the field and the age of the invitees; the caterer can help you with this number). It takes only about fifteen minutes to create an e-vite with Paperless Post, but you will need a day or two for your boss to review what you've created, so you must complete it by, let's say, October 2. You get the idea. All the dates and details go into your "plan." Keep track of certain details on your calendar.

Determine your concentration threshold. Morgenstern says that this is essential. If you try to do too much on any project in one sitting, you may end up procrastinating. Break down a big task, such as writing a report into three sessions, for instance— one for the draft, one for the revise, and one to review.

If you hit a roadblock, try jumping ahead a few steps in your plan. Sometimes you can end up stalled on a project not because you're procrastinating but because there's a sudden impasse or someone isn't getting back to you. A trick I like to use in those situations is to proceed to step 4, let's say, instead of staying stuck at 3.

Here's an example of what I mean. For two years I tried to arrange for Rihanna to do a second *Cosmo* cover. We'd been the first major magazine to feature her on the cover, and the issue had sold brilliantly, but then everybody else wanted her and we had to wait our turn again. We were due for another cover, but after Chris Brown assaulted her, she decided to keep a low profile. My project was to score another Rihanna cover, but I wasn't having any luck.

So I decided to get out ahead of the situation. I told my photo editor to see if she could find some great shots of Rihanna that had appeared on a European magazine but hadn't been released in the United States. I thought that if we went to the singer and said we had a cover-worthy photo and she had to do only the interview rather than the interview plus a photo shoot, she might be tempted to consent. We had never gone with a cover photo we hadn't commissioned, but I wasn't opposed to doing it once.

Well, we found a nice set of photos that had been shot for a European magazine and were available for purchase, as long as Rihanna's publicist agreed to let us use them. So we asked Rihanna's publicist and, sure enough, she agreed to let us use one of the photos for the cover and arranged for us to interview the singer. But then, a few weeks later, we found out that Rihanna had decided to do a summer tour. She would need publicity. We went back to her publicist and said that as long as she was now doing the interview and she had the tour, why not let us shoot her? Things were already in motion, so it was easier now for them to say yes—and they did. We'd jumped ahead a step, and it had paid off.

Inform your boss of your progress. Even if your boss isn't asking for in-person updates, send her periodic e-mails about the project. That way she can get a sense about whether there's any kind of problem you might not recognize, especially if you're new at the game. Better to have her course-correct than have the project later blow up in your face.

Keep close tabs on what other team members are doing. If you're working on a project with your peers, you must stay abreast of their efforts and make sure no one is screwing up, which could end up making *you* look bad in the long run. And what if someone isn't carrying his weight or is doing his part badly? You don't want to be a tattletale, but you can't ignore the problem either. One strategy is to suggest to your boss that everyone on the team meet with her and give a progress report. That way she'll see first-hand what's going on.

As you progress in your career, you'll have projects where you supervise team members, and you'll want to inspire the best from them. Peggy Schmidt, an independent college counselor in Silicon Valley, supervises students as they apply to schools. Her advice: "Get a handle on what your team's strengths and weaknesses are. If you know what to expect in advance, you can modify how you work with a particular team member—for instance, what incentives or parameters are likely to produce results. People are surprisingly candid about their work habits."

She also feels that people are more invested in completing a task if they have the autonomy of selecting days and times for turning in work as long as those deadlines fit into the larger picture.

Leave room at the end, says Lili Root, to "sprinkle on some fairy dust." Always plan to finish a day early or, at the very least, a few hours early. This allows you to step back, look at your finished project with fresh eyes, and tweak it if necessary. It can also give you time to add a magic touch or two.

{ Develop a Golden Gut }

At one point in my career, the magazine company I worked for was sold, without warning, to a large European corporation that took over with all the aplomb of a blowtorch. Management treated my staff and me as if we were summer interns who were just learning the business, asked zero questions about U.S. consumers, and immediately redid the entire magazine, with a young guy on the business side supervising all the layouts.

It was a terribly unsettling experience, one of the worst I've ever been through professionally. Every day meant new changes and new instructions to follow. I felt worried about my own career but also concerned about all the turmoil and uncertainty my staff was going thorough. Fortunately, about five months later, I was offered a job as editor in chief of another magazine at a terrific company, and I fled the scene with just a few singe marks on my butt. Yet I don't regret the time I spent in those stressful, unpredictable conditions—because it was there that I learned to listen to my gut.

I'd always respected my gut, but I'd never put it to work the way I did during that time. At first I didn't even see how much I was relying on it. I did know that since the ground underneath me was shifting every day, I needed to do my best to anticipate what might be coming next so my staff and I wouldn't be caught off guard. I found myself saying things to my managing editor such as "Let's do *a*, because *b* will happen and we'll be ready." Or "Don't do *c*—it will only create problems tomorrow." My decisions turned out to be right on. One day as my managing editor and I were strategizing, she narrowed her eyes and asked, "How do you *know* all this stuff?"

At that moment I realized that for the past few weeks I'd been paying heed to my intuition on an almost primal level. And it was helping save my ass, big-time. It was as if I were in a survival-training camp and I had no choice but to use my instincts. Later, after I was ensconced at my new job and had caught my breath, I analyzed what I'd been doing so I could always have those skills to fall back on. Since then I've relied on them through thick and thin.

It's never too soon to begin developing your gut. Here are the tricks that have served me best.

Know how your gut likes to talk to you. Vowing to trust your gut won't do you any good if you can't tell when it's sending you a message. You have to learn to tune in. For many people, me included, a gut reaction is just that—a rumbling feeling in my stomach. A gut reaction, however, may not actually occur in your *gut.* I've heard some people say that they've learned to pay attention when their pulse pounds or they feel a tingle all over. (A *Vanity Fair* writer once remarked that when Tina Brown was the editor, she knew an article was right if her nipples got hard when she read it!) You might not even have a physical reaction: perhaps you just have a niggling sense in your mind that something's really good or really off. Doesn't matter how it occurs. What's key is to begin to note when you feel different in some way and ask yourself *why.*

If you're not sure if certain sensations really mean anything, keep track of them and see if you can validate them later. Let's say that when you leave dinner with a friend one night, you end up with a nervous feeling in your stomach on the drive home. When you arrive at your place, write down your impressions. What could have happened during the night that made you feel that way? Was there something subtle about your friend's behavior that suggested she was troubled though not admitting to it? Did she arrive seeming that way, or did her behavior shift during the meal? Later, if she confesses to a personal problem or admits that you pulled a move that upset her, you'll have an idea that your tummy was definitely talking to you that night.

Just shut up. Even when you learn to trust your gut, you may sometimes not hear when it's signaling you. The secret is to listen. One of the smartest, most intuitive women I've come to know from writing mysteries (and I love the fact that she is now a great friend) is Barbara Butcher, the chief of staff and director of Forensic Sciences Training Program at the New York City Office of Chief Medical Examiner. Barbara spent years working crime scenes as a medical death investigator, investigating 5,500 death scenes and 680 homicides. It was at those death scenes, she says, that she learned to develop a golden gut.

"Everything we need to know is around us for the taking as long as we are truly taking it in," she says. "As a death investigator I learned to open my senses to what was around me and abandon preconceived notions of what I was going to find. I learned early on that if I was told that I was going to investigate a homicide, then that is what I would find, but if I reminded myself that I was going to investigate the cause of death, then I would find the truth."

Her advice for honing your gut instincts? "Take your hands off your ears and put them over your mouth," Butcher says. "Learn to listen, see, smell, and absorb everything around you without speaking your thoughts first. If you practice these skills, you will get all the signals you need to be able to trust your instincts."

Trust your gut but teach it first. Your gut is directing you based on what it knows, so be sure it's well informed about what matters. Experts who swear they make gut decisions often have years of training, and their response is an automatic one based on their reserves of knowledge.

A few months after I began at *Cosmo*, I took a bunch of mocked-up covers out to a shopping mall, showed them to young women, and asked how they liked them. Based on all the covers I'd done over the years, I was pretty sure the women would automatically pick one particular cover because the model was gorgeous and the background color was a yummy shade of yellow. But before they gave their answer, woman after woman asked me the following question: "What month is it for?" Until then, I hadn't realized how important the *seasonality* of the cover clothes was to *Cosmo* readers. Knowing that enabled me to better use my gut when picking cover shots.

Connect the dots. You just saw two coworkers whispering furtively in the hallway. Is something up that you should be concerned about? Maybe—though it *could* be that one of them has hooked up with a guy in accounting and is simply sharing the steamy details with her office pal. Your boss didn't make eye contact with you when she passed you in the hall. Is she annoyed with you? Maybe. But then again, she might just be having a bad morning or got reamed by *her* boss earlier that day.

Little moments don't always mean anything, but sometimes they do—though it may not be exactly what you think. So how do you know what to pay attention to and what to ignore? You play "connect the dots." If one thing catches your eye in an odd way, make a note but don't go insane with concern. But if two things relating to the same person or same situation grab your attention, it's time to sit up. In your mind, run through a list of things they could suggest. Ask yourself how it might relate to you and whether you should be concerned.

Guard against your gut's biggest enemy. Even if you've learned how to tune in to your gut, there may be times when you end up stupidly ignoring it. Why? Because other people pressure you to—directly or indirectly.

I've seen the potential for that kind of thing to happen with magazine covers. When you're a magazine editor, sometimes a cover shoot comes in and for some reason just isn't strong enough. Maybe the clothes didn't work or the celebrity felt awkward (or was hungover!). Your gut will tell you you've got a loser on your hands, but you feel pressure not to say the word "reshoot." People *hate* that word. It's difficult enough to coordinate the celebrity's and photographer's schedules the first time, let alone for a reshoot. But you can't allow your gut to be silenced.

This happened with the second Kim Kardashian cover we did at *Cosmo*. In order to make this cover look different, we had decided to shoot Kim in jeans and a bathing suit top and mist her body with water, even wetting her hair a little. I loved the idea—until I saw the results. Kim was her gorgeous self, but she looked in the photos as if she'd been hosed down with Wesson oil instead of water. It was like a *Maxim* shoot run amuck. My gut was rumbling big-time, and when I started talking about needing to do it again, everybody turned ashen. But it was totally the right call.

We reshot Kim in a salmon-colored minidress made of sweatshirt fabric, and the cover was the biggest seller of the year.

Know that you shouldn't necessarily take your gut at face value. That rumble or knot is telling you something, but it may not be the obvious thing. In a *Cosmo* interview, Laura Day, the best-selling author of *Practical Intuition*, pointed out something I've found to be true. "When you have an instinct," she says, "it doesn't mean you should blindly follow it. It's a message that you should examine the situation a little bit more."

{ *Always* Ask for What You Want }

I probably don't have to tell you that it's vital to ask for what you want. You know that, right? Whenever I give a career talk to a woman's group, I stress the value of asking, and lots of women always nod their heads in agreement.

The reason I think that there's so much vigorous head bobbing isn't simply that I'm telling them something they know. It's because they're trying to drive home the point to themselves. Women realize that they should ask—and ask for *more*—but so often we don't do it. According to a study by Linda Babcock, a professor of economics at Carnegie Mellon University's John Heinz III School of Public Policy and Management, men initiate negotiations between four and eight times more often than women. It's no surprise, then, that in another Babcock study, the women received average annual starting salaries that were 8.5 percent lower than the men's.

Why are we such scaredy-cats when it comes to asking? We're afraid that if we ask, it will seem as if we're overstepping our bounds. The other person might get mad, or stop liking us. If someone's offering us a job, we may even fear that if we ask for a higher salary than the amount being named, the offer might be snatched back from us. We may also hesitate because we lack experience in asking and it makes us self-conscious. "Guys," says a business friend of mine, "grow up calling for the ball."

But if there's one thing I've come to accept with certainty, as both an employee and a boss, it's this: *the squeaky wheel definitely gets the grease.* One of the most important things you must learn to do in your career is ask—*in the right way.* You must ask for money, responsibility, opportunities, title changes, benefits, bonuses, and perks. And don't worry about the other person becoming ticked off. Bosses or prospective bosses may seem annoyed that you've asked, but they expect the best employees and job candidates to do it. They will get over their annoyance soon enough. And trust me, you will be glad you spoke up. The actress, comedian, writer, and producer Whitney Cummings put it perfectly when we interviewed her for *Cosmo*: "I learned this magic trick at an early age. If you ask for something you usually get it."

And the sooner you learn to do it, the better, because gains that seem small at one point can actually have a compound effect over time. Consider this amazing statistic presented in a 2009 study by Michelle Marks of the School of Management, George Mason University, and Crystal Harold of Fox School of Management, Temple University: assuming a 5 percent pay increase each year over a forty-year career, a twenty-five-year-old employee who starts at $50,000 would earn $634,198 less than an employee starting at $55,000 by the time she reaches the age of sixty-five. And it's not just money that is compounded. Let's say you ask your boss if you can travel to an annual industry convention, and she says yes. You end up making some key contacts who down the road introduce you to others. *That's* a compound effect.

Does reading this section make you feel slightly nauseated? If the answer is yes, it may be because you're already established in your career and realize that you've missed more than a couple of chances to ask. But it's not too late to learn how to do it. Let me tell you a funny story from my own life. After I was tapped to be the editor in chief of *McCall's* magazine and had accepted the job with a rough idea of what the salary package would be (bad move on my part), a meeting was set up for me to discuss the details with the top two executives in the company. We were going to gather in a small lounge on the executive floor of the company that owned the magazine.

There were two things I knew for sure about that upcoming meeting. One was that it would be nerve-wracking. I'd be negotiating with two powerful men who had far more experience doing that sort of thing than I did. The other was that I probably wouldn't be brilliant at handling the situation. By that point in my career I'd come to see that if you don't ask, you don't get, but I didn't yet feel comfortable speaking up and declaring exactly what I wanted.

So I did something that even to this day shocks me: I talked my accountant, Bob, who'd always preached to me about the value of asking, into coming with me and acting as my *agent*. You see, my husband was in the TV news business at the time, and like other newscasters he had an agent who handled salary discussions on his behalf. I thought, why not steal a page from that playbook? I explained to one of the executives in advance that my accountant would be joining me at the meeting so that I could review the numbers with him, never revealing the exact role I intended for Bob to play.

Bob seemed a little nervous that day, though I could hardly blame him. He took a ton of notes at the meeting, working with what seemed to be endless sheaves of paper. I saw the other two men exchange a dismissive look once—they clearly thought Bob was in over his head. But Bob asked great questions and pointed out a few gaps in the deal that the execs acknowledged and agreed to fix. After about thirty minutes of going through the numbers, one of the executives said, "Why don't we give you two a few minutes to review everything in private. We'll pop back in afterward."

They returned about fifteen minutes later. "All set?" one of the guys asked. I could tell by their manner that they thought things were going to be wrapped up shortly.

"Well, we've read everything over," Bob announced. The two men nodded, obviously pleased. "And now we're ready to negotiate."

I'll never forget that moment. I swear I saw the two executives' jaws drop. They hadn't seen that coming at all. Over the next fifteen minutes Bob explained how "we" would like to see the deal enhanced, and he dickered back and forth with the men. I ended up leaving with a package much more lucrative than the original offer.

I told that story a while back to several young women who worked for me, stressing to them how essential it was for them to ask for what they want in life. When I finished, one of them wailed, "*We* need a Bob."

Unfortunately, only people in certain fields—like TV news, acting, and sports—generally have agents. You have to learn to "be your own Bob." Asking is a skill you can acquire, and it actually becomes easier the more you do it. But as I said before, you have to ask in the right way. Here are my favorite "BYOB" strategies for getting what you want.

Never try to talk yourself out of asking. Because asking is such a bitch, we sometimes convince ourselves that there's really no need to do it. We think, "If my boss had the money to pay me more, he would" or "They know I want that promotion. My work speaks for itself."

But guess what? Your work *doesn't* speak for itself. You're the one who needs to do the talking. With money, for instance, your boss is under pressure from his or her boss to lowball you, so unless you speak up, you won't receive more. And when a better job opens up in your department or area, it's not your boss's job to read your mind and know that you'd kill for it. In fact, employers often wait for people to go after a job as a way of seeing how hungry they are. Recently someone told me that a former employee was really upset because I hadn't promoted her into a key position. But she'd never said boo to me about it. And to me that was proof she didn't have enough gumption for the job.

Make sure you deserve what you're asking for. It just makes it easier. A few weeks after I told the group of young women the Bob story, one of them went to her boss at the magazine and said she wanted a fifteen-thousand-dollar raise. She had recently been given a big new assignment that involved not only editing a series of special sections but also promoting them through other platforms. Well, I was touched that she'd been inspired, but there was one little problem: *she hadn't done anything yet to deserve a raise*.

You shouldn't ask when you have nothing to show yet. A few months' worth of doing more than you've been told to do doesn't necessarily deserve a raise or promotion. Not only are you unlikely to score anything, but you'll also undermine your credibility for when you're really ready.

If you *do* have plenty to show, pull all the info together and be sure of your facts and stats. Profits are up in your area? Great, but by how much exactly? You don't necessarily have to go in with a PowerPoint presentation, but have a fact sheet with you and a copy for your boss to follow.

Know the ZOPA. ZOPA stands for "zone of possible agreement." It's a term I first heard from a woman who'd attended business school at Wharton, and it reflects a strategy that's recommended for negotiating. When you head in to ask for something, you need to be aware of the range of what will satisfy you—in terms of money, perks, and opportunities. Knowing what your range is in advance allows you to respond effectively and not settle for something that you'll later regret.

But here's the other half of that strategy: you also have to have a sense of what the *other* person's range is. That helps point you to what "middle" or zone the two of you could meet in. I think a lot of women get so nervous or focused on their own needs that they don't estimate what numbers and terms the other person has in mind. And that can lead to trouble.

Consider what happened to a former colleague of mine who was up for a job as a deputy editor position at a new magazine. This woman, let's call her Allison, had taken time off from her career to be with her young kids, and it was proving tricky to reenter the field. The job would be perfect for Allison, and she wanted it badly. Toward the end of the interview, the conversation started to skirt the topic of salary, and Allison announced the amount she was looking for (a no-no, which I'll talk about later), based on what she thought was the going rate for a deputy editor. The editor in chief nearly flinched. She said they were paying significantly less than that amount. Allison felt put off by that info—she thought she was being taken advantage of—and realized later that she'd probably shown it. From that moment on, the conversation never got back on track.

Later, after the job went to someone else, Allison found out through the industry grapevine that the magazine was being done on the cheap as a kind of an experiment and no one had been insulting her by throwing out such a low number. Though the salary wasn't what she had envisioned, she could have leveraged the job into a better-paying one later. Not knowing the ZOPA cost her.

So how can you figure out both numbers—yours and theirs? Use the Internet to determine a ballpark idea of what comparable jobs pay. Up for a raise? If your company always gives 3 percent merit raises, you might be able to nab one higher, but something like 12 percent is probably *waaaay* out of the question.

To determine the bottom amount you could accept, figure out your fixed living costs—your rent or mortgage, commuting fees, food, clothes and accessories, and quality-of-life costs, such as vacation travel. But regardless of what you could live on, aim high. Take the number you think you could snag based on the job and your skills and pad it, knowing you'll probably be negotiating.

Be clear and concise—and leave the emo at the door. With your prep work done, you're ready to ask. If you are angling for a raise and/or promotion at your current job, don't ambush your boss. Set up a meeting with him instead, and be sure to do it far in advance of raise time (if you do it too close to the day raises are announced, your boss may have already submitted a number for you). Get right to the point. Perhaps you've been the assistant manager of a restaurant for a year and business is up 20 percent. You've suggested some changes to the menu that worked and also found clever, inexpensive ways to promote the restaurant through social media. Here's what you could say to your boss: "I love my job here. I appreciate all your support with my efforts, and it's been exciting to see the results. As you know, business is up twenty percent over last year at this time [hand her the memo sheet now]. I'd like you to consider changing my title to [fill in the blank] and taking my salary up to [fill in blank]. I'd really like to show you what I could do in this new role."

If you are interviewing for a new job and have just been offered it, let the *interviewer* name the salary number. It could be higher than what you had in mind. And then, no matter what figure the other person names, *always ask for more.* (This is generally true with raises, too, unless they hit your mark.) That's because a prospective boss is almost certainly lowballing you, hoping to take the smallest bite possible out of his budget. Let's say, for instance, that a prospective employer has just offered you $50,000. And hey, $50,000 is actually in your zone. But don't accept it. Instead tell him, "I'm very pleased to be offered the job. I would love to work here, and I think I have a lot of to contribute. But I was hoping for $60,000." (That number allows him to find something in the middle that could still make you happy.) Then sit there with your lips tightly zipped. There's a more-than-decent chance that the person will make a counteroffer. If he says, "I can do that," great. If he offers $53,000, give it one more try. Say, "Is there any chance you can do a bit better?" He may say he'll have to get back to you. Remind him you'd love the job and tough it out (a frozen margarita that night can help!). When he comes back with $55,000 the next day, it will all be worth it. And if thcy insist you name a number? Be both realistic but generous to yourself, and add that you're open to discussion.

Give the person across from you a nod. One nice (and important touch) when you're asking your boss for something is to acknowledge the issues he's facing at the moment. It's easy to become so wrapped up in taking care of your own needs that you don't consider what's on the other person's mind. And generally what's on his mind is "What about *me*?" He's wondering how your request for more money or more time working from home or whatever is going to affect *him*.

Try saying something such as "I know you've got many challenges right now." It helps if the other person senses that you're not seeing things only from your own perspective. But be sure not to look like you're caving.

Do not mention your personal woes when asking. Trust me, an employer doesn't care about your college loans or the fact that your landlord just jacked up your rent. All discussion should center on why professionally you deserve what you're asking for and what great things you'll be doing in the months ahead.

Know that asking is always easier than asking again. Sometimes women are so timid about fully stating what they want that they make their request too vague. Then, when they're displeased with what they receive, they have to try again and this time clarify their request. And it's much harder to get something the second time around. The other player views the situation as water under the bridge. Avoid ever having to ask again.

A few months ago I bumped into a friend and business associate of mine, Carol Fitzgerald, founder and president of Bookreporter, at the registration desk of a luxury hotel in Miami. The desk clerk had just explained that Fitzgerald's room was ready and was about to print out the key. In a sense, when you register at a hotel, it's an asking moment. If you've booked a room, they give it to you but some rooms are better than others.

Right then, I saw Fitzgerald do something very intriguing. She lightly tapped her credit card on the counter five or six times and asked the desk clerk nicely. "Am I going to really like this room? Or do you think I'll be down here ten minutes from now trying to change it for another one?" The desk clerk smiled, typed some things into her computer, and then said, "Why don't we put you in this room instead?"

Fitzgerald made it clear up front that she wanted the best room available—no need to traipse back downstairs later and attempt to ask for a better one.

Anticipate the negatives in advance and deal with them on the front end. That's something I learned later than I would have liked, but once I caught on, I never stopped using it.

Here's why. If the other side comes back to you having learned about the negatives, it puts you on the defensive. You can still dig yourself out, but it's tougher. Plus, once they've considered potential problems, their minds may be made up. You don't want them to go there without your framing the situation.

This trick came in handy when we were negotiating to get Adele on the cover of *Cosmo*. As an artist she burst onto the scene in a huge way in 2011, and once I learned more about her, I was sure our readers would love to see her on the December issue.

Adele hadn't done any U.S. covers yet, so I doubted that we'd have trouble booking her. Wrong. Though Adele's publicist responded enthusiastically to my entertainment editor, there was one hitch: Adele was booked to do the March 2012 cover of a competitive magazine. The publicist said he would have to go back to that magazine and make sure it was okay for Adele to do us in advance. I knew in my bones that the other magazine would demand to go first.

Of course, there had been plenty of times when that competitor had followed us with cover girls. But if Adele's people came back to us with "Sorry, we can't," we'd seem defensive if we suddenly said, "Oh, but they *often* follow us." The decision would have been made, and they probably wouldn't want to change it.

So here's what we did. I had my entertainment editor make a list of all the times this competitor had followed us with cover subjects and send it to Adele's reps before they went back to our competitor. The entertainment editor told the rep, "As you can see, they often follow us, so it shouldn't be a problem." That way if the competitor said they didn't want to let Adele pose for us, her management would have viewed *them* as being difficult. I don't know what happened in the conversation; all I know is that Adele posed for the December cover.

Here's what you do when they say no. Never scurry away with your tail between your legs. Remember what Bob said: "Now we're ready to negotiate." *You want to walk away with some-*

thing. If you don't get the raise you want, ask for a title change, an extra week of vacation, the chance to attend a key event, a spot bonus, or another review in six months.

The trick is to have your backups clearly in mind so you can bring them up at the right moment. That's what comic Amy Schumer did. She'd been on the short list to be one of the four comics who wrote the Charlie Sheen roast for Comedy Central. In the end the committee decided not to go with her. What did she do? "I told them, 'Well, can I be *on* the show, then?' " *Done!*

{ Success Style: 10 Easy Steps }

A photo editor I used to work with was a fantastic but obsessive dresser who sometimes went home to change at midday if he felt that his outfit wasn't really working. He told me that one of the most embarrassing fashion moments he'd ever experienced was when he was walking down the street in head-to-toe Gucci, thinking his ensemble was perfectly *fabulous*, and two male fashionistas approached him coming the other way. He sensed he was about to get a nod of approval from them, but instead they shook their heads in unison, and one of them exclaimed, "No, no, *no!*"

Fortunately, most of us are never going to have strangers commenting on our workday style that way, but how you look really does matter. People will judge you on your appearance, sometimes consciously, sometimes without realizing it. The standards will vary, too. In some fields, it's all about how stylish you are, in others it's how *un*stylish, and still in others it's how well you manage to look professional without your clothes seeming to say a peep.

Here are ten style strategies to follow in most work situations.

1. It's absolutely true what they say: dress for the job you aspire to. There are a lot of workplaces where you can dress casually or even totally grunge. But just because everyone in your pay grade is doing so with management's blessing, it doesn't mean you should. How does your boss dress? That's who you should be modeling yourself after, not your peers. Even pay attention to what your boss's boss wears. And just because your workplace supports casual Friday doesn't mean you have to adhere to it. I never, ever have.

2. Invest in a killer handbag. Yes, a designer bag if you can swing it, and if not, something great from a place such as Coach or a bit pricier, such as Tory Burch. If you can't afford a pricey bag at the moment, purchase a good-looking budget one but not a cheap purse that has just any logo on it. Those generally look lame. (The brands are meaningless, so why the logo?) Ariel Lawrence, a fabulous stylist I've worked with who has both TV and private clients, says that you can also find great designer bags cheaply on eBay or even at resale stores. There's also the website Bag Borrow or Steal, where you can rent a designer bag by the week. It's not very cost-effective, but it can make sense for a week when you've got a bunch of important interviews lined up.

3. Buy great-looking shoes, too. Most women you interact with professionally will notice your shoes. And though guys *say* they don't notice, on a subliminal level they're certainly picking up on things such as run-down heels and scuff marks, and even whether you seem really pulled together. The great news about shoes, as Lawrence points out, is that companies such as Guess and 9 West knock off designer shoes almost instantly, so check out what's being shown in magazines and online and then buy the knockoffs.

4. If you're building a new work wardrobe because you're right out of college or entering a new field, devise a clothing budget and plan for yourself. Start by purchasing the absolutely best classic and interchangeable basics (pants, skirts, dresses, jackets) you can afford. Add trendy accessories and tops at lower price points because those don't have to hold up as well—and in those categories, inexpensive is less likely to translate as cheap.

Lawrence's suggestion for a starter wardrobe: a black dress, a fitted black jacket, black pants, a black skirt, a camel-colored skirt, a white blouse, a trendy-looking cardigan in a color (red could be good, for instance), several cool, inexpensive blouses (from places such as H&M or Zara) that pick up or work with the color of the cardigan and will go with your pants and skirts. For shoes, go for black heels and a pair of colored ones (they will make one of your all-black outfits look totally fab). Then build from there.

5. Buy clothes that fit you. Clothes that don't fit right or flatter your shape look unprofessional, and that's the biggest mistake that Lawrence sees women making. "Unfortunately, saleswomen often lie to get the business," she says. "They'll encourage you to buy a certain skirt, for instance, and though the skirt is cute, it's the wrong length for your height or makes your hips look too big. If possible, shop with a great friend who'll be honest. The main thing you're looking for are the styles that really work with your shape. I had a client who wanted to buy this Michael Kors maxi dress, and I had to remind her, 'You're *five two*.' Once you've nailed down the clothing shapes that flatter your body shape, it's easier to shop on your own."

From there you can even begin to develop a fab signature look that you're known and remembered for in a great way. I love how *Morning Joe* cohost Mika Brzezinski has made a signature look of gorgeous, sleeveless shifts that show off her amazing guns!

6. Do not wear a puffer coat to work in winter. Okay, if it's really, really cold, that's one thing. But if you want to look professional, you need a classic coat in black or camel. For warmer weather or climates, Lawrence swears by a khaki trench.

7. Get a serious haircut. You should have a cut that says you mean business, that you do more in the morning than roll out of bed and toss your strands out of your eyes. Through word of mouth, find a good salon (many salons offer free cuts by young, upcoming stylists), and if it doesn't give you a cut that's super, go someplace else the next time. In many workplaces—particularly anyplace that's creative— you can get away with wearing your hair long if you want. Just make sure it's trimmed of split ends, conditioned, and never straggly-looking. If you work in a conservative environment, you probably shouldn't wear it longer than just below your shoulders. It screams coed or boho.

8. Have your eyebrows professionally shaped. After looking at tons of pictures of models and celebrities over the years, I realize how important good brows are to making your face look gorgeous and your appearance pulled together. (If you don't believe me, go online and compare pictures of Angelina Jolie now to when she was married to Billy Bob. People thought the vial of blood around her neck was all wrong, but that's nothing compared to the eyebrows she had then.) Women who do their own brows often shape them incorrectly without even realizing it. (Hint: Do yours bear any resemblance to commas, hockey sticks, or sperm? They *shouldn't*.) So find a salon—via word of mouth is the best way—that will do a good job (the one I love in New York City is Sania's Brow Bar; Sania is masterful!). It's worth the price to have them done professionally. Warning: Don't let someone make your brows too thin, because overplucked eyebrows often don't grow back. If someone scalps you, find another salon. And once you have the perfect brows, pencil them every day with a Shobha eye pencil (www.myshobha.com). It's a fantastic tool.

9. Develop a signature look with your makeup, too. That doesn't mean you can't experiment and have fun, especially at night, but calling a look your own really adds clout. I always found Kim Kardashian striking in her photos, but when I had lunch with her in Manhattan I realized how jaw-dropping attractive she is in person. Okay, she's got great hair, great eyes, great bone structure, but it's also about her makeup. I especially love what she does with her mouth: nude or pink lipstick with lots of gloss on top. It's not right for everyone, but on her it's totally arresting and you never forget it. Whatever you choose as your trademark doesn't have to be complicated. One of my favorite editors in chief wears just one item of makeup as far as I can tell: red lipstick. But it looks awesome and is very much *her* look. As for fragrance, I'd worry less about finding your signature scent and focus on being very, very subtle. A lot of people hate being subjected to fragrance in the workplace. And it can really put a damper on a job interview or meeting.

10. Don't hesitate to dazzle. In some jobs you still have to dress conservatively. But to me there is nothing more mind-numbingly boring than a matching jacket and skirt, particularly if it's navy blue, and I think there's plenty of wiggle room in most fields today. If you look fantastic and fashion forward, you'll feel more confident and people will notice and remember you.

{ Why You Should Get in Touch with Your Bitch Envy }

There is an interesting phenomenon that sometimes happens when you're finding your way in a career and trying to make your mark. You come into contact with a chick—maybe she sits a few cubicles away or down the hall—who can only be described as a bitch. She brownnoses the boss in a gag-worthy way he fails to see through, hogs the limelight at meetings, and sneakily secures little perks and opportunities that no one else manages to score. And it annoys the freaking hell out of you.

I first had that kind of experience when I was working in the articles department at *Glamour*. About two years after I moved into the department as a writer, the articles editor who ran the department hired a recent college grad—I'll call her Jackie—as her editorial assistant. The young women who worked as junior editors and writers in the department were all generally nice and thoughtful, and everyone graciously welcomed Jackie when she arrived. But it was soon clear our new coworker was a different type of player. Jackie was loud, brash, and utterly intent on getting everything she wanted.

There were two things in particular that I found irksome about her behavior. Right after college she had attended a fancy six-week intensive publishing program, and not only had it left her with this smug sense of entitlement, but she'd also met tons of cool, dynamic people there who were all now in entry-level positions like her. She was constantly dropping their names and where they worked and where they'd be having drinks that night. She made it sound as though they were the Bloomsbury group.

The other annoying thing: She soon convinced her boss to let her try her hand at editing articles, something that I, as a writer, wasn't even doing yet. And to make it worse, she always provided every-one in the department with a verbal play-by-play of her efforts—"I can't right now," she'd say. "I have to edit this *huge* health feature we're doing this month." How freaking pushy, I remember thinking. Clearly her boss didn't know how to say no to her.

Years passed before I saw what truly bugged me about Jackie. Yes, she was unpleasant to be around, but the main source of my ir-ritation was that she was doing stuff that deep down I knew *I* should be doing. And that's the thing you need to recognize about the work bitch. Part of why she galls you may be that you secretly *envy* her. She's making moves and winning points in ways that you wish you could pull off yourself.

Envy can seem like such a nasty feeling that you may find your-self trying to squelch it when it rears its ugly head or even refram-ing it. But envy has lots of benefits if you acknowledge it and use it right. First, you have to redirect envy—away from the other person and back to yourself. Instead of telling yourself, "I can't stand that bitch," realize that deep down what you may be thinking is "Damn, I want some of what *she's* got."

In my own case, I sucked at networking. I was envious of all those contacts Jackie had and how she used them. And I wanted to be editing. I just hadn't had the nerve to ask.

So if there's a bitch in your midst, instead of hating on her, start taking notes. Do you wish you had some of her skills, nerve, gumption, and butt-kissing talent? Do you secretly admire her ability to go big or go home, ingratiate herself, speak up, or massage the boss's ego? Envy can be a good thing if you flip it around and see what it's telling you about yourself.

Something I need to add: This book is loaded with tips on learning what you need to know, promoting yourself, going big, breaking the rules, and even engaging in the right *kind* of butt kissing. Read them and use them. But being gutsy doesn't have to translate, as it did with Jackie, into being tough to be around. It's good to have your coworkers' respect even if they don't always like you. That prevents them from trying to undermine you and helps creates allies for down the road. Some good rules of thumb:

- **Go after what you want but not if it clearly belongs to someone else.**

- **Dazzle your boss but don't make your colleagues listen to the details.** And avoid humble bragging, which involves showing off while couching it as some sort of self-deprecation. (I.e., this is a tweet that showed up on the @humblebrag hall of fame: "What the heck does one wear to a meeting at the Style network? Seriously.")

- **Go big but not if it means throwing someone under the bus.** One way to judge how colleagues view you is to pay attention to their interactions with you. If they exclude you from conversations and group lunches, if they often seem hostile, it may be because your actions have become galling rather than simply gutsy.

{ 4 Tips for Masterfully Managing Your Boss }

I have had both good bosses and bad bosses in my career, which I'm sure is true for many people. There was, for instance, Art Cooper, who went on to become the legendary editor of *GQ* and who once sent me to interview Helen Gurley Brown because he said he could picture me as editor of *Cosmopolitan* one day (good boss!). And then there was the boss who asked me to come by her apartment one Saturday and, once I arrived, seemed to be hinting that I try a threesome with her and the smoking-jacketed married man she was seeing (ugh, bad boss!).

Within days of starting to work for someone, you will have a visceral sense of whether you've signed on with a good boss or bad boss. Does your boss listen? Give clear instructions and challenge you to really go for it? Inspire you? Praise what you do well? Critique you fairly? If yes, good for you! This is going to make it easier for you to succeed. But if you've been handed a bad boss, don't despair. A bad boss can be a ticket for success as well. Of course, it will be tough to achieve much of anything if your boss has created a toxic work setting or is failing at *her* job, and the only real rule to follow in that kind of situation is to escape as quickly as you can—go to a new department, new company, whatever. But if your bad boss is simply a lardass, that can be a real asset for you because she may turn over all sorts of projects to you that will advance your skills and reputation.

So at the end of the day, it doesn't matter if your boss is good or bad, as long as you end up with the opportunities and credit you need. You just have to be smart about how you handle the situation.

Let's start, then, with the premise that you are working for either a good boss or a good bad boss. I'm going to tell you four little things you need to know to manage your boss effectively and gain all you can from the relationship. At this point you may be thinking "Wait, isn't doing a great job enough?" Unfortunately, it isn't. Bosses are human, and little things can get under their skin and rub them the wrong way.

1. Your boss has both *sweet spots* and *hot spots,* and you need to determine what they are. Sweet spots are the little things that he responds to positively, such as punctuality, fast turnaround, or frequent updates. Hit those sweet spots as much as you can. Of course, it's a given that you are doing your job well. But seemingly little things matter to bosses, too.

His *hot spots* are the behaviors that seriously piss him off, such as tardiness or long-winded answers or even something minor, such as your wearing your iPod at your desk. Avoid touching those hot spots.

How do you know what his sweet spots and hot spots are? Dr. Mark Howell, a New York psychotherapist who has helped me a lot in my research over the years, says that "you have to play the scientist" in the landscape of your office, gathering the data you need. "First," he says, listen to the gossip around your workplace. That can tell you so much. If there are negative aspects to your boss, you'll learn about them if you pay attention to what people say."

Sometimes you have to listen between the lines, though, because coworkers may be too nervous to be blunt. Note their tone of voice and loaded-sounding phrases. A comment such as "I wouldn't go in there just now" can tell you your boss gets moody or difficult at certain times of the day or when he hears bad news.

Next, says Dr. Howell, make an effort to register when your boss is pleased *and* displeased." For instance, does she just stare at you when you walk in at 9:30 A.M.? That probably means she wants you in earlier.

You can learn a lot just by paying attention to comments your boss makes about others. I had a boss who on several occasions mentioned receiving a handwritten note from someone. This kind of gesture was important to her and she was sharing that information indirectly.

Once you've gathered your data, act accordingly. If all this seems like common sense, trust me, it isn't. One of the biggest mistakes I see people make in the workplace is ignoring both a boss's sweet spots and hot spots or behaving based on what their own needs are or how they acted with a former boss. Your boss isn't you, and the same things might not matter to her. And no two bosses are alike. In fact, what might be a sweet spot for one boss can be a hot spot for another. For instance, some bosses like you to hover; others hate it.

One of my annoying traits as a boss is that when I ask for info, I tend to want it ridiculously soon. Anyone who has worked for me and has taken the time, as Howell suggests, to register what pleases and displeases me would discover this easily. Because if I've asked you for something and haven't heard back in a day or two, I will ask again. And that should be an oops moment for you—as in "Oops, I should have given her an update." But it's shocking to me the number of young staffers I've had to pester with e-mails and phone calls, asking "Do you have that info yet?"

When I look at the people I've promoted, they're always the ones I never had to chase down for information but rather who were always bursting into my office with news.

Unfortunately, sometimes as much as you play the scientist, you may not see a boss's hot spot until she calls you into her office and chews you out. That happened to me with Art Cooper. I was his senior editor at *Family Weekly*, and I sensed that overall I was doing a good job. But after lavishing praise on me in my first review, Art shocked me by adding a criticism. He said I had "a tendency to dig in my heels." You won't believe what I did right then and there. I started to say, "But it's *not* digging in my heels. I just always want you to know why I made a certain decision." Fortunately, at twenty-eight, I'd learned a few things, and I shut my trap after "But." Then, a second later, I told him, "I understand. I will definitely correct that in the future."

And that brings me to:

2. Bosses really want to be heard. They want to know that you're on board with their mission and are going to execute it. Listen carefully. Listen, too, between the lines. Pick up on any recurring phrases. Nod when your boss is talking. Take notes. Seem enthusiastic about the mission.

When your boss makes suggestions about your work activities, follow up on them. In discussions, make references to his mission for your area or department. (As you move up the ladder and have people reporting to you, make sure they know your boss's mission, too.) When your boss does something nice for you, don't simply smile, assuming you deserved it. Act grateful, write a note. (Gratitude can also help prevent a boss from feeling threatened.)

What if you disagree with your boss on a particular decision? First ask yourself if you think there's a chance you can change his mind because if the answer is no, it may not be worth the effort to try. But if you sense that he will—maybe because he simply hasn't digested all the relevant info—and you don't want him to make a bad decision, choose your words carefully. Avoid using blunt phrases such as "I disagree," or suggesting he's wrong. Cast the situation in terms of simply offering more info. You could say something like "I hear what you're saying. But can I show you some additional information? It throws an interesting light on the situation." That will allow him to reconsider based on new information rather than having to admit he was wrong. If he doesn't seem interested, back off. You beat a dead horse at your own peril.

3. Bosses want your loyalty. Do not be seen whispering with coworkers—your boss will assume you're talking about her. Never go around her. Do not, under any circumstances, violate a confidence. If you are looking for another job, be as discreet as you possibly can. Don't allow a friendship to develop between you and your boss. That situation can be loaded with land mines. If your boss confides details about her personal life, don't share back. So you don't seem impolite, bring up a juicy article you just read or a show you watched. This makes it seem like you're dishing.

4. Bosses like to have their butts kissed.

Sorry, but it's true. Let your boss know that you like her ideas, appreciate her support, and are excited to be in her presence. Be sincere by focusing on the things you really do like and/or respect. Years ago someone told me that certain staffers were concerned that I didn't realize that one of their colleagues was always trying to kiss my ass. I laughed. "Of course I know she's an ass kisser," I said. "And I appreciate the fact that she's smart enough to do it."

Special Advice for Dealing with a Boss Who Takes Over from Your Old One

Employees sometimes make the mistake of thinking that since they're already established in the company, the new boss is the one who has to prove herself, and that they're fairly well protected. *Wrong.* New bosses frequently have carte blanche to overhaul the department and get rid of anyone who doesn't appear to be on board.

Let a new boss know right away that you are excited to have her there. Look enthused about her mission when she shares it. (If you're not, fake it until you can find another job.) And—this is important—ask what you can do to help her to transition. That will carry a huge amount of weight with her.

{ How to Dazzle at a Meeting }

Not long after you start a job, you will probably be asked to attend your first meeting there. Meetings are a great opportunity for you to impress your boss and peers. But if you aren't prepared, you can also come across as a boob. I've probably held way over a thousand meetings in my career, and I've loved watching some of my staffers really strut their stuff in them. They've also been a perfect way to get a closer look at those on staff who don't report directly to me.

Yet unfortunately, for every person who's dazzled me at a meeting, there have been many more who have never volunteered a single solitary idea and have sat there with their jaws totally slack, as if I were up at the head of the table reading the instructions for installing a plasma-screen TV.

Never miss the chance to shine at a meeting. Meetings may sometimes seem very casual, and you may not even be called on to participate, but your boss is paying attention to how you perform. If you contribute and look engrossed, it will raise his opinion of you and may even lead to new assignments. If you do poorly, you will lose ground—and you may not be invited back.

Here are ten fail-proof strategies:

1. Be sure you know what the meeting's about. Reread the e-mail. If you are new, ask around to see what's generally expected, and come prepared.

2. Never be late—and get there early enough to grab a good seat. If you're not one of your boss's top people, don't sit right next to her like a big brownnose, but find a spot close enough to show you're delighted to be one of the participants.

3. Arrive with a game-on attitude. Seem enthused, excited about the agenda. This really sends a good message. When a promoted *Cosmo* staffer was suddenly included in a monthly meeting, I loved that she came in full makeup.

4. Always bring something to take notes with—your iPad or a pad and pencil. Turn your cell phone off. And I wouldn't think I'd have to say not to use your iPhone or BlackBerry during a meeting, but I've often seen people make that dumb mistake.

5. Lean in. Women sometimes come across as tentative at meetings. One reason for this: they don't belly up to the table. If you hang back, other participants may not hear you when you speak—or may even ignore your remarks because you don't seem fully engaged. The body language expert Janine Driver recommends that you sit on the first third of your chair during a meeting and lean in when you speak, indicating that you have something important you want to get across.

6. When you do have something to contribute, don't just blurt it out. Instead, lead into it with some kind of introductory statement. That helps grab people's attention. Pause a moment before continuing—you want to make sure people are looking your way and know you are about to speak. Otherwise, someone may trample over your idea verbally and you'll have to start again—awkwardly.

What kind of introductory comment works? If you're established in your job and feel comfortable with your boss, I think it's fine to gain the floor with a gutsy statement—such as "I have an idea that I think could save us at least twenty-five thousand dollars a year in shipping costs." But Andrea Kaplan, the head of Andrea Kaplan Public Relations and one of the most brilliant people I know at idea pitching, cautions about being that bold when you are first starting out. "Early in your career, part of what you're doing when you're first pitching ideas is gaining a confidence level," she says. "So you want to do everything possible to get a good response. If you announce, 'I have a great idea,' it puts too big a spotlight on you, and if everyone turns up their noses, you can feel deflated." Instead, she suggests making your intro statement a bit subtler, such as "Here's a thought. What if we were to . . . ?"

7. Avoid a lot of warm-up with your actual idea. I've noticed that women often have a tendency to explain their thinking first ("I came across a study that said . . .") rather than get right to the point. By the time they describe the actual idea, they've lost people's attention despite how good the concept may be. Then some guy brings the same idea up succinctly two minutes later, and everyone gushes over it.

When you speak, also be careful not to use fillers such as "um" (practice delivering your ideas ahead of time), or end statements so they sound like a question. "We could do it in *California*?" Studies show that women are particularly guilty of these habits. And lock your hands to the table so they don't flail around or touch your hair.

8. If you were asked to come to a meeting with ideas, do not, under any circumstances, arrive empty-handed and try to blend into the surroundings. Your boss will notice if you don't volunteer anything. And don't think of your ideas ten minutes before you dash in the door. I can always spot those lame-ass ideas, as well as the ones made up on the spot based on what someone else just said. The best time to begin thinking of your ideas is as soon as you receive a notice about the meeting. Rather than putting off the task until you "have more time," tell yourself you're going to take thirty minutes ASAP to come up with some initial ideas. This will actually save you time in the long run because over the next few days your subconscious will be on the lookout for ways to flesh out and add to what you've come up with. It also allows you the chance to polish the good ideas and dump the stupid ones.

9. Get a sense of your meeting face. I can't tell you how many people look bored at meetings or even kind of sad. I had a staffer at one magazine who never sat at a meeting without looking as though her kitty cat had just been crushed by a Mack truck. I'm sure that most people have no idea that they appear that way, but though they may be blameless, the damage is still done. They come across as unengaged, and they can even end up sucking the energy out of the room, which bosses hate. So try to catch your reflection in the window or the flat-screen monitor during the meeting—or, when you're alone later, reassume the expression you think you were wearing and check it out in a mirror. Do you seem invested, interested, enthusiastic? If not, fix it!

10. Compliment your colleagues' winning ideas. It spreads goodwill. Don't, however, go overboard complimenting your *boss's* ideas. You'll seem like a major butt kisser in front of your coworkers. You should, however, nod at her good comments, really taking them in, and smile when appropriate. Later, you can shoot your boss an e-mail and comment positively on the new strategy or ideas she suggested and say you are eager to implement them. She'll appreciate any additional thoughts you have.

{ 12 Ways to Get Buzzed About }

These days it seems that people are always talking about buzz—the secrets of getting it, the importance of keeping it, the danger of losing it. I even gave the name *Buzz* to the celebrity magazine in the Bailey Weggins mystery series I write. (I hope you don't mind that I just gave a buzzy shout-out to something I do!) We often think of buzz now in regard to media—both traditional and social—but there's also tremendous value to good old-fashioned word of mouth.

Is buzz really necessary? Yup. It is if you want news to travel about you and/or what you do. And buzz isn't just for those in high-profile jobs. You want to start creating buzz about yourself *now*.

But you want the right kind of buzz for your field and your particular job. If you're a young associate at a conservative law firm, for instance, you don't want party pictures of yourself in a drop-dead sexy dress all over the Internet. But you do want people in the office buzzing about how sharp you are.

Pretty much everything I've learned about buzz has come from the absolutely amazing publicists I've worked with—not only publicists who represented the magazine I was running at the time or me as an author, but also lots of terrific Hollywood publicists. They include the woman brilliant enough to talk Hugh Grant into going on *The Tonight Show* and offering mea culpa after he was arrested for engaging in a lewd act with a prostitute in 1995. Those talented gurus (mostly women but some men, too) have not only given me a glimpse of how buzz is created and kept alive but have also shared a few tips about quieting buzz when it's bad.

1. Start close to home. Yes, you want to be buzzed about in the outside world, but first and foremost you want your boss and coworkers to be gabbing about the awesome things you're doing.

2. Learn to take credit for your successes. This can be tough for women to do. And, yes, it can be tricky to strike the right balance. You want to make people aware of your latest accomplishment, but you don't want to sound desperately needy of praise.

One age-old strategy for not sounding too show-offy is to present your triumphs as part of a group effort. You burst into your boss's office and announce, "We did it! We figured out where the problem was." There's nothing wrong with that approach sometimes. It gets the big news across and makes everybody feel good. But if you always make it about "we," your boss may lose sight of exactly how much you're contributing.

How can you go there without sounding obnoxiously braggy? Try discussing your achievement in terms of the *process* that it involved. Bosses are often interested in the backstory of exploits and achievements—I know I am—because that info can prove helpful to them as they direct future efforts.

Perhaps you're in sales and you just landed business that involved a monumental effort on your part. You don't want to take your boss through every meeting you had with the client and every presentation you made, but perhaps the client revealed something surprising about the company's new direction, a detail you then used to help make the sale. *That* could be valuable for your boss to know. So tell her you have something important to share. Explain how you'd been trying to get the business for a while and finally, after snooping around, you found out this one critical piece of information. The client had no idea how your organization would be able to leverage it, so you did a presentation specifically around that. You want your boss to know because it's going to change how your company approaches the client in the future. She'll appreciate the insight, and indirectly you've given her a sense of how much you kicked butt to get the business.

It's not easy to stand out when much of what you do is teamwork, so find ways to separate yourself from the pack. An up-and-coming female attorney told me, off the record, how she does this: "I've found the best way to make a name for yourself can be through nonbillable work, such as pro bono cases. You usually have a lot more responsibility on those cases, which translates into more opportunity to stand out. It's also a good idea to join committees, like the hiring committee or the associates committee, and to volunteer for roles on them that make you a liaison to partners."

3. Develop a digital strategy. "That's one of the best ways to self-promote today," says Marisa Ollins, the director of public relations at Henri Bendel. "Start a website, a blog, a Twitter feed, a Tumblr feed."

If you don't own a Web domain name yet, get one. Your own name may still be available. Even if you don't plan to use a domain name right now, it doesn't cost much to keep the name, and then you'll have it when you need it someday. Sophia Stuart, the executive director, digital, at Hearst Magazines International, points out that if you only want to blog right now, you can use a blogging platform for free.

You want to be sure, however, that whatever you do digitally doesn't bite you in the butt. According to Stuart, one of the smartest and safest strategies is to update your website or blog with fairly neutral material, such as the latest articles in your profession. "That way, she says, "you can be seen as a fabulous curator of news and views but careful about opinions."

Always check with your boss before doing a blog or website. Not every boss is cool with it, and it's not appropriate in many fields.

Should you tweet? Again, you have to be sure what's appropriate in your company, your department, and your field. You'll want to check with your boss first.

Twitter can be a real asset if you take the time to do it right. Let's say you're just out of veterinary college and have started working as a vet at an animal clinic. You need buzz to build your business. With Twitter, you can create a hashtag such as "#healthypets" and regularly tweet helpful animal-care tips. This will create a clickable link where Twitter users are able to see who has been using that hashtag in their tweets and hopefully reply, thanking you for your advice. Ideally some will even decide to take their pet to you when it's time for a check-up. Websites such as www.hashtag.org

track the frequency that a hashtag is used on Twitter and provides details about the hashtag.

Just as with blogs, it's possible to tweet without getting too personal. "Talk about the great speech you heard or the book you just read about leadership," says Ollins.

You should also follow people on Twitter, particularly those who are in your line of business. They are probably tweeting about relevant trends, articles, and ideas that may be of interest to you and important for you to be aware of. Learn from their style of tweeting. What are they tweeting about? What seems important to them? For example, if you're an aspiring food blogger, you should be following other food bloggers, chefs, restaurant critics, restaurants, food publications, and so on.

And retweet. You should do this with any tweets from the reliable sources you are following. As an inspiring food blogger, you can retweet something from a food magazine editor because you think it might be interesting to your followers. This lets everyone know that you're keeping up with trends and want to be associated with brands that can help your own. If the editor retweets nicely, you have now been exposed to all of his or her followers.

If you're not sure about how to use Twitter, there are books you can find online that provide all the info you need.

4. Be out there—in person. "Though Facebook and Twitter are important," says Zoe Weisberg Coady, a partner in Brandstyle Communications, "face-to-face time is still incredibly valuable. Talk to as many people as you can. Continue to do informational interviews. Tell people, 'I want to know as much as I can about your business.' " (See "Advanced Networking [Never Say You're Too Busy to Do It]" in part II.)

5. Volunteer to be on committees, task forces, and panels, both inside and outside your company. This not only exposes you to tons of new people but clues everybody in to your growing expertise on certain topics. And when you do it within your own company, it's a way to impress coworkers without seeming braggy. And stay active on LinkedIn. It's not just for when you're searching for a job.

6. Don't be a whiner. When you talk to people, frame what you say positively. If you trash-talk your job or your boss, even to people you think of as pals, that info can leak out and create a negative buzz about you. I mentioned earlier how a European company once purchased the magazine where I was working and suddenly everything was in a terrible upheaval. If I ever felt like whining, it was then. One day a *Wall Street Journal* reporter was invited to sit in on a meeting with me and the man now running the show. I knew it would be hard to disguise how dreadful I felt, but I told myself I had to. When the reporter got me alone for a moment, he told me, "This must be a hard time for you." "Actually," I told him with a smile, "I find it very exciting." That quote of mine ran, and the next day a headhunter called. I had sounded like a winner, not a whiner. Within a short time, I had a great new job.

7. Develop a signature look. Steal a page from the editors of fashion magazines. They get a certain hairstyle, for instance, and work it. If you do this, people will absolutely be more apt to notice you and remember you.

8. Start a "big-mouth" e-mail list. It should consist of former bosses, former coworkers whom you want to stay in touch with, anyone who has mentored you, people you've met who seem interested in your career. When you have important job news—such as a promotion—share it with this list.

9. Create a network of women who are mutually supportive and want to create buzz for one another. I heard this idea from Rachelle Hruska, the dynamic and gorgeous founder of Guest of a Guest, the online media site that features social news and tons of party pictures. "Women are far less likely to talk about their accomplishments than men," says Hruska. "Having supportive peers to boost you up makes it easier to brag without feeling badly about it. Why do women ever feel bad about bragging? Men don't seem to."

Hruska is part of Women in Tech, an e-mail chain group. "Just becoming aware of other women and their struggles in the workplace has inspired me in my own job," she notes. "I have stopped feeling badly about tweeting an accomplishment or asking for a favor to extend my brand further. If something similar doesn't exist in your field, start one. Find a handful of women peers and encourage them to invite more, and before you know it, you'll have a powerful support group that will be nominating you for your next big press story."

10. If you can't afford a publicist and must pitch something to the media yourself, develop a clear, precise strategy. "Good PR is not about a gazillion placements anymore," says Ollins, "or throwing a lot of stuff out there to see what sticks. That's the old way. Do your research and determine the key outlets that will make the most impact, and then customize your pitch just for them."

Over the years I've received pitch letters from hundreds of publicists and individuals who clearly had not taken a look at the magazine and had no idea what columns or features were carried. Your pitch will have a shot only if the outlet feels you *get* it and its needs.

And keep social media in mind when you write any kind of press releases. Use the best search optimization terms to help you pop up on Google.

11. Before you do a press interview, create your own call sheet. That is what publicists do for their clients. It lists the topic to be covered, contact info for the reporter or producer, and possible questions, so that you are completely prepared. Research the reporter or blogger so you're familiar with other stories she's done. And rehearse your responses beforehand!

12. Shut down any nasty rumors. There was a time, not all that long ago, when if there was an ugly rumor spreading about you, you left it alone hoping it would soon burn out. But things can go wide (and viral) quickly today, and you must react proactively to rumors. *Cosmopolitan* entertainment director Tracy Shaffer offers two strategies. "One, use your actions to show it's not true," she says. If there's a rumor, for instance, that you and a colleague are feuding, have lunch with her in the company cafeteria.

"Secondly, you need to talk to a few key people and enlist their support," she continues. "They should be people you trust, people in your field. Don't be defensive or act freaked out that your reputation is on the line, but tell them in a confident, genuine way what is happening and that you're concerned about it. Those people then become like soldiers who quell the rumor when they hear it referenced."

{ Be Grabby! }

One of my favorite stories about success involves Linda Eastman, the first wife of Paul McCartney, who died of breast cancer when she was only fifty-six. Maybe I love the story so much because I was pretty young when I heard it, newly arrived in Manhattan, and she'd done something I probably wouldn't have ever thought of, let alone dared to try.

Linda, a single mother with a young daughter, was working as a receptionist for *Town and Country* magazine, though she had a serious interest in becoming a professional photographer. One day at work she deftly intercepted an invitation—meant for a senior editor—to the U.S. press launch of the Rolling Stones on a yacht in the Hudson River. She took her camera along with her, hoping that there would be an opportunity to shoot pictures. She ended up being tapped by the Stones to photograph them at the event, and that gig helped launch a successful career as a photographer (which, of course, later led to her meeting McCartney).

I talked earlier about how important it is to knock your boss's socks off with dynamite ideas that you end up executing brilliantly, but there's another way to go big or go home that you should include in your repertoire as well. You have to be grabby.

By grabby I don't mean pinching your boss's invitations. But there are things you can take and leverage into a win for yourself, even if they haven't been earmarked for you. One of the absolutely best things I ever grabbed was a yellow turtleneck. I'd just won the *Glamour* Top 10 College Women contest and was in New York City with the other winners, preparing to be shot for a special portfolio in the magazine. I was thrilled to be a winner, but deep down I also longed to be the lucky girl whose photo would appear on the cover.

The day before the shoot, we were all taken to a photo studio filled with racks of clothes, and told to pick out a fall outfit to wear for our picture. Most of the clothes were in the muted shades that the fashion director told us were popular that season—such as heather and sage. But way at the end of a rack, almost like an afterthought, were a bright yellow turtleneck and matching orange-and-yellow skirt. I made a beeline past the muted outfits and grabbed the bright one instead. Why? Because I'd looked at enough magazine covers by then to know that they had to "pop" at the newsstand. And you know what? I ended up on the cover. I never look at that old shot of me in the yellow turtleneck without thinking how wise I was to grab it.

Things you should routinely grab in your career include:

- A moment of time from someone who could advise you or provide you with key info.

- The chance to introduce yourself to someone powerful at a party or event.

- The opportunity to raise your hand for a project that's just been announced (even though you may tick off the good girls who just sit there hoping to be tapped for it).

- A peek at something insightful that's lying out on someone's desk. (Hey, if they've called you in and it's on the desk, isn't it fair game?)

- A chair close to someone important at a meeting.

- Power or control in a void—as long as you won't be seriously bitch-slapped by someone higher up. (Once, when my executive editor had to step away before the start of a meeting, I was about to say, "Why don't we wait?" But the deputy editor said nicely, "I think we can start. I can run through the first part." She knew her boss wouldn't mind, and I was totally impressed by the way she took command.)

- An offer from someone to introduce you to a person you're dying to know but have no access to.

- A diamond-in-the-rough project that no one else wants to touch because they don't see the potential.

It was taking on a diamond-in-the-rough project that made all the difference for Jane Buckingham, the founder and CEO of Trendera, whom I hired as a contributing editor the day after I started at *Cosmo*. "I was working at an ad agency in Boston not long after I graduated from college," she explains, "and we were pitching the Massachusetts Anti-Smoking Campaign. No one wanted to work on this project because it was unsexy and funded by the government. But I was very antismoking, so I poured my heart into the research and we won the business. The campaign was a huge success, and we got a ton of buzz. And that led to me starting my own business."

Remember: just because no one has invited you to grab something doesn't mean you shouldn't.

{ What You Need Even More Than a Mentor }

When she gives speeches, Sheryl Sandberg, the brilliant and charismatic COO of Facebook, often mentions how critical it is for women to have mentors in their professional lives. She has had some terrific ones herself, including former secretary of the Treasury Larry Summers.

Most women would second Sandberg's comment. A recent LinkedIn survey of nearly a thousand female professionals found that 82 percent of women agree that having a mentor is important. By definition, a mentor shows you the ropes, offers feedback, and provides strategies for success—all very good stuff. Mentors are often at a higher vantage point than you are, so they can provide insight you can't develop from yours. And if your mentor is in your own organization, she can help you understand where the land mines are.

A common misconception about mentoring is assuming you have to wait for a mentor to find you. According to LinkedIn, almost 20 percent of women have never had a mentor, and more than half of those said it was because they hadn't encountered anyone appropriate. But you can't sit around waiting for a mentor to find you.

You have to search for them, and that may mean looking beyond your immediate department or area.

Your own organization may actually have an internship program. Intel, General Mills, and Procter & Gamble are just a few of the Fortune 500 companies that do. Check with your HR department. Also consider your college. Even if you've been out for a while, see if it has any kind of mentorship program. If not, you could use LinkedIn's advanced-search platform to determine if there is someone from your alma mater in your field whom you can connect with.

But don't get too locked into the I-need-a-mentor mind-set without considering these two points.

First, one mentor rarely has all the answers you need. If, for instance, your mentor is a single woman, she may not be able to relate to your dilemma of whether you should leave your job and follow a serious boyfriend to Chicago, the only city where he was admitted into law school.

To me, better than a mentor is a group of advisers, which you can begin to put together early in your career. Michele James, a partner in James & Co. and former chief talent scout for AOL Time Warner, wholly endorses this idea and even has a name for it: *your personal board of directors.*

"Think of your PBOD just as you would a real board of directors," she says. "You need about five people, with different capabilities. On a real board there's someone who runs the audit committee, and you'll need an audit person, too—someone who can help you evaluate compensation. There needs to be someone in charge of brand strategy and so on."

When you need advice in one area, you ask the appropriate person; when you need advice in another area, you ask someone else. One of the people on my own PBOD is a guy I met in my twenties who later became the head of a major media company. I'm lucky to have a friend like him, and he gives the most sage advice about any career decision I need to make. But if I'm struggling with a quality-of-life decision, I turn to an old friend who started a small company out of her home. She's got a different take from many people on work-life balance.

Second, and it's a biggie: though mentors—or your PBOD—can give you advice, they don't necessarily help you succeed. A recent *Harvard Business Review* article, based on a Catalyst study of MBAs, pointed out that there wasn't a strong correlation between a woman having a mentor and receiving a promotion. But get this: *men* with mentors were more likely to receive promotions. Why? Because in the case of many men, their mentors are what you'd actually call *sponsors*. A sponsor tends to be more senior in an organization than a mentor and, rather than simply offering feedback, he uses his influence with senior executives to advocate for the sponsoree. A sponsor opens doors and works to get a candidate promoted. Women, unfortunately, tend to be overmentored and undersponsored.

So what you also want is sponsors, people who are going to sell you to people higher up in your own organization and others.

How can you find a sponsor? Well, an obvious candidate is your boss. You want to be sure you're working for someone who will advocate on your behalf and isn't going to try to keep you in your same old spot—out of selfishness or envy.

But you'll want to find other senior people, both inside and outside your organization, who can be sponsors for you, too. Start with due diligence. Check out company websites to find out who the important players are and what they are focusing on. Go to company and industry events. According to communications and body language expert Lillian Glass, at professional cocktail parties, power players are generally standing just off of the center of the room with several people around them. Get to know their names. Also attend company and industry conferences and talks. Are there speakers you admire? And ask around among peers and friends—who are the standouts in an organization, who is being buzzed about?

Once you've identified people who can be both mentors and sponsors, you need to make contact. Don't hesitate to introduce yourself to a potential ally at an event or in the elevator and say you admire her work. If the person is spearheading a committee or drive, volunteer to be on it. You can also request an informational interview. You could say something such as "I've heard so much about your work [or latest venture] and would love to know more about it."

But don't come right out and ask someone to be your mentor or sponsor. Shellye Archambeau, CEO of MetricStream, which helps companies meet compliance standards, says that can freak out a busy person. Her strategy early in her career was simply to adopt people as mentors by gradually treating them that way. "Look for a person who you feel a real connection with when you speak," Archambeau says. "With mentors, you have to be able to let your hair down. It's not a business relationship."

If you've just had a brief conversation at an event, ask, "Is it all right if I drop you a note?" You can follow up with a question in writing. Also, periodically send your potential mentor or sponsor information that she will find insightful. When you have an accomplishment under your belt, let her know about it—not as part of your big-mouth list (see "12 Ways to Get Buzzed About") but in a personal e-mail. Just don't be nuisance.

Do *not* turn to a sponsor for advice the way you might a mentor. You don't want her to have even a glimmer about any work dilemmas you're facing or doubts you may be struggling with. You want her to see only your strengths, because her role is to *sell* you.

Once that person has a sense of you, she may begin to volunteer to make introductions. But if she doesn't, you're going to have to *ask* for her help. If a job opens up that she could "sell" you for, tell her, "You've been such a valuable resource for me. I would really appreciate having your help on something. There's a terrific position open at Company A, and I'm hoping you would be able to advocate on my behalf." Don't be shy about also asking a sponsor, "Do you know anyone I could talk to?"

Yes, it can be hard, but you know what? Guys do it all the time.

I hope this is stating the obvious. You *must* send a written note to a mentor or sponsor when she helps you. Perhaps even a gift. And here's a great tip from Archambeau: When you take someone's advice, let her know it and how it worked out. So few people ever do that.

{ Career Breakthroughs: The Very Simple Formula }

Y ou're just about done with the first part of the book. I've offered you the best lessons I've learned about figuring out what you really want to do professionally, landing the job you want, and knocking your boss's socks off. But let's face it: that's not all you're looking for. You want your efforts to *pay off*. You are hoping that your hard work and go-big-or-go-home undertakings will lead to a terrific promotion or fabulous new job up the ladder. In other words, you want the success you've been gunning for.

So let's talk about how to guarantee that happens. Career breakthroughs occur at the intersection of *readiness*, *opportunity*, and *hustle*. If you are itching for your first big breakthrough (and I'd say that, early in your career you should never be at any job longer than a couple of years before questioning if you've been there too long), you need to create that intersection.

Ask yourself these three questions:

1. Are you really ready? If you're hoping you'll be promoted when a job above you opens up, have you been mastering the skills you would need for that job? Have you been impressing the hell out of your boss by going big with your ideas and doing far more than you've been told to do? If not, get busy. If the right job outside the company opened up, would you be ready for *that*? When I was a young feature writer at *Glamour*, it finally dawned on me— later than it should have—that if I wanted to move up (at either *Glamour* or another magazine), I was going to have to master a whole new skill, one I hadn't even begun to develop in my current job. I loved being a feature writer and seeing my name in print, but it was really a dead-end job. The positions directly above mine at the magazine were associate editor and senior editor, and as the titles implied, they involved *editing*, not writing. Luckily, around that time, the articles editor started giving me pieces to edit in order to lighten her own burgeoning load, but if I'd been less naive, I would have already volunteered to take on that task. At least I was smart enough to see how fortunate I was that she'd asked. I stayed late every night doing as much editing as possible, developing this necessary skill and making certain I did a good enough job so she'd keep giving me more.

In some cases you can learn what's required in your own workplace, but there's also a chance you'll need to take a class or program outside. I signed up for a couple of classes in copyediting to bolster what I was learning on the job.

2. Are you creating enough opportunities?

Look, sometimes opportunity really does knock, and that's a beautiful thing. But that happens the least when you're first starting out because you have so few connections. One of my best friends when I was younger landed two amazing jobs during her twenties, one just a couple of years after the other, because in each case her boss got a great new job elsewhere and took my friend along, but nothing like that ever happened to me. You can't wait around for that kind of luck. You've got to:

- Make sure your boss knows how eager you are to move up, by both your performance and the messages you give.

- Network your butt off, inside and outside the company (see "Advanced Networking [Never Say You're Too Busy to Do It]" in part II).

- Watch job boards and your company website for opportunities.

- Introduce yourself to senior people in your organization who may be in a position to hire you one day. And continue to develop sponsors.

- Sign up for LinkedIn if you haven't already (see "Ballsy Strategies for Finding a Job" for more about using LinkedIn). Study how it works and maximize it, using the advanced search options.

- Get job news from companies you're interested in by signing up for their Twitter and Facebook feeds.

- Read trade journals and websites devoted to your field.

- Shoot periodic e-mails to former bosses and colleagues, updating them on what you're up to and sharing a link to something they'd be interested in.

- Keep a folder of clippings or a computer file about new companies or people doing things that intrigue you. (I still have that kind of folder!)

- Check in with your college career office even if it's been a few years since you graduated.

- Stay in regular contact with friends in your field, particularly those who seem to know all the gossip.

- Allow for serendipity and opportunities beckoning from whole new directions.

3. Are you ready to hustle? As soon as you learn about an opportunity, go for it in as big a way as possible. Don't just send your résumé. Make a call introducing yourself. Use a sponsor to open a door for you (see "What You Need Even More Than a Mentor"). And do not hesitate!

Part II

{ Success: How to Go Big with It }

Congratulations! You're obviously reading this section because either you've achieved a significant level of success already or you have every intention of doing so. It's a fantastic stage to be at in your career. Your skills and efforts have begun to pay off, and the work you're doing at this point is probably more interesting and exciting than some of the stuff you were required to do when you first started out.

In my career, my first real success was being hired to run the articles department at *Mademoiselle*. Though at *Family Weekly* I'd eventually been promoted to the number two position, this was a much bigger deal at a much more prestigious company, and it was a fun time for me. I assigned pieces to writers such as Jay McInerney and Tama Janowitz, had a cute office with an actual couch (well, love seat), and oversaw a staff of seven or eight, including my Harvard-educated male assistant. After I'd been there about a year, the magazine ran a four-page fashion story about me as a single girl in Manhattan. If there'd been a Carrie Bradshaw on TV then, I would have felt I was having a Carrie Bradshaw moment.

Yet first success brings many challenges. As you handle plenty of day-to-day demands, you must also focus on the larger picture in a way you were not expected to do as a junior player. You need to come up with even bigger ideas and run with them. Office politics can be intense, sometimes even brutal, at this stage of the game. And there's a good chance you are overseeing staff now—perhaps only one or two people, but still, managing *anyone* takes understanding and skill. At this stage I sometimes felt as if I was flying by the seat of my pants. And I probably looked more confident than I was.

This is a period when you also should be paying serious attention to your career as well as your job. Where do you hope to go from here? What moves should you be making to help you reach the next level even if you don't feel ready to jump right this second? Some opportunities may open up all on their own, but if you want to guarantee that you'll go big with your success, you need strategies and you must work them. In some ways you have to think of your career as a living, breathing thing. It needs nurturing!

Plus, timing can be critical. At *Mademoiselle* I was becoming pretty certain that I really did want to be an editor in chief one day. But I also could see that I didn't have all the time in the world. From my vantage point, it seemed that most editors in chief of women's magazines had secured that title by the time they were in their early forties, if not sooner. I was in my mid-thirties, so that meant I had a window of about five or six years for it to happen. Many fields have this kind of window. Do your homework and figure out at which points you should be going after certain jobs.

This section of the book is jam-packed with strategies for supersizing your success, including tips on how to generate winning ideas, handle office politics shrewdly, use information as your secret weapon, develop your personal brand, and navigate setbacks (because they happen to even the best of us). I'll also share advice on how to manage your career—and finally land the BIG JOB.

{ Get Some Eye of the Tiger }

I have a confession to make. When I was the editor of *Redbook*, one of the group publishers in my company asked if I would have lunch with a woman who had really impressed him. The woman had developed a cooking concept that she was now peddling, and the executive thought there might be a way for *Redbook* to feature her, perhaps even monthly. Sure, I'd be glad to join them for lunch, I said. We were always looking for new ideas and new voices.

We met at a Midtown restaurant, and though the woman seemed polished and determined, I quickly decided that there was no way I could use her for *Redbook*. To me there was nothing appealing about the concept she was championing: using store-bought foods such as pudding mix to create partially homemade meals.

Okay—wait for it—the woman I had lunch with that day was Sandra Lee, the author of the *Semi-Homemade* cookbook series, which by now has sold millions of copies, spawned other products, and led to her not only hosting her own show on the Food Network but creating a whole line of home products. Guys obviously like her cooking, too, since her live-in boyfriend is Andrew Cuomo, the current governor of New York.

Okay, clearly I'm pathetic at spotting talent in the chefs-Middle-America-will-love category. Still, I can't help but admire Sandra Lee's success and the gritty resolve that helped her achieve it. She knew what she wanted and went after it single-mindedly, not allowing herself to be discouraged when she met someone like me who didn't go gaga for the concept. *She* liked it and sensed that many busy women would. Recently I came across an interesting comment she made about the secret of success. "You have to want it," she said. "You have to have the eye of the tiger, and you have to do it every single day."

The eye of the tiger. It means you're focused, steadfast, and fierce. Sandra Lee's point was that you absolutely must have those attributes in order to be truly successful. Though I still don't appreciate her food philosophy—to me eating a chicken dish made with frozen haricots verts and condensed soup seems about as fabulous as hand washing a week's worth of panty hose—I have to agree with Lee's philosophy of success.

Helen Gurley Brown certainly had the eye of the tiger when she ran *Cosmo*. I didn't know her well then, but everything I saw, heard, and read indicated that she was utterly focused and that she watched out for her brand like, well, a killer big cat. A major media executive told me a story that perfectly illustrates this. Years ago, he was sometimes invited to attend the monthly luncheons at the "21" Club where Helen would preview each issue of *Cosmo* for a round-table of advertisers. At one particular luncheon this guy ended up talking the whole time to a gorgeous advertiser seated next to him, even though he knew he should be working the table more. When it was time for the preview, Helen asked him if he would hold the display book—it was customary practice to have someone do that. Right before she started to speak to the group, Helen leaned down, put her hand onto the exec's neck, and whispered something into his ear. He told me that anyone at the table would have assumed that she was saying something wonderfully flirty to him. But what she was really doing was digging her nails into his neck while telling him "Don't you *ever* monopolize one advertiser again." Now, *that* is some awesome fierceness.

To take your career from "Hey-isn't-this-nice?" success to major, fabulous success, you need the eye of the tiger. Where does that come from? Sandra Lee is clearly hardwired that way, and her tough upbringing ended up making her even more determined. In other words, a combination of nature and nurture creates that kind of drive. You actually can't just go out and *get* the eye of the tiger.

But even if you didn't wake up this morning with the urge to take down an antelope or a wild boar, do not panic. It doesn't mean you aren't cut out for big success. I think that focus and fierceness can sometimes take a while to fully bloom—and that they also require a bit of cultivation. That was certainly the case for me. By my late twenties I was a senior editor at *Family Weekly* magazine, reporting directly to the editor in chief and overseeing all the articles that ran in the magazine, including the celebrity cover stories. But in no way did I have the eye of the tiger. I wasn't sure yet what I wanted professionally. Though I'd fantasized about becoming an editor in chief and was on a path that *could* lead there, I also sometimes toyed with the notion of being a freelance writer. That's because the thought of becoming an editor in chief scared my pants off.

If you don't feel full-throttle fierceness yet (but wish you did), the first thing you need to do is ask yourself if you are in the right place. I mean, do you *love* what you're doing? Essie Weingarten, the founder and creative director of Essie nail polishes, which is now owned by L'Oréal, told me, "The one sure way to be totally focused is to be passionate about what you're doing." Essie ended up creating nail polishes because she was captivated by fashion and style (plus she adored getting her nails done). Loving what she was doing made it easier to work long hours, push the envelope with creativity, and cold call on hundreds of salons, introducing her polishes to them. Sometimes the reason you see other people charge by you is that you've stumbled into the wrong workplace or wrong field.

If it *does* feel like a pretty good fit (at least for now), one way to fire up your fierceness is to get a taste of what big success feels like. I still remember the moment that happened for me. After I'd been a senior editor at *Family Weekly* for several years, my boss, Art Cooper, was tapped to be the editor in chief of *GQ*. I was named executive editor and given the task of running the magazine while management searched for the new editor (they told me I was also a candidate). I was so nervous at first—28 million people would see what was published under my direction each week—but of course I couldn't say no. Then all of a sudden, after I'd been running the magazine a few weeks, a funny thing happened: I discovered that I found the whole experience absolutely exhilarating. I loved being in charge, loved deciding what the cover stories would be, loved telling people what to do. I even loved having the buck stop with me. I realized that some of the stress I sometimes felt at work involved reporting to a boss, and when I didn't have one—at least a direct boss—I actually was much happier. (When the editor in chief job went to a man, Art said he'd heard that had been the intention all along. But I tried not to let it bother me. I'd had an epiphany from the experience, making it all worthwhile.)

So give yourself a hint of what major success in your field would feel like. If a leader in your company or field is giving a speech, for instance, go hear it and watch the attention that is paid to her, see how nice it is to command a room.

Another way to hone the eye of the tiger is to define your goal in a sexy way for yourself. You may not be a hundred percent certain of what it is, but decide on something that feels right at the moment and go with it for a while. Saying it to yourself not only gets you jazzed but also helps guide your choices.

The wonderful crime novelist Karin Slaughter, who has sold more than 30 million books worldwide, used to own—are you ready for this?—a sign-painting company. But she secretly wanted to write. She finally found an agent to shop her first book, but it took a while to sell, and by the time she was close, she had written another book and had an idea for a third. When the agent asked her what she hoped for, Slaughter suddenly heard herself say, "A three-book deal." Just saying that phrased crystallized things for her—and she ended up with exactly that from a publisher.

Don't be afraid to think big. I had the chance recently to work with a dazzling duo of women who run the PR and marketing firm Brandstyle Communications. One of them, Zoe Weisberg Coady, told me that from the time she was in her early twenties, she would tell herself, "One day I want to have my own company," and that phrase helped propel and direct her.

"Having that phrase in my mind helped me make certain decisions," she says. "I worked for one of the big agencies when I was younger, for instance, and my boss was *crazy*, but I stuck it out because I knew it was good for me to be there because of my long-range plan. I was learning things I would need to know when I ran a business one day."

Coady has always done something else that also helps hone the eye of the tiger: she uses envy as a motivator. "It's so easy to get bogged down in the day-to-day," she says. "But when I read about someone else doing something interesting or being really successful at something, it's a real kick in the butt. I think, '*I* need to do that.' "

No matter how fierce you become about your goals, at times certain things will steal your focus and possibly diminish your fierceness: setbacks, for instance, or crushing criticism. Experiment and find the tactic that gets it back for you. The comedian Amy Schumer, who parlayed being a finalist on *Last Comic Standing* into a very successful career as a comedian, had a trick that worked for her when she was first trying to make it. "When I felt like it was an uphill battle," she told me, "I reread the positive feedback I'd received in e-mails, on Facebook, and on Twitter. That always kept me pushing ahead."

{ How to Come Up with Bold, Brilliant Ideas }

One of the reasons for the success you have today is that along the way you must have had a few damn good ideas. Perhaps you suggested to your boss some clever way to trim costs, or you came up with a compelling tag line to use in the company's marketing brochure. Being a good idea person helped you do your job and blast ahead. But now that you're poised to go big with your success, you need to go big with your ideas, too. You need to come up with not just good ideas but *bold, brilliant* ideas, the kind that these days are called "game changers."

Think for a moment about some of the most exciting products and companies you know. Facebook, for instance, or Netflix, or lash-lengthening mascara or those spinners that dry your lettuce, or—one of my personal favorites—Paperless Post, whose online cards are as fabulous as anything in traditional stationery. They've made your life better or easier (or possibly even more exciting), and now you may even feel you couldn't live without them. Each began with a bold new idea.

Great ideas are the currency of big success. No matter whether you're a product developer in Silicon Valley, a high school teacher in Kansas, or a private wealth manager in Pennsylvania, if you're going to make your mark and make a difference, you need to be a strong idea person. Your concepts may not change the world or make you millions, but you want them to have an impact in the work you do.

The ability to generate ideas comes easily to some people. I also believe that you can *learn* how to do it and make it a regular and exciting process in your job. Though I started off as a decent enough idea person, I've gotten much better over the years, not only by working at improving my own techniques but by studying how supercreative people seem to do it.

Here are the tricks I've used—as well as a few I've stolen!

Find your idea-creating zone. It took me years to realize that though I'm basically a night person, I have my best ideas early in the morning. That meant I needed to become a morning person, too. (I know—this *could* be called burning the candle at both ends.) Though it took getting used to, hauling myself out of bed at 5:30 A.M. made such a difference for me. And don't be afraid to book creative time into your schedule. I read once that Madonna scheduled creative time each day. It's a little like scheduling sex. It may not sound so erotic, but just wait until you're in the throes of it.

Give your brain something to spark off of. Ideas don't happen in a vacuum. They occur when your mind encounters something and suddenly catches fire with a creative thought. Ideas are often about associations. The Swede who invented Velcro began to develop the idea after finding burrs stuck to his pants leg following a walk in the woods.

Sure, sometimes people come up with stupendous ideas by letting one thought in their brain spark off another. But why not give your brain some help? In my home office I keep a huge folder of crime stories I've clipped from magazines and newspapers or down-loaded from the Internet. Whenever it's time to start thinking about a new novel, I make a cup of tea and sit for an hour going through those clippings. One of the best plot twists I've ever had was sparked by an anecdote I found on the twenty-fourth page of an article I'd downloaded.

Dari Marder, the chief marketing officer of Iconix, has a great approach she uses. She regularly has what she calls a "ten slides meetings." Everyone in attendance must give a PowerPoint presentation of ten images that have really grabbed them over the past few days or weeks. Those images often trigger amazing ideas.

Don't become stuck to your desk. Clippings and images are helpful, but you also need to be out in the world. The more you encounter, the more there is to spark ideas. Walk in nature, as the Velcro inventor did. Go to museums, galleries, shows, events, theater. I once came up with an interesting idea for *Cosmo* when I was viewing an Asia Society exhibit on Marco Polo and the Silk Road ("What to Do When Your Guy Won't Stay Put"—just kidding). Essie Weingarten told me that one of her nail colors was inspired by the plaid shirt she had seen on someone at a soccer game.

Put the question to the universe. I know this is going to sound crazy, but it's something I learned from Laura Day, author of *Practical Intuition*, and it really, really works. Decide on a question ("What end-of-the-year project can I give my students that will enthrall them?" or "How can I encourage more people to come to the open houses my realty company gives?") and say it a few times in your mind. The answer eventually will come to you. It's not a weird ESP kind of thing. You prime your subconscious to be ready to receive great input. I use this constantly not only for my work with *Cosmo* but also when I'm writing my books. When I was gathering ideas for my second mystery, I posed the question to the universe and scheduled a pamper-myself-into-a-pound-of-butter day to help things along. While I was waiting to have a facial done, I looked at the instruments and thought, "You could kill someone with that!" Then suddenly I decided to set my second mystery in a spa.

Think about what's *really* needed. Remember that statement I included in part I from Paperless Post cofounder Alexa Hirschfeld: "You have to consider what the world wants from you, not what you want from the world." In other words, if you hope to make money and be a success, your idea has to be marketable. Step away for a minute from your concept and consider whether it's really going to be in demand.

Put your wildest, craziest thoughts onto the table. Years ago, I read an essay by Cynthia Heimel called "How to Be Creative." I still have a tattered clipping of it, and I reread it from time to time. One of my favorite parts: "There is only one way to be creative—and that is to have the courage to examine all our secret convolutions, hopes, and jokes and transform them into art. To hell with what the other guy thinks! The odder and more personal we get, the more everyone identifies. It's magic."

So let your wacky ideas see the light of day. Others can probably relate to them.

Brainstorm. In recent years, some experts have pooh-poohed brainstorming, saying it's not an effective way to generate ideas, but I find it works great in many cases—and it can be a lot of fun. The key is to work with a small group of people (four or five) who feel totally comfortable together. And though this sounds ruthless, over time you may have to drop people from the group if they suck out the oxygen and don't produce.

But also channel your inner loner. According to Susan Cain, the author of *Quiet: The Power of Introverts in a World That Can't Stop Talking*, research suggests that people are more creative when they enjoy privacy and freedom from interruption—and that solitude is a catalyst for innovation.

Riff on it. When you see something that wows you or another person says something that you find intriguing, hold on to it mentally for a few beats and then kick it around in your mind. Why did it catch your interest? Could some permutation of it work in a presentation you're doing or a new product you're developing? That's what the Velcro creator did. And it's what I often do when I'm writing a mystery. There's one kind of kooky example that comes to mind. Around the time I was finishing my first novel, *If Looks Could Kill*, I attended a three-day conference for work and ended up sitting next to Laura Day. Day explained to me that she was an "intuit," meaning she intuited ideas for companies. I told her I was struggling a bit with the final two chapters of my book and asked if she could intuit for *me*. "I don't know why," she said after a minute of reflection, "but I'm seeing a lottery ticket."

Well, as much as I tried, I wasn't able to think of a way to use that lottery ticket in the ending. But I hated to let it go. And then suddenly I had a thought. Bailey Weggins, my amateur detective, had broken up with her husband because he was a scoundrel of some kind, and though I'd yet to decide what his problem was, I knew I didn't want the standard "he cheated on her." I decided at that moment to make him a compulsive gambler.

Sometimes your brain snags on something interesting but you can't use it right then and there. But if you get into the habit of paying attention and mentally storing good material, you can come back to it. The PR guru Andrea Kaplan says that one of her best ideas occurred from an observation she made—and then returned to—when she was doing PR for *Family Circle* magazine. "During one of President Clinton's State of the Union addresses, I noticed that Hillary Clinton was sitting next to Dr. Berry Brazelton, a *Family*

Circle contributor," she says. "A week later in a brainstorming meeting, the editor in chief asked what we could do celebrate Dr. Brazelton's ten years as a columnist. My synapses started firing, and I said, 'Let's do a Salute America's Children campaign with Dr. Brazelton and Mrs. Clinton.' It all came together, and I even booked them on *Oprah*. It was Mrs. Clinton's first time on that show."

Ask yourself "What if . . . ?" That's a technique that's recommended for novelists as a way to develop plots. You see a lone glove lying on a sidewalk. You ask, for instance, "What if the woman wearing it hadn't simply dropped it but was kidnapped and forced into a car? What if she had stumbled on information in her job that put her in jeopardy?" And on and on. You can use that same trick at work.

When I had lunch with reality star Bethenny Frankel, I learned that that's basically how her multimillion-dollar Skinnygirl Margarita business happened. On an episode of *Real Housewives of New York*, she'd asked a bartender to make her "a skinny margarita," and gave him a recipe she'd concocted. After the show aired, lots of women went online and asked for the recipe. Rather than simply share it, Bethenny asked, "Since so many women like it, what if *I* create and sell the mix myself?" Bethenny said that you have to look at everything and see what you can do with it. "If I were Faye Dunaway," she said, referring to the star of *Mommie Dearest*, "I would have created a line of clothes hangers."

Try thin slicing your concepts. Sometimes making an idea tighter or more specific actually makes it much stronger. That's been one of the tricks I use with cover lines. To me a great cover line deals with a universal issue but hooks you by addressing a specific aspect of it, thus making it seem an even more intriguing concept. Compare "9 Stress-Busting Tips" to "What to Do When Stress Keeps You Up at Night." The second is just grabbier (you can't help but wonder, How do they *know*?). Two of my all-time favorite *Cosmo* lines are "The Most Crucial Thing to Ask Your Gyno" and "Why Guys Cheat in August."

I think this same approach works with ideas in general. So when you're letting your mind play, don't be afraid to thin slice.

Never ignore the pebble in your shoe. When you're playing with information, look for patterns, too. Not long after I arrived at *Cosmo*, I began to notice all the e-mails from guys saying how much they loved sneaking a peek at the magazine because it was like "having the other team's playbook." That eventually led to the iPad app CFG—*Cosmo* for Guys.

Once you have an idea, don't overly perfect it. When you try to hold on to an idea too long in order to make it perfect, you can miss the moment. So put it out there. "Even if your product isn't as perfect as you'd like, perfection in your hands isn't relevant," says Paperless Post cofounder Alexa Hirschfeld. "You need to know what your *consumer* thinks. When you put it out there, you can begin to collect data to make it more perfect."

Stumped? Step away. Brandstyle's Zoe Weisberg Coady says that when she is stumped for an idea, she does something totally different. "Then later, I come back to it," she says. "If you're too pressured, it's never going to happen. But if you step away, your brain solves it."

Press up on the bottom of your desktop or a table with your fingers. This comes from a study done by the *Journal of Personality and Social Psychology*. Apparently the motion flexes the muscles you use to bring things closer to your body, which your brain associates with openness and creativity.

And always ask yourself, "Did I go big or go home?" You've got a winning idea. But could it be bolder? Could you take it further? Hold your ideas up to a phrase that nudges you to go bigger. When I met Colin Cowie, the lifestyle guru and party planner who put together *Cosmo*'s fortieth-anniversary party, he told me that everything he created needed to be a "jaw-dropping moment." What a great phrase to use! From the moment I started writing *Cosmo* cover lines, I tried to use a similar tactic: I asked myself if they were fearless enough. That's how lines such as "Heinous Break-ups: You'll Want to Slap These Jerks" turned into "The Most Heinous Break-ups in *Cosmo* History: You'll Want to Bitch-slap These Jerks."

{ You, the Brand }

Several years ago I bumped into a professional model I knew who was now over age thirty and was beginning to get involved in other projects, including being a product sponsor. We caught up, and then I asked if she was still doing any modeling. "No," she told me. "I'm really more of a *brand* now."

We're constantly being told these days that we *all* must turn ourselves into brands. We need brand identities and brand statements and brand promotions. It may seem silly to think of yourself the same way you would a bag of coffee or box of tampons, but it can actually be helpful to define your professional brand identity, especially now when you've begun to achieve some success. It forces you to focus your efforts before you go too much further down the road, helps you market yourself for jobs, and enables you to create buzz about what you are doing.

What does a brand identity mean? Here's insight from advertising executive Bobbi Casey-Howell: "I was brought up in the world of advertising, and the idea I most cling to and believe in is the one Donny Deutsch, CEO of Deutsch, taught me: a brand is a set of values. Values are your beliefs and what make you *you*. Your brand isn't how you wear your hair, what color your eyes are, or how you dress. Values are at your core. Your brand values actually inform your dress, your look, and how you act."

You can begin to think about your brand identity by considering how you live your life and the kind of work you're drawn to. "You make decisions every day based on what your brand is," says Casey-Howell. "Let's say you're deciding where to have dinner with friends. What values are reflected in your choice of restaurant? Energy? Friendliness? Creativity? Consistency? If you make a list of brands you prefer and purchase—detergent, shampoo, computer, cell phone, et cetera—you can probably find similarities among them and get an insight as to what your own brand is about."

Casey-Howell says that when she looks at the brands she prefers and what she values, it's easy for her to see that her personal brand is all about no-nonsense.

After you've defined the values that matter to you, begin to think about the professional skills that you want to develop and showcase that will reflect those values. Early on in your career you may want to experiment and try your hand at a bunch of things, but before long you'll want to start narrowing it down.

"You need to find your focus and stick with it," says Emily Heyward, partner and director of strategy at Red Antler, a branding company that believes in designing from the inside out. "A friend of mine who is a high-powered advertising executive gave me great advice, which was to stop trying to be good at things I don't enjoy doing. Of course, every job is going to have unpleasant tasks associated with it. But instead of trying to be good at everything, work on being great at a few key things. By completely owning a few core functions, you become indispensable in those areas, and everyone knows your value—versus the brand that tries to be all things to all people and ends up standing for nothing."

Casey-Howell also stresses the importance of focusing. "It's almost impossible to be a generalist today," she says. "As a consumer you want to work with a specialist. You want someone who specializes in what you're paying for. Your hair, for instance, or an exercise class or the software you use. The same holds true in your career. Your brand can be your specialty or how you get something done."

But be aware, says Casey-Howell, that at the rate things are moving, your specialty may not be a specialty forever. Always keep an eye out for how you can adapt. And, of course, one day you may want to change directions altogether.

Even if you think you've focused, ask yourself if it might be smart to go ever tighter. A strategy in one of my favorite marketing books, *The 22 Immutable Laws of Marketing*: if you can't be number one in a category, set up a new category you can be first in. Example: Amelia Earhart wasn't the first person to fly solo across the Atlantic, but she was the first *woman* to do it. Look for a void that needs to be filled.

Once you have a sense of your brand, boil everything down into a sound bite that you can use as a measuring stick. This is especially true when you're creating any kind of product or service. Recently I went to a breakfast to hear designer Tory Burch speak, and she defined her wonderful brand as "upscale flair at an accessible price point." All her designs are held up to that statement. She also described the piece that had crystallized the concept for her: a tunic she saw in a Paris flea market, one that reminded her of a lovely tunic her mother had worn. Tunics are still a key part of her collections. It can help with *any* brand to have a visual in mind. Try making a board of images to help you focus.

As your career progresses, you will need to make choices that keep you true to your brand. "The agency I work for is no-nonsense, just as I am," says Casey-Howell. "And at this stage in my career, I hire people I believe possess that value. Since I want everyone I hire to be successful, I ask questions to uncover that value."

Take on as many assignments as possible that will enhance your specialty. And learn what you need to make it even stronger. Just as important as saying yes to what fits your brand is saying no to what doesn't.

Pay attention to your gut, too. It will help inform you when things are off brand for you. But you have to take the time to listen and question yourself. One of the things I eventually realized at the end of my first year at *Cosmo* was how much better of a fit the magazine was for me than either *Redbook* or *McCall's* had been. I've always been drawn to what's kind of edgy (um, maybe that's why I write mysteries), and I'd always felt weirdly constricted in those other jobs. But I hadn't done enough thinking at the time to put my finger on it and wonder if there was something better suited for me. Luckily I found my way there.

What you want to strive for is consistency. "The reason Lindsay Lohan has had such a hard time making a comeback is because she went from being America's sweetheart to a hot mess," says Jo Piazza, the author of *Celebrity, Inc.: How Famous People Make Money*. "A lesbian, then not a lesbian. She's a brand flip-flopper. Consumers don't know what they will get, so that's why they are no longer willing to invest in her. On the other hand, Charlie Sheen's fans didn't abandon him when he had a breakdown because his brand had always been consistent. You know he is a bad boy, and the badder he is, the more successful he is."

Once you're sure of your professional brand identity, you need to *advertise it, promote it, market it*. "You want to make sure you're communicating your key point of difference—your positioning—

at every occasion," says Heyward. "When you create a résumé, for instance, it's not about listing every single role and responsibility you've had. Instead it's about highlighting accomplishments that all ladder up to your overall positioning, expressing a clear point of view. You're taking control of the impressions you make by doing the work for them."

You should also have a bio that plays up your brand—this will be used for any kind of press or speaking engagement. Make it jazzy and exciting, and don't be afraid of language that really touts you. For instance, Rita Hazan's online bio doesn't simply call her a hair colorist; it refers to her as "one of the most sought-after colorists in the world."

Keep reinforcing your brand at every opportunity—on your website, in blogs you write, in speeches you give, in interviews.

You've got to have the guts to say no here, too. If a particular activity isn't going to reinforce your brand, it may very well be a waste of time. Sometimes, though, things can be tweaked to your advantage. Let's say you're an environmentalist who specializes in saving lakes, and you're asked to be on a panel on global warming. Does that support your brand? It does if you speak specifically about how the warming of northern lakes makes them more susceptible to invasive species and the lack of snow cover threatens the replenishment of lakes.

Think about the details, too: the way you dress, the accessories you use, your stationery. One day when we were chatting at her salon, Rita Hazan showed me the screen saver on her iPhone. It was a close-up shot of the back of Katy Perry's hair, dyed the most fantastic shade of blue by Rita. Her screen saver wasn't a shot of her dogs. It was a shot of her *brand*.

One last point about brand: go big or go home with your brand whenever you can. Ask yourself with each step: Can I go further? Can I push the envelope here? Can I make a bigger statement? When the dermatologist and surgeon Ellen Marmur decided to leave her offices at the Manhattan hospital where she practiced and open up her own office, she decided not to call it Dr. Marmur's office but rather Marmur Medical. Thinking big. I just love that.

{ My Best Rules for Being a Boss }

When I was sixteen years old and eager to make more regular money than babysitting provided, I took a job as a part-time dental assistant, working on Saturdays and every weekday during the summer. The dentist taught me something he called four-handed dentistry, where we slapped the dental instruments back and forth into each other's hands like you see on shows such as *Grey's Anatomy*. While other girls were cheering at football games on Saturday, I was securing bibs on patients, assisting the dentist as he filled their cavities, and vacuuming debris out of their mouths afterward. In many ways it was a good experience (though there's something creepy about hearing someone say "Miss White, get me the bone file" when you are only sixteen). The only major problem: my boss, the dentist, was a total meanie.

He was charming to patients, but he constantly snapped, barked, and even yelled at the staff, often in an ego-crushing way. In the three years I worked there, something like fifteen receptionists came and went; one never even returned from lunch on her first day on the job. Because I wanted the work, I stuck it out, always doing my best to keep a stiff upper lip. The worst moment for me was when, just before we closed the office one summer day, a star athlete from the rival high school came in for an emergency filling. The dentist reprimanded me harshly in front of him, totally humiliating me. To this day, I can still picture myself leaving the office later. I slammed the door as hard as I could (the dentist obviously felt the walls shake because he called me at home to apologize), and on the front stoop I made a vow to myself: I would never, *ever* be that kind of boss.

I've been in charge of people for several decades—starting with one person and eventually overseeing more than sixty—and I would give myself decent marks for keeping my vow. Wherever I've gone, I've tried to create a supportive and easy atmosphere that people thrive in. I've enjoyed nurturing talent (I love the fact that at least seven people I've hired have gone on to become editors in chief), and I think most people would say I'm a fair and encouraging leader, bearing little resemblance to a *The Devil Wears Prada* type. I've given a huge amount of thought to what makes an effective boss, and when I've stumbled—far more times than I'd like—I've tried to analyze what I've done wrong. Here are the rules I've tried to live by.

Rule #1: *Study good bosses—and lousy ones.* Though some companies offer management-training programs, most places are not going to provide you with any instruction in being a boss. What I'm trying to say is, girlfriend, you're on your own. But don't just wing it. Watch your boss and her boss and other bosses around you, and try to articulate to yourself what they do right and what they do wrong, which behavior you'll want to emulate and which you'll want to avoid. What are their tricks for inspiring and motivating employees? Or not? How do they handle pressure? What do they do that works your last nerve?

One of my best bosses was a guy who had a Zen-like calm and handled everything with near-perfect equanimity. Though I knew I wasn't hardwired to be exactly like him, I still learned so much from being around a man who saw the advantages that came from not overreacting. One of my worst bosses was a guy who actually sneaked my idea folder out of my tidy file while I was at lunch one day (I found out because my lunch date didn't show and I came back early). He was terrified of losing his job, worried that everyone had more ideas than he did. From this dude I learned that desperate feelings can lead to desperately stupid actions if you don't pop a chill pill.

Over time, think, too, about your own strengths and weaknesses as a leader. And though it's important to work on your weaknesses, it's also smart to keep polishing those strengths. Look, you can't do everything, so make your mark in what you excel at.

Rule #2: *Tell your team what your mission is (even if your team is only one person, i.e., an assistant).* Besides the fact that people need to know what they're doing, they love to work with a mission in mind. It's totally energizing. Tell them that you want to "kick the butt of the competition by increasing sales by 15 percent" or "be the standout department in the high school by boosting student test scores by ten points."

You should also be sharing a set of values. What are the standards you want your employees to adhere to?

Rule #3: *Tell people what you want them to do and when you want them to do it by.* In "4 Tips for Masterfully Managing Your Boss" (part I), I stressed the importance of clarifying with your boss what your responsibilities and deadlines are. In an ideal world, it's the *boss's* job to arrange those sessions. So when you are the boss, do it. Be clear with your employees. Spell out their assignments and their completion dates. It might prove valuable to hold a quick daily or weekly meeting with your staff at which you review what's going on. People, I've found, like the ritual (and when done right, the *fun*) of regular catch-up meetings, as long as they aren't a time suck. Consider making meetings "stand up"—where everyone remains standing while quickly running through what they're focusing on.

And don't just tell, *teach*. Let staffers try new stuff. The smart people want to learn what you know so they can have a job like yours, and this will help keep them engaged. One of the best compliments I ever received was when a former staffer said in an interview, "Working for Kate was like going to editor in chief boot camp."

Just don't share *all* your secrets. Those people may compete against you one day!

Rule #4: *Give feedback regularly.* If it's criticism, say it calmly, but don't sugarcoat it either. Nobody learns from that. On the flip side, praise a job well done. Some bosses operate under the premise that too much praise will turn you into a lardass, and yet I've always found that the right kind of praise (authentic and for accomplishments that really matter) is incredibly motivating. Say it in person, but it's also great to sometimes put it into writing, too— not just in e-mails but also handwritten on nice stationery. Trust me, people will save those notes. And if good work deserves praise, fabulous work deserves a reward: a bonus, a perk, dinner out, a chance to handle a great new project.

Rule #5: *Listen.* Not just to your direct reports but to those on the front lines and new staffers with a fresh point of view. Part of listening is going deeper with good questions about the topic at hand. It's not only intoxicating and gratifying for an employee when you, as a boss, listen to him or her; it also helps to ensure that you will learn worthwhile information and behind-the-scenes dirt—about how a project is really going, a new approach to doing business, emerging trends you should be aware of, little problems in the workplace, *big* problems in the workplace, a troublesome staffer, as well as rumors about the company and coworkers.

And don't just listen at your desk. Years ago I heard someone say that smart guys who ran manufacturing companies knew that it was key to "walk the factory floor." Not only do you increase your visibility when you pop in on people, but when you ask them questions, they aren't tied to a prepared script.

By the way, being a good listener also helps you build the kind of inner circle every boss needs to really go big with a mission. When people know they're *heard*, it helps inspire a fierce devotion.

Unfortunately, the people capable of offering helpful insight aren't necessarily going to come right out and volunteer it, despite how inclusive you may be as a boss. They may believe you don't really need to know certain details or you'll get miffed if they butt in. So when something's on the table, ask for their opinion. Say things such as "What do *you* think?" or What's *your* gut telling you on this one?" Or "If it were up to *you*, would you go with A or B?" And under no circumstances dis their reply. Even if you disagree, say something like "Interesting" or "I hadn't thought of that." And most important, leave your ego at the door and actually consider what they say, even if it's contrary to your initial instinct.

That said, you don't want to make choices by committee or give everyone a vote. Learn what your staffers know, and then *you* make the decision.

And when a staff member does contribute a powerful idea that you decide to run with, share credit. Let your boss know who on your team has contributed big ideas or important tactics. This doesn't take away from you. And your subordinates will begin to learn that you promote them this way. Some of your staff are aiming for greatness, and they want you to help them get there.

Rule #6: *Encourage people to present you with solutions, not just problems.* When they come running in all crazed and saying stuff such as "No one's calling me back" or "They just shut down the whole thing" or "Mandy is blowing a gasket and threatening to quit," tell them to figure out how to fix the situation and then come back and present the plan to you.

Rule #7: *Eschew the too-big idea meeting.* In addition to running regular catch-up meetings like the one I described previously, you will probably need to sometimes have idea meetings, too, or in-depth catch-up meetings.

Please keep those meetings on the small side. I don't think I've ever been in a brainstorming or strategy meeting of over five or six people that I could say was productive. When meetings are bigger than that, people tend to become tongue-tied—maybe they're afraid of speaking up in front of that many people—and as you stare at their slack-jawed expressions, you will find it harder and harder to articulate what you need from them. Small groups produce far more energy and creativity. If you have more than six people whom you need to hear from, schedule meetings with a few at a time.

Rule #8: *Change your mind sometimes.* People hate indecisiveness in bosses, but even more they're aggravated by bosses who frequently make a decision and then change their mind. That kind of flip-flopping makes you look weak, plus people have busted their butts implementing your *first* decision. If you find you are constantly rethinking things, sit down alone with a cup of coffee on a weekend morning and review how many of your rethought decisions have turned out to be right. If it's most of them, try to figure out what prevented you from making the right choice initially. Did you not have enough information? Were you afraid to trust your gut? Did you listen to the wrong person? Then figure out how to make sure such things don't get in the way in the future.

That said, I think it's good to change your mind *sometimes*. It keeps people on their toes when you are a little unpredictable and prevents them from being complacent. I remember once changing my mind twice on how a fashion story should be written and I could tell the copywriter had her panties in a twist about it. But it was a good thing.

Rule #9: *Expect total and complete discretion.* As far as your subordinates are concerned, working for you should be on the same level as being a member of the Pitt-Jolie household staff—everything is confidential. Let them know up front that this is what you demand, not after someone has gossiped and it's gotten back to you.

Rule #10: *Nip bad behavior in the bud (sometimes I wish it were "butt").* There is a law of what I call "work physics" that you absolutely must know: the bad behavior of people who work for you never, ever goes away on its own. In fact, if it is left unattended, it will most likely get *even worse*. By bad behavior, I don't mean poor job performance (I will tackle that in a minute). I mean naughty stuff such as eye rolling in meetings, muttering under one's breath, showing up late, playing hooky, visiting www .prisonpenpals.com during office hours, talking too long on personal calls, bad-mouthing other employees, and so on. Sooner or later people who work for you will do crap like this because they get frustrated or bored or are jerks to begin with.

Now, when you are first a boss, you may be tempted to let this conduct go unnoted initially because it's awkward to bring it up and you may not even be a hundred percent certain that the muttering or eye rolling actually happened (betcha it did, though!). But if you don't address this behavior, it will happen again, trust me (this falls under the heading "If you give someone an inch, they will take a mile").

So here's what you need to do the very first time naughtiness occurs: ask the person to step someplace private with you and tell him you never want to see that kind of behavior again. If he denies doing it ("I wasn't rolling my eyes"), say, "Good, because that kind of action is totally unacceptable."

What if someone just isn't doing her job well? She's lazy or unfocused, for instance. You may feel the urge to wring the person's neck or chew her out, but I've found those strategies, though momentarily satisfying, do not produce effective long-term results. In fact, when you really take someone to task, she often ends up panicking, perhaps not having ever realized how badly she was perceived. Her performance starts to spiral downward, getting worse rather than better.

Better, I think, is to call the person in, calmly state your concerns, and ask *her* how she thinks she can best address the issues. By involving her in the process, you give her more of a sense of control.

Rule #11: *Never let a staffer tell you something while he or she is sitting down and you are standing up.* There's a type of bad behavior that can occur when you are a new boss and someone who works for you resents your hiring or promotion or if you're younger than someone reporting to you: the person may challenge your authority and even try to undermine it. If this occurs, you will probably be stunned initially. You will wonder how someone can have the balls to act that way to a superior. Well, the rage they feel over the fact that you are their boss has rendered them stupid.

It happened to me when I was given the job of running *Family Weekly* while the publisher searched for an editor in chief. A woman on the staff, who was now reporting to me, suddenly turned very bratty. One day when I was dropping off a file in her office, she asked me to close the door. Dutifully—and idiotically—I did so. As I stood in front of her desk—where she was *seated*, by the way—she told me that she had the publisher wrapped around her finger and could make things easier for me. I muttered something like "Of course I need everyone's support" and left.

As soon as I got back to my office—and reassured myself that no, I wasn't in a 1940s movie starring Joan Crawford or Barbara Stanwyck—I realized how dumb I'd been. I'd let her act if *she* were the one calling the shots. And it had been made worse by the fact that she had been sitting at her desk (in the power position) and I'd been standing in front of it (in the supplicant position).

When you're first establishing your authority (you won't need to worry so much about stuff like this when you're firmly in charge), be careful about ending up with the wrong feng shui for a boss. Don't allow yourself to be cornered or placed in an awkward seating or standing situation. The moment the woman told me to shut the door, I should have told her, "If you have something you want to discuss with me privately, you need to set up a time to do it. Call me later when I have my calendar in front of me." And then I should have had the discussion in *my* office. If she'd still had the nerve to make her little comment, I should have said, "All I need from you right now is to focus on doing your job and doing it well. You shouldn't be spending time on inappropriate things, like trying to wrap someone around your finger."

One successful woman I know believes that, with resentful employees, it helps to put things on the table. You can say something such as "You seem to have an issue with me. Let's talk about it."

It would be nice if those with a big chip on their shoulder eventually sweetened up. But over the years, I've found that people who feel totally wronged by someone else's hire rarely get over it. Your best bet is to eliminate them from your staff as soon as possible.

Rule #12: *Hire passionate people whose strengths compensate for some of your weaknesses—and who won't just tell you what you want to hear.* One of the worst bosses I had, an editor at a woman's magazine, hated it when you didn't agree with her. Not long after I started, we were doing a one-page story on improving your public speaking skills and the art department had picked a photo of a woman wearing a dress so short you could practically see the crack in her ass. I suggested to my boss that we use another shot. But my boss allowed the photo to run, in part, I think, because she'd hated being contradicted. After that I learned to keep my mouth shut. That woman, I came to see, was surrounded by yes people, and that is partly why she failed in the end.

Second opinions are so often worth hearing. They can wake you up and make you aware of new trends and insights, which in the end leads to better decision making. So hire smart people with minds of their own and fire in their bellies. Yes, they must endorse your mission, but let them talk, let them run with projects. (How do you find these people? When you interview job candidates, ask them to describe something they're passionate about and times when they've taken risks.)

If one of your star players seems to run out of steam or lose his way after being there a while, don't just decide that it's over. Give him a brand-new project to do—it may help him get his mojo back.

Rule #13: *Make people ask (even beg a little) for their promotions.* I absolutely love promoting from within. When I arrived at *Cosmo*, I discovered that most editorial assistants in the articles area eventually left the magazine after a couple of years because there were no positions for them to be promoted into. I created two associate editor positions to solve that problem, and over time we promoted many assistants into those jobs and then even into senior editor and deputy editor positions. But here's what became clear over time: if we waited for someone to come to us and ask for the job before promoting her—rather than simply announcing to her that she was getting it—things turned out better.

The new editor would be more likely to feel that she *owned* the job, and work hard at it. For some idiotic reason, I occasionally did not follow my own advice and almost always regretted it.

Rule #14: *Never underestimate the power of giving someone a title.* Yes, people want raises—*good raises*—and they want promotions, too. But sometimes neither is yours to bestow at a given moment, so upgrade the person's title. Trendera CEO Jane Buckingham says that early on in her business, when she couldn't afford to hire extra people, she recruited interns and gave them fancy titles. "I let an intern put 'trend specialist' on her business card, for instance," she says. "And there's a bonus that comes with this. So often people totally take off in the role. They rise to their titles."

Rule #15: *Fire intelligently.* Sometimes you have to let people go for economic reasons. Maybe times are tough, or it could simply be that your company is restructuring. Regardless, there's nothing you can do about it (except to offer whatever support and job leads you can).

But as a boss you'll also have to fire people for cause sometimes— because they're not capable of doing their jobs or doing them the right way. This gets a bit trickier. It's not always black and white, and no one is giving you a deadline. I've had to do my fair share of this kind of firing, as well as guide people on my staff as they terminated people under them. And as you might imagine, it's an easy process to mess up. The two most common mistakes I see people making—and I've made them myself—are firing too quickly and not firing quickly enough. This sounds contradictory, but let me explain.

Sometimes people fail at their jobs not because they are incompetent or lazy but because they don't know what they're supposed to be doing or perhaps have been miscast. Before you let someone go, it's important to ask yourself if you have been absolutely clear about your expectations with this person and what he is doing wrong. (If you do feel someone's performance is suffering and that it may lead to termination, be sure to contact HR to determine the steps you should be taking.) Also, could there be something getting in the way of this person's performance that you could possibly fix? I once had a high-level employee whom I thought I was going to have to fire. She was very capable in some areas, but there were critical aspects of her job that she didn't do very well. But after thinking about it for a while, I shifted her job so that it involved doing mostly what she was good at and gave someone else the other responsibilities.

But once you are sure that you've been clear with your subordinate and she can't pull it off, act swiftly. You are torturing yourself, the rest of your staff, and even the subordinate by dragging out the situation.

Rule #16: *Have fun, be easy.* From the start at *Cosmo*, I tried in little ways to encourage a sense of fun and ease. I let people know that they could always bring their kids in if the babysitter failed to show. I also started organizing salons for the staff every six weeks with guest speakers—authors and experts of various kinds. Animal Planet star Dave Salmoni did two salons, one with a tiger and another with a cougar.

Rule #17: *That said, be sure there's an invisible line drawn between you and your subordinates.* You can be friendly without being a friend. If you cross that line, it opens a door for employees to take advantage in little ways, and it can be hard to play boss when situations require it.

Rule #18: *Be a bit of a mystery.* Don't share important details about your personal life. Don't always say where you're going. You don't want to be so mysterious that people start gossiping

that you're having an affair, but intriguing bosses are just m
interesting to work for.

Rule #19: *Last but not least, YOU DO NOT HA\
TO BE A BITCH.* I think women who make people feel li
stripped cars are either narcissistic or pathetic at handling stress, s
they take it out on others. Despite what you may have been led t
believe, being nice and fair will not undermine your success; in fact
I think being a nice, fair boss rather than a raging bitch will bring
out the best in the people who work for you, thus improving your
chances of achieving great success.

{ Arrive at Work Before Everybody Else }

'm sure there are plenty of successful women who don't arrive at work early, but my unscientific opinion is that you significantly increase your chances of success if you do. "Early" generally refers to early in the morning, but what I'm really talking about is at least an hour ahead of most everybody else—whenever that is.

You will discover very quickly that this strategy gives you a fantastic edge. By the time everyone else hauls butt through the door, you will have answered your e-mails, gone through the dregs of your in-box, written up your daily to-do list, and ticked off at least a few items on it. You will be firmly in charge of your day rather than at its mercy. You'll avoid that awful gotta-catch-up feeling that arriving later tends to cause or, even worse, the sense that the day is getting away from you.

Besides, though they may never admit it, many bosses have a weird thing about the time people arrive for work. They secretly *want* you to show up early. It suggests to them that you're really committed to your job.

I came to this wonderful success strategy fairly late in the game.

In my twenties I was an incorrigible night owl and rarely rolled into work before at least nine thirty (but never, I swear, in the same outfit I'd worn the day before). In my early forties I had to drop my kids off at school, preventing a well-timed arrival. But once my kids were older—and I saw my workload expanding like a Chia Pet—I decided to head in to the office before eight each day. And wow, what a huge difference it made. I wished I'd discovered the benefits years before.

If in your case arriving early at work means that you will have to wake up at some ungodly hour, please resist the urge to bitch-slap me because of this strategy. Instead, buy one of those wonderful alarm clocks that gently pings you awake instead of emitting a horrific blaring noise. That's what I did. It makes waking up early almost tolerable!

{ Beware of Sudden Promotion Syndrome }

From the moment C. arrived at *Cosmo* as a writer and editor, I was superimpressed by her skills. Her writing was not only very accomplished for someone her age, but it was also really witty and perfectly on the mark for *Cosmo* readers. I still remember one of the lines she wrote, and it makes me smile even now: "Granny panties are what you wear on the days that your butt needs a hug." When a senior editor position became available, we decided to give it to C. even without her asking. To our annoyance, once C. learned about her promotion, she pressed and pressed for a particular office that we'd earmarked for a deputy editor position yet to be filled; we finally caved, despite my better judgment. C. seemed thrilled with the decision.

But a funny thing happened to C. after she was promoted. Within weeks it was clear that some of the steam had seeped out of her. She continued to write and edit, but she didn't offer up the kind of killer ideas that the new job required. She stayed in her office for long stretches, mostly with the door shut. And when she felt under pressure, she cried.

I've promoted tons of people over the years, and I've mostly been thrilled with the results. In some cases there was an initial awkwardness or difficulty as the person got up to speed, but soon enough he or she took off.

But there have been more than a few who responded to their promotions the way C. did. They seemed to freeze, or their energy fizzled, and they never rose to the challenge of the new job. Or they completely botched their new responsibilities. I think of it as Sudden Promotion Syndrome.

Why does this happen? I asked that question of Adele Scheele, PhD, the pioneering career coach and the author of *Skills for Success*, who wrote a terrific career column for me at *Working Woman* and now does the same for the *Huffington Post*. Scheele knows a lot about how we handle change—she got her doctorate in it—and she has some definite thoughts on SPS.

"Winning a job promotion isn't so different than being a marathon runner," she says. "You cross the finish line but may end up crashing afterward. You used a lot of time, effort, and strategy in order to be recognized enough to land the new title. But after you realize the goal that's been driving you, things start to sink in: Do you deserve it? Do you want it? Are you going to be found out?"

Part of the problem, says Scheele, is that although we want more, we also, at the same time, want to know the territory, to feel comfortable in some basic ways, and not to have to learn everything all at once. "A new job or promotion can be such an overwhelming change," she says, "that some people—more women—don't even try. Those who do still have to internally process the chaos, turbulence, and the unknown."

In hindsight I think that C. was pretty overwhelmed. That would explain the tears and shutting herself away behind a closed door for hours. I also believe she may have imagined her career only up to the point of *becoming* a senior editor, and once she had the title (and that sweet office), she went into idling mode.

I've also noticed over the years that women sometimes feel more panicky in new jobs than men do. Whereas men view being in a situation where they don't know everything as simply "a stretch," a woman might start thinking "Yikes, I'm in over my head." And that can lead to paralysis. Or, in her anxiety to prove herself, she goes full-tilt boogie without really thinking about what she *should* be doing.

Though Sudden Promotion Syndrome has the potential to undermine your career, it *can* be treated effectively. Just recognizing that it's begun to take hold is half the battle. Here are some key steps for dealing with it.

Upgrade your image immediately. Buy new clothes, new shoes, a new coat, and a new handbag—all fitting your new position. And have your hair trimmed and newly styled. "To be the part, you have to *look* the part," says Tracy Shaffer, my terrific entertainment director at *Cosmo*, who was once the publicist for celebrities such as Johnny Depp and Denise Richards. "That's why stars wear lipstick when they take out the trash."

Those kinds of style upgrades also help you *feel* the part. Now, you may hesitate to indulge in a minimakeover like this because you're afraid people will assume you're now Miss Smarty-Pants. And guess what? Some *will* think that, especially people you left behind or those you are now competing with. But it's generally only out of envy. Trust me, the benefits far outweigh the negatives here.

Set up an appointment with your boss to discuss exactly what he expects of you. You must do this with any new job, but it's especially important when you've been promoted. Because you're already on the "inside," your boss may assume you know what you should be doing next—but how *can* you know all the ins and outs of someone else's job? Besides, your boss may have rethought—consciously or unconsciously—how he wants the job to be handled this time. So make an appointment with him, show up with your notepad or iPad, and hear everything he's got in mind. Ask questions such as "What goals would you like me to hit in the next three months—and by the end of the year?" and "Are there things you'd like me to accomplish that weren't being addressed previously?"

Listen between the lines, too. Bosses sometimes haven't yet articulated to themselves what they think was missing, and you may have to tease that information out. Go back to your desk or workstation, and reread the notes you took. Do that every week, in fact, to be sure you're not straying from the mission. Having the responsibilities and goals in front of you in black and white will not only guide you but also ease any panicky SPS feelings.

Now make a plan. Or if your job is fairly advanced, you might need to develop a real mission statement. Let's say you're now in charge of PR for a small company and your boss wants you to create more buzz. Your mission would involve garnering more coverage via print, TV, online, and general word of mouth. But try to come up with a tight angle and focus for your overall goal.

I was handed a terrific mission statement when I arrived at *Cosmo*: Fun Fearless Female. It was a slogan created for an ad campaign several years before I started, and it fit both the magazine and the reader perfectly. Everything needed to match those three little words. And though they served me well for anything I was doing at a given moment, they were also directional. As the world became edgier, *Cosmo* could never seem less than totally fearless.

You then have to consider what projects will help fulfill that mission (your boss will have probably shared some thoughts but it's up to you to figure out others). Again, if you're in PR, those projects might include everything from securing profiles of people in your company to organizing tent-pole events that will get talked about. Determine, based on your notes, which projects take priority and set deadlines for them. Block out times on your calendar to concentrate on what must be accomplished. Keep a to-do list.

Accelerate your learning curve, even if no one is telling you to do so. In almost any new job, you're going to need to learn new things. You'll step into the job with some of the skills and knowledge required (unless you've totally snookered your superiors) but not necessarily all of them. That's okay, that's the way it works (guys tend to get this better than we do). If you had every skill and piece of knowledge that was required, you'd be ready for the job *above* your new one. Besides, a job isn't exciting if you're not learning in it. That said, you must master new skills and acquire knowledge as quickly as you can—even if you're not feeling any direct pressure to do so.

Sometimes you can find the information you need right where you are. Ask your boss for any relevant material she'd like you to take a look at. Go through any material or files that were left by the person you were replacing. (I've found this extremely helpful on several occasions!) If part of your new job is receiving reports from people in support areas, ask if they'd please do a follow-up call or meeting with you to run through the info. Some people like to strut their stuff this way, and it will give you the chance to delve deeper. If there are people from other areas or departments that you'll now be working with, take them out for coffee and ask for info. You don't want to sound needy or unsure, but saying something such as "I'd love to hear how your department works" will provide great intel.

In some cases, you may have to go outside to improve your skills. That's what Dr. Holly Phillips did after she took a job as a health reporter for a New York City TV station. Phillips, a graduate of Williams College and Columbia University College of Physicians and Surgeons, was a practicing internist in Manhattan who was frequently asked to appear on TV and discuss medical issues. Working with an agent, she made a demo reel of her many TV appearances and within a short time landed the job as a reporter. Because she'd never been an actual reporter before, the station provided her with a producer who offered her lots of guidance. But Dr. Phillips felt she'd have a huge leg up if she went further than that, so she hired a private media coach on her own dime. "It cost me the first three months' salary," she says, "but it was worth it. There are aspects of being on television, like the cadence you need to speak with, that I couldn't have picked up on my own." She's now the medical contributor for *CBS This Morning*.

Prepare to wow them. You've figured out a plan to accomplish what your boss wants, and that's good. But remember, you need to do more than they tell you. In part I, I talked about the importance of noting what may be missing or what needs to be fixed. Keep an eye out for that sort of stuff and run with it.

Don't hide in your workspace or office. Most of the people I've worked with who had Sudden Promotion Syndrome burrowed into their offices like chipmunks or moles. They clearly concluded that if they hid out, they'd (1) be out of the line of fire and (2) get their work done better and faster. But to a boss, burrowing makes you look unengaged or scared.

Own your new power. Sit where someone of your stature is expected to sit at meetings, and use the perks that have been given to you. There's no reason to be modest. And *delegate*. If you have an assistant for the first time, work it, even if you feel awkward initially. Really successful people can answer their own phones, but if you're at midlevel, having an assistant do it or grab you lunch occasionally helps establish your clout with the people around you.

If you've been promoted from one job to another in the same workplace, distance yourself from office pals who aren't on your level, at least at the office. I know, I know, it sounds really bitchy and mean. But if *your* boss sees you still chatting at their workstations or eating with them in the cafeteria, it will make you look "junior" to her. If you're actually close friends with someone, tell her that you are crazed with the new job and will have to focus on catching up with her after hours.

{ 18 People Principles: Because Now You Really, Really Need Them }

No matter how well you handle your actual job, you won't be able to optimize it if you don't learn to handle people well, too. I've already talked about how to deal effectively with both your boss and the people who report to you, but there are all sorts of other people you come into contact with each day, including colleagues on your level in your immediate area; coworkers in other departments who are below, above, or equal to you in rank; your boss's boss; people outside your own company, such as clients, whom you must interact or do business with; and support personnel both inside and outside your workplace. If you travel for business, that includes everyone from flight attendants to desk clerks at hotels.

Though those people—let's call them coworkers just to make it easier—don't leap out of bed each morning thinking of ways to make you a star, they often play a key role in how successful you will be in your job and your career.

In many ways, coworkers help make a job exciting and fun (some of my closest friends are men and women I once worked with), but, let's be honest, they can also present plenty of challenges. Unlike with a boss, there's no strict protocol you can fall back on, and, unlike with people who report to you, you generally don't have a lick of authority with them. That's why you need to master people skills. And it's especially important as you reach the first levels of success. The more power and responsibility you have, the more you will be interacting with people outside your area—people you hope to collaborate with, for instance, or people you may need something from but who aren't necessarily required to give it.

Unfortunately, there also may be more people gunning for you once you're a success. If you have something they want, such as power or a killer idea, they may not hesitate to come after it. The workplace *can* be a jungle at times—filled with tigers, snakes, and jackals!

The good news is that once you master some basic people skills (aka rules of the jungle), you can rely on them forever because people tend to be fairly predictable. Here are the best rules I know for interacting with coworkers based on what I've learned by trial and error and from watching people better at it than I am.

Principle #1: *Almost everyone wants to feel good about him- or herself.* It's a very simple principle, and acting with it in mind will make you much more effective—whether you're negotiating with your boss's assistant for time on his calendar or you're part of an interdepartmental committee of people who are all on your level. Whenever possible, acknowledge the other person's expertise and your respect for it. It's the difference between saying "You gotta figure out what's wrong with my AV setup!" and "You're such a whiz with this stuff. I'm sure you can figure out what's wrong." But they will know if you don't really mean it. "People want to feel important and valued," says Dr. Dale Atkins, a psychologist with whom I sometimes appear on the *Today* show, "but the key in communicating is to show a genuineness and sincerity when you say something rather than sound like you're just complimenting them because you want something."

Principle #2: *People who approach you generally have an agenda, and you should figure out what it is.* When people contact you at work—whether in person, by phone, or by e-mail—there's almost always a purpose. They need something from you, for instance, or they want to pass along information. Sometimes, though, the agenda is not what it seems, and you need to discover it. Ask questions. Listen carefully. Ask yourself, too, whether the agenda the person announces to you may not be the *true* agenda.

Principle #3: *Sugar lips can get you what you want.* When I was the editor in chief of *Redbook*, I gave a luncheon to honor some of the outstanding members of Mothers Against Drunk Driving, and we asked Elizabeth Dole, a former U.S. senator and then the head of the American Red Cross, to present the awards. As I was reading up on her before the event, I discovered that she was sometimes known as Sugar Lips. Why that nickname? She was apparently a master at getting her way by sweet-talking. The day of the luncheon, I was able to see the sugar lips in action. Dole was strong and impressive but also very warm and incredibly charming.

Up until I read the articles about Senator Dole, I hadn't heard the term "sugar lips" (though it's apparently an old southern expression), but I'd certainly seen the technique before. In my neck of the woods it was known as "You can catch more flies with honey than with vinegar." Regardless of what you call it, it works.

By sugar lips I don't mean acting all gushy. I'm talking about using a little charm to persuade people rather than acting like a bully or a bitch. The phrase "I could really use your help," said with a smile, can work brilliantly.

When I was first starting out in the work world, women were encouraged to talk tough, act tough, and take no prisoners. But there are several problems with this approach. One, it can be very threatening, especially to men, and the other person ends up becoming defensive rather than cooperative. Two, it leaves you with nowhere to go if things *aren't* working out. And last, as that became the modus operandi for many women and men, too, it lost all its wallop. If everyone is bitching or barking, it's not going to grab attention as it might have before.

When Lady Gaga's publicist called a week before our *Cosmo* cover shoot with her and reported that she wasn't feeling up to it, I wondered briefly if I should try to go into a hard-ass "We had a deal" mode. But I knew that that would do nothing to help my case. So I called one of the top people at the record company and asked for his help. I told him that I knew that the cover would be important for both of us—an issue of *Cosmo*, I told him, generally sold more on the newsstand than *Glamour*, *Vogue*, and *InStyle* combined—and I was hoping he could do all he could to turn the situation around. He did just that. The cover shoot went great, and the issue was a top seller.

Principle #4: *Sometimes you need to kick butt and take numbers.* Unfortunately, sugar lips don't always work. In certain instances you have to get tough. But by tough I mean firm, direct, no-nonsense, giving a hint of anger without raising your voice. Not shrill or strident—it makes you seem weak. No name-calling or idle threats, such as the lame "I'll have your job!" That kind of remark only backs people into a corner. When you're talking about anything from bad behavior to a pathetic hotel room, a great phrase is "This is unacceptable, and it's important that you fix it immediately."

Principle #5: *If you tell someone something under the legendary "cone of silence," there is about an*

85 percent chance that he or she will repeat it. People are very bad at keeping secrets. They swear that they will place your secret "in the vault," but guess what? *There is no vault!* In some cases people blab just because they're compulsive gossipers; while you're still speaking, they're thinking of whom they can spill to. You can learn to spot those people, by the way; they're the ones who tell *you* something they heard in confidence from someone else, claiming they're sharing with just you.

Other people don't *intend* to blab, but a moment arrives when sharing the secret will make them seem wonderfully in the know, and they go for it. When I was pregnant with my first child, I wanted to wait to tell my boss until I was safely past the first trimester. I sensed that my pregnancy might throw her a curveball, and there seemed no point in shaking things up unnecessarily. Just before I was planning to break the news, I flew to San Francisco for a business trip with several people from the advertising sales team. One of the women on the trip looked at me after I'd ordered my third Caesar salad in two days (I had such a pregnancy-related food craving for Caesar salad that at times it seemed I might end up giving birth to a head of romaine lettuce!). I whispered to her that I was pregnant. It was nice to share the news, and I felt no qualms she'd tell. No one, I decided, would betray that kind of secret. WRONG. She told her boss, who then told my boss. It clearly made the chick feel important to relay that kind of news. And my boss, as you'd expect, was pissed off that I hadn't told her first.

That's when I realized that no secret is entirely safe, even personal ones (it's best, by the way, to *always* leave those at home). When people don't out-and-out spread the story, the info may still leak out from them indirectly.

Does that mean you should never confide anything to anyone? No. Because you sometimes *have* to share sensitive work info with your team. But help them understand the importance of discretion. Start with "I really need everyone to keep this information confidential. Can I count on you?" But be prepared that it still might get out.

Principle #6: *Secret keepers go far.* It's hard to keep a juicy secret. But if you promised you would, you must. One way to resist telling anyone is to *relish* the secret. Be like the cat that ate the canary, and delight in the fact that you have something no one else does. If you're good at keeping secrets, you'll earn a reputation for it, and people will share info of value. What you can share instead is industry gossip that you've overheard or read about. That will prevent you from seeming prissy.

Principle #7: *You can learn a lot from people's body language if you pay attention.* I'm fascinated with body language. I've not only written articles on it myself but also published lots of pieces with some of the top body language experts as sources. Reading a book by someone like Janine Driver or David Givens is worth the time, but you can also gain a lot just by tuning in to the gestures and expressions people use. Those movements are often quite literal. When someone can't meet your eyes easily, trust me, he's uncomfortable for some reason. When someone touches her lips or nose, she may feel awkward about what she's saying (it could even be a lie). One gesture I've never read anything about but find quite revealing is when someone who is seated kicks his or her foot up a little—especially when you've just asked a question. It seems to signal that you've hit a nerve somehow. In fact, it's almost the same thing that happens when a doctor taps your knee with a reflex hammer!

Also look for recurring patterns, or what poker players call a "tell." I had a boss years ago whose eyes watered slightly when she didn't like where the conversation was headed. That was so useful. I knew when to change the subject!

Principle #8: *When you're trying to get into sync with someone, mirroring his or her body language works almost magically.* While doing research for an article for a magazine I was editing, I stumbled on information one day about the power of mirroring people's body language. It seemed awfully New Agey, but I found it intriguing. That same day I was having lunch with a writer I was trying to woo as a regular contributor and decided there was no harm in trying the technique. The lunch went well, and the writer accepted the offer. As we were leaving the restaurant, she stopped in her tracks and said, "I can't quite explain it, but this was one of the best lunch meetings I've ever had."

I felt a little guilty having used that lovely writer as a guinea pig, but I learned the value of mirroring that day. Lots of research backs it up—it's simply a way to get into sync with someone you're meeting with. If he puts his left hand into his lap, put your right hand in *your* lap. But wait a beat or two so it doesn't seem obvious, and don't mimic every gesture exactly.

Principle #9: *Sometimes the best way to extract information from people is to say nothing.* There will be times when you sense that people have something to tell you but are reluctant to do so. Do not pounce; it will only make them clam up. And don't try getting aggressive. That generally doesn't work either (unless you are working with a weapon or a water board, and I assume you are not). There's a much better technique that's sometimes called the "pregnant pause." Just sit there and wait patiently.

Lawyers use this, including Cumberland County chief deputy district attorney Jon Birbeck, who is a great source for me when I'm writing my thrillers and mysteries. "Silence is an effective tool in getting anyone to talk," he says. "Witnesses on the stand are uncomfortable with silence, so after a suspect answers a question on cross-examination, rather than jumping into the next question, count to eight silently while staring at your prey and then wait for him or her to start talking again. People are very, very uncomfortable with silence and a look, so they frantically try to break the quiet by rambling on and on."

Principle #10: *To succeed in most fields, you have to demonstrate you can be part of a team.* Secretary of State Hillary Clinton reportedly linked the State Department to the Pentagon, trading staff members and ideas as part of an initiative connecting diplomacy, development, and defense. That sounds like some sweet teamwork. One part of teamwork entails being willing to compromise. My brother Jim, a hedge fund professional, taught me that the trick is to focus on areas of agreement. Each player should rank different points on a scale of one to five in terms of priority. When you discover all the points you agree on, it makes it easier to hash out the other stuff.

Principle #11: *When you need to make a point with someone (such as the desk clerk at the hotel that doesn't have the right room for you), use the broken record technique.* This is an approach I learned during my twenties when I was writing a lot about consumer rights, a hot topic at the time. If you're not making headway, repeat your message again (and again), varying the words slightly each time but never raising your voice ("I understand you are full, but I requested a room on a nonsmoking floor, and it's essential that I have one"). It's very effective at wearing the person down. And because you don't sound angry or emotional, you don't make the other person defensive.

Principle #12: *People, even nice ones, will sometimes do something not very nice to you at work.* In certain instances you see it coming—perhaps the person has a rep for a type of behavior and you know it's only a matter of time before you end up on the hit list. But other times it comes out of nowhere and you experience the double whammy of not only being snakebit but also being blindsided.

There are a bunch of different ways people can mess with you at work. There's passive-aggressive behavior, for instance. The person "forgets" to tell you important info, such as when a meeting is scheduled, and you end up arriving late. Then there's sneaky stuff: a coworker goes around you on a matter you should be dealing with or takes credit for an idea of yours. In certain instances this is done in a very subtle way—what you could call a "soft assault"—that (1) makes you wonder if you might have imagined it and (2) leaves you thinking that it might be best just to let it go. Here's an example of what I mean. I was at a big meeting once where someone who dealt with my area in a marginal way made a comment about the terrific results of a project a staff member of mine had worked on. There was technically nothing wrong with what she said—it was totally positive—but by talking about it, she took ownership in an indirect way, and I'm sure some people at the meeting assumed she was involved.

Unfortunately, there's also behavior that's on a practically vicious level: you find that someone has been backstabbing you, spreading a rumor about you, or even undermining your efforts.

Why do people do bad stuff like this? Usually, I've found, it's because they feel threatened on some level. You're earning good marks, for instance, and they resent you for it. Or it may not have anything to do with you directly. They may feel anxious about not having any winning ideas, so they poach one that just happens to be yours. Idea stealers, I've found over the years, are almost always people who suck at coming up with good ideas themselves and are afraid it will catch up with them. (By the way, when you have a good idea, don't go blabbing about it to coworkers; send it in an e-mail to your boss.)

When I started writing this book, I intended to have a whole chapter on all the types of bad behavior you might encounter from people and how to deal with each. But the more I thought about it, the more I realized that though there are many transgressions that can occur on the job, you must deal with almost all of them in basically the same way: you must let the other person know that you disapprove of what just went down, and it had better not happen again. Dr. Atkins concurs. "In most cases," she says, "this will mean that the person's actions are now 'public,' even if you and she are the only people who know what's going on. There's a better chance of the offender taking responsibility and watching their actions if they are aware that what they did is not going to be tolerated."

Confronting the person will be awkward and you may try to talk yourself out of it, mentally reassuring yourself that it probably won't happen again. Oh, but it *will*. That's because by not saying anything, you've indicated to your coworker that you don't mind her naughty behavior or are too much of a weenie to do anything about it. And what I've found is that the next time is often worse.

When you speak to someone about his or her behavior, avoid going in with your guns blazing. That can put the person so much on the defensive that you end up accomplishing nothing, except perhaps leaving a trail of bloodshed. Instead speak calmly and avoid making a direct accusation, as in "You've been complaining about my strategy to anyone who will freaking listen." Dr. Atkins suggests something along the lines of "It's come to my attention that you may have some issues with my project." A pregnant pause can work great here. Give the person a chance to respond, even if it takes a minute. If he admits the truth, you can discuss the situation. End with a comment like, "We're all working toward the same goal. If you have a problem in the future, please speak to me directly about it."

If he denies the whole thing, don't contradict him but instead say something such as "Well, I think it's important for you to be aware that this is what people are saying." This will not only prevent you from getting into an ugly back-and-forth but also put him on notice that you're on to him and won't accept further bad behavior.

When someone's behavior just barely crosses the line, asking him or her a question can be a good way to show your displeasure or concern without causing things to heat up. With the woman who seemed to be trying to own my staffer's idea, I called her after the meeting and said, "I'm curious. Why did you decide to bring up L.'s project?" She muttered something about simply wanting to compliment our efforts. "I think it's best to leave it to L. to discuss in meetings," I replied. "I don't want anyone confused about how much work she did on it."

Principle #13: *When you find yourself seriously annoyed by someone at work, it can often mean that you're actually annoyed at yourself.* Perhaps because you don't like the way you responded in a situation. Or because the other person did something you wish *you'd* thought of.

Principle #14: *If someone pisses you off, it's always better to count to ten (at the very least) before responding.* When you need to address someone's actions, avoid doing so until the steam stops coming out of your ears. Count to ten. Or if possible, sleep on it. The discussion will go far better, other coworkers will be less likely to get wind of the problem, and you won't feel stupid afterward. If possible, handle the situation in person. E-mails have an ugly habit of blowing up in one's face—and then there's that awful trail. If you must respond to someone's behavior by e-mail, write a draft without the person's e-mail address in the "to" line. And imagine other people seeing it, because they very well might. Give yourself at least a few hours before sending it.

As *Morning Joe* cohost Mika Brzezinski told us for her *Cosmo* column, "If I'd known years ago that being calm leads to the most effective conversations with men (and women!), not only would I have spent less time getting upset, but I'd also be making a lot more money now."

Principle #15: *Unless it's absolutely essential, don't drag your boss into a problem you're having with a coworker.* The bottom line: if you tell your boss you're having issues with someone, he's probably going to assume that you are part of the problem. I learned that the hard way when I worked for Art Cooper at *Family Weekly*. A young female editor who'd been in charge of a failed special section of the magazine had to eventually be absorbed into my department, which meant she was now loosely reporting to me after having been fairly autonomous. She bristled when I gave her assignments and rolled her eyes at my comments in meetings, so I strode into Art's office one day and told him what was going on. He shook his head in dismay. "The last thing we need here is the battle of the blondes," he said. I cringed at his words. He was practically calling me a member of Female Jell-O Wrestlers of America. I knew then I should have done everything possible to sort out the situation myself.

Sometimes you have no choice but to involve your boss. If that's the case, ask for his advice on a very professional level or suggest possible solutions that you want her input on. That way you come across as a grown-up rather than a tattletale or someone hopelessly out of her depth. What I should have said to Art was "Can I ask for your advice on something? K. is not used to having a top editor on her work, and she seems unhappy with the system as is. How would you suggest we handle it?"

Principle #16: *Even in the sanest workplaces, you can come face to face with a psycho.* Idea stealers, land grabbers, backstabbers, they all pale next to a coworker who is a psycho—someone totally unethical or narcissistic. Now, you may be lucky enough never to interact with one—I've met only a couple in my whole career—but unfortunately they do sometimes rear their ugly heads.

How do you know if you've encountered a psycho? Initially it's tough because psychos often appear fairly normal (experts call this "wearing the mask of sanity"). But then one day he or she does something that's the tip-off, something that, as Dr. Atkins says, leaves you slapping your head and silently asking "Wait, what just happened here?" Psycho behavior is totally out of line and over the top compared to anything else you've experienced.

Consider what happened to a friend of mine after law school. She went to work for a government agency, and not long after she started, she wrote an article she planned to submit to a trade journal for publication. First, though, she gave it to her boss—a sane-enough seeming guy—for his opinion. Weeks passed, and her boss didn't return it. Since my friend was new on the job, she hated to nudge, so she bided her time. Finally she offered a gentle reminder, and her boss nodded in understanding. More time passed. Then lo and behold, my friend discovered her article published in a journal under her boss's name!

"With this type of individual, it's all about them, not about you or the goals of the company," says Dr. Atkins. "They often stop at nothing and don't see what they're doing as wrong."

If you work for a psycho, get out as soon as you can because the situation will never improve. If you have a psycho for a coworker, avoid that person if you can. Not possible? "Then have people with you when you meet with the person," says Atkins, "and do as much interacting as possible by e-mail so you have a paper trail." If you must address any bad behavior with him, keep your tone totally neutral, and be prepared for the fact that he will never, ever admit to having done anything wrong.

I met my first workplace psycho years ago at a very nice company. The guy—let's call him Dexter—worked in another area, but occasionally our worlds overlapped a little. One day I learned that for reasons I would never understand, he had tried to use his clout to dismantle a project I'd put together. I felt totally out of my element with him—it was like being put into a tiny room with a puma—so I went on instinct. First, I avoided any kind of discussion with Dexter himself over what he was doing (I kept reminding myself of that old expression "When you get in a wrestling match with a pig, you both get dirty—and the pig likes it"). Instead I dealt with several people in corporate, trying to reinforce with them the value of the project. And I never backstabbed the guy. But after the corporate executive relayed updates on Dexter's efforts, I would ask questions such as "Why do you think he would say that?" I think those questions were key. They seemed to help her see that Dexter's crusade was about his own ego and nothing more.

Principle #17: *Men can still feel threatened by women.*
When women first began entering the workforce in big numbers, plenty of guys felt confused and threatened, and they sometimes responded hostilely, inappropriately, or just plain stupidly. When I was on a business trip as the editor in chief of *McCall's*, a male executive from my company spotted me in the breakfast room of the hotel and hollered across the room, "Hey, Kate, was that you pounding on my door late last night?" What a jerk, right? Over the years things have improved greatly, especially in female-dominated fields, where the men coming in generally have an appreciation of women—but you can still encounter problems. Sometimes it's in the form of sexual harassment—inappropriate comments or behavior of

a sexual nature. Sometimes it's what I call guerrilla chauvinism, such as not making eye contact with you in a meeting or not including you in a key activity.

With guerilla chauvinism, you could try saying something to the guy, but he will probably pull his head back, scrunch up his face, and act as if you're *nuts*. I've found that a better way is to try to humanize the situation. Suck it up and ask him to coffee. Share some info that will help him out. He'll see that you're not out to neuter him. Of course, if you are both on the same promotion track, his behavior may not change. Focus on your work and your relationship with your boss, make sure your ideas are in writing, and watch your back.

With any type of sexual harassment, address it immediately—because this is the kind of bad behavior that will *absolutely* happen again if you don't shut it down. Say something like "Your comment made me feel very uncomfortable. Please don't say anything like that to me again." You're entitled to go to your boss or HR because sexual harassment is illegal, but that can ratchet the situation up, so many experts believe it's best to try to deal with it person to person first. If you correct it that way, you will avoid unnecessary drama and the awkwardness that can follow.

Principle #18: *You must check company policy before you take your work crush to the next level.* Some studies show that more than 40 percent of couples meet at work. And why not? It's less clunky than blind dating and less risky than meeting someone at a bar. And in closed quarters sparks can fly. Years ago, when I was single, a boss of mine who was leaving the company totally surprised me by taking me into his arms, kissing me, and telling me "I've wanted to do that since the day we met."

But some companies have policies against dating anyone on staff, and it's important to discreetly check it out before the first drink. It may appear in the company policy guidelines on the web-site. If there's no prohibition and you take the plunge, never bring your relationship into the office. Even if coworkers are aware of the romance, avoid references to it at work or any displays of affection. And know that even if you decide you want to keep the relationship under wraps, probably no amount of discretion on your part will prevent coworkers from finding out. They *will* know.

What if you're hot for a boss or a subordinate? That's always a no-no. Oh, it can be wickedly fun, but there could very well be consequences—including utter awkwardness at work, damage to your stature and rep, and even dismissal (yours!).

{ The Secret Weapon That Will Make You a Winner (and Save Your Butt) }

About a week after I landed the job as editor in chief of *Cosmopolitan*, I sat down for a meeting with a man named Chris Butler, the consumer marketing person I'd be involved with on a regular basis. Chris oversaw subscription and newsstand sales. I'd worked with him while I was at *Redbook*, and I was pleased that our partnership would continue. Not only was he very smart, but he'd been on *Cosmo* for a while and already knew the ins and outs of the magazine.

Chris was one of the few people I felt comfortable admitting the truth to—that I was more than nervous about my new job, a job I'd never even *applied* for. "I don't know a freaking thing about the audience," I said. "And there's just so much at stake."

"Don't worry," he said. "Editing *Cosmo* is unambiguous. You'll see once you get to know more about the reader. It's very clear what they're looking for from the magazine."

And he was so right. As soon as I started seeing e-mails from readers and hearing them talk at focus groups, I discovered that they were gutsy and fun, and they came to the magazine for very straightforward reasons—to be informed and entertained about men, sex, fashion, beauty, health, and living life to the fullest. If I paid attention to what readers were telling me about their needs, I'd be okay. In fact, there was a chance I'd thrive.

What Chris was reminding me of that day is that knowledge really *is* power. When you are making any kind of key decision or move in your job, information is your secret weapon. Of course, it seems stupid to call it a *secret* weapon. In many jobs we're encouraged to constantly acquire info, and thanks to technology, that's easier to do than ever. Yet we often fail to use knowledge to our advantage. We either don't gather it on a regular basis, or we reject what we discover.

"Just like in love, people in business tend to hear what they want to hear—or discredit where it's coming from," says Trendera CEO Jane Buckingham. "Sometimes bad news is too hard to take, so people just pretend they didn't hear it. One of our clients once was a TV network that had a show by a great producer and writer, but unfortunately it just wasn't a good show and everyone who saw it disliked it. But the network really wanted to be in a relationship with the writer and producer and ignored what viewers of the show were saying. The show was canceled four episodes in."

The other reason people don't use knowledge is that they don't program their minds to really consider it. They let their eyes skim over what might be of value without gaining any traction. You have to set your brain on "inquiry" and make it a habit to seek and question.

Though I regularly listen to my gut to make decisions, I also rely on research, and from the moment I began at *Cosmo* I did a ton of it. And over the years that information guided how I evolved the magazine. For instance, I saw from studying the ratings that the health column that was running in *Cosmo* when I arrived scored poorly, except when gynecological or breast issues were addressed. That made perfect sense, actually. Readers were hardly coming to the magazine to learn how to handle a head cold or dig a splinter out of their foot. Their *mothers* could tell them that. What they craved was info about sexual health and facts about their bodies they couldn't find elsewhere. So I started two brand-new health columns, one called "Gyno" and the other called "Your Body," where the main item would be breast news. They became two of the highest-rated columns in the magazine.

I also began to see through research how much readers liked it when we explained the male mind to them. Yes, they wanted info on how to navigate their relationships, which had been a staple of *Cosmo* for years. But they also yearned to know what made men tick. When I was in my twenties and thirties, there seemed to be a sense that if we forced men to drink enough chardonnay, they'd become more like us, but the new *Cosmo* readers knew that was never gonna happen. They accepted that guys were hardwired differently from them but wanted to understand the differences. The four-page section called "101 Things About Men," which I started in 2011, quickly became the highest-rated section in the magazine.

So turn knowledge into your secret weapon. Here's how.

Make information gathering a regular part of what you do. It shouldn't simply be a matter of conducting an annual survey or holding an occasional feedback session. Always be picking people's brains, listening, investigating. Train your brain to be on the lookout for info relevant to your field, and snag what might be essential for you. Sue Leibman, the president of Barking Dog Entertainment, who manages the careers of many celebrities, worked for Warren Beatty early in her work life. She said Beatty is a brilliant, always inquisitive man, whose favorite line was "Tell me what you know."

Accept info only from people who have a freaking clue what they're talking about. I'm sure you've noticed this by now. People love to weigh in on all sorts of things—even when they know absolutely nothing at all on the subject. In my business this is particularly true when it comes to covers. From the time I started booking celebrity covers—as far back as my early thirties—I read everything I could about celebs, tracked box-office results, and researched magazine sales. Unfortunately, there's no science to picking a cover subject, but when you've educated your gut, you at least have a hint of whether someone's image will sell.

But people with no expertise, people who *haven't* done their homework, will happily volunteer their opinion and perhaps even try to force it on you. With everyone who offers info, ask yourself: How much does he know on the subject? Where is he getting his information? Can I really trust what he's saying?

Set up a Google alert or get the Flipboard app to provide you with a regular flow of information on any subject you should be informed about. Things are moving too fast today to simply count on the right information finding you.

When you hear or see something intriguing, don't just note it: Think about how it could be used effectively. Dari Marder, the chief marketing officer of Iconix, which designs and markets products for companies such as Candies and London Fog, is a master at gathering info and using it to design awesome campaigns for her products. She used those skills superbly after she'd signed the model Gabriel Aubry to appear shirtless in bed for a campaign for Charisma Bed & Bath products. "At the same time we were shooting Gabriel," says Marder, "I was trying to book his ex, Halle Berry, for another campaign. Someone on her team mentioned that she had just shot the September cover for *Vogue*, which is usually a pretty closely guarded secret. I decided to hold the release of my Charisma campaign until the same period, and then time my PR strategy to a day or so before the *Vogue* cover was released. My hope was that every time the media did a piece on Halle's cover, the news of what her ex-boyfriend was up to would be folded into it. It worked. The launch of the campaign garnered about 250 million PR impressions. Not bad for a campaign about sheets, towels, and comforters."

Toughen up. Yes, the truth can hurt sometimes, but tell yourself to get over it. You want to be not only open to what's negative but also willing to seek it out. As Bill Gates put it, "Your most unhappy customers are your greatest source of learning." Then listen carefully. Write down what you've heard. (Yes, even if it makes you cringe.) Writing it down not only gives you a sense of control in the moment, but also guarantees you won't miss anything important. Ask questions. Get below the surface.

This is especially necessary when you need to orchestrate a turnaround. As much as info may sting, it can also guide you out of the woods. Shortly after I started running *Child* magazine, a parenting magazine for upscale parents, two researchers from the parent company visited me to present a study on the market they'd been asked to conduct. And talk about info that stings! They'd discovered that the number of parents who had high incomes and kids under the age of two was actually very low. I mean *really* low. Too low to make a magazine for. But after accepting that number for what it was (the ugly truth), I immediately refocused the magazine for parents who were educated and successful but not super affluent. I doubled the newsstand sales the first year.

Know that some info is just plain wrong. When I was at *Redbook*, women in focus groups sometimes told us that we should put women such as Sandra Day O'Connor on the cover. I guarantee you, if I'd followed that advice, I wouldn't be sitting here giving you tips on success. Sometimes it's hard to spot a phony "fact." But the more of an information gatherer you become, the easier it will be.

When you have a setback, double your research efforts. But recognize that the sources you've been using may be wrong. Get new sources, new voices. Dare to ask a whole other set of people.

{ How to Own a Room—and Be Great on Your Feet }

The more successful you become, the more confident and sure of yourself you will be—whether you're talking to people at a cocktail party or a meeting or making a formal presentation or speech—and that's a fabulous feeling. It's also nice for the people in your midst. Confidence is sexy and exciting. People want to be around someone who has it, to hear what she's got to say and learn what she knows.

Confidence is also compelling. When I arrived at *Cosmo*, one of the first things I did was try to analyze why some covers sold better than others. The particular model on the cover obviously played a role, and so did the cover lines, of course. But I soon realized that on the best-selling covers, the model or actress almost always had a certain expression on her face. It wasn't a smile, and it wasn't a "Take-me-*now*" look. It was an expression of utter confidence. It was as if she was standing in a doorway thinking "I *own* this room." That look helped guarantee that women bought the issue in droves.

I'm not talking about haughtiness or smugness. Those qualities, I've always found, tend to spring from insecurity and are totally off-putting. Real confidence is both authentic and inviting. And, as your confidence grows, you also tend to be gutsier and less afraid of taking risks. You believe in yourself, trust your instincts.

But here's the tricky thing about confidence: it can seem fluid at times. One minute you're on top of the world, the next minute you're unsure of yourself. Various factors can trigger a temporary confidence outage. A new job, for instance: you may question your skills, worrying that you're in over your head or that you're even an imposter.

What I find fascinating is how even *little* things can make you go off your game. Maybe you're in a job interview and you see the interviewer glance at your skirt. You suddenly realize that it may be a little too short, and then you can't get back on track with the interview. Or you're giving a presentation and someone yawns, and now you are freaked that you're being a total bore. A year or two ago I was asked to be the afternoon keynote speaker at a big women's conference. I do a lot of public speaking, so I felt no qualms about addressing the thousand-person crowd. Just before I was introduced, I noticed that the woman who had been the morning keynote—a leader in her field—had come into the room and taken a seat at a table right in front. I felt flattered that she'd decided to return for my talk, and I was looking forward to meeting her later.

But a funny thing happened. As I spoke, the woman didn't do what people ideally do when you're giving a speech: she didn't nod or smile or laugh. Instead, through most of the speech, she wore a perplexed expression on her face, as if I'd lapsed into an ancient Incan dialect and she couldn't understand a damn word I was saying. She was like a speech "cooler." I realized that if I had been younger or less experienced, her behavior might have sucked the mojo right out of me.

The fascinating thing about a confidence outage is that nothing has changed about you from one moment to the next. You have the same interview or presentation skills you had before the person noticed your skirt or yawned while you spoke. Confidence is a state of mind.

During my first years at *Cosmo*, we featured models on five or six covers a year. One day we shot a model I adored and whom I knew would be fantastic on the cover, but my design director, returned from the shoot saying that the girl had been incredibly nervous. I suspected that the importance of the shoot had thrown her, though that was hard to fathom—she was gorgeous and had done many major ad campaigns. But sure enough, when the pictures came in, her terror was evident. She looked like someone who had just been stopped by customs agents at JFK airport and was waiting for them to find the kilo of cocaine she had in her luggage.

I remained certain, however, that she would be a perfect *Cosmo* cover girl, so, rather than give up, I decided to try to restore her confidence. I had the model editor call the agency and say the girl was absolutely amazing in the pictures but we'd like to redo the shoot because we were unhappy with the clothing choices we'd made. The next shoot was awesome, and the issue sold 2.3 million copies on the newsstand. Nothing was different about that model from the first shoot to the second—except that the second time she was convinced she had what it took.

Experience and a growing belief in your own ability will help your confidence grow. Here are some tactics to nudge it along.

Own plenty of confidence clothes. Chances are you have at least a couple of outfits that people always compliment you on, that make you feel like a million dollars when you wear them. Figure out the common denominators of those wow outfits—the colors, the shape—and buy more of them. And wear them when the stakes are high. I know it sounds a little silly, but looking like a badass can give you badass confidence.

Instead of focusing on how you might screw up, think about what good things you can bring to the moment. That's something that the actress Natalie Dormer, who stars as Margaery Tyrell in *Game of Thrones* on HBO, pointed out to me. I first discovered Natalie when she played Anne Boleyn in *The Tudors*. It's hard to take your eyes off her, and once her character lost her head, the series was never the same. After we featured Natalie in a fashion story in *Cosmo*, I gave a small dinner for her. She has the most fabulous presence, so I thought she'd be the perfect person to ask about maintaining confidence.

"I was once told something by an older actor that often comes into my head before I walk into an audition room," says Dormer. "They *want* you to be the solution. Whoever is waiting in there for you—interviewer, examiner, casting agent—is hoping you are the answer to their search. Our fear or self-doubt can persuade us that those waiting in the room want us to fail, but that means you carry that closed or victim energy in. People get into the negative habit of preempting the worst-case scenario as a misplaced way of protecting themselves. Try to walk in instead with an 'I can be the solution to your problem' attitude. Not arrogant, just open. The rest is out of your hands, but the positivity in itself is empowering."

This advice works almost across the board—at meetings, interviews, presentations, and speeches. What's so interesting is that in almost all situations, the people you're interacting with are worried about *their* needs and how *they're* doing—even when you wouldn't expect it. One of my very favorite TV shows to be on is the *Today* show's fourth hour with Kathie Lee Gifford and Hoda Kotb. They're fun and charismatic, and they also make *you* look good. Hoda told me that whenever they have a guest host on, they make a point of chatting with the guest host about his or her current projects and interests in order to calm the person's nerves (you wouldn't think that guest hosts would need this, but they do). When you focus on the other person, it actually ends up benefiting you by giving you a sense of control and making the overall experience much more positive.

Know what you need to know at the moment. "There's one thing in particular that gives you a real aura of success when you're interacting with other people," says Julie Kampf, the founder and CEO of the executive search firm JBK Associates. "It's when you say something incredibly smart."

Having the information you need in a situation—whether you have to share it verbally—will help you feel on your game and therefore as confident as possible. Always do background research when you're going to be interacting with people. If you're attending an important meeting, be sure you know the agenda beforehand. What's going to be discussed? What questions might you be asked? What should your answers be? When you're giving a presentation, know exactly what you're supposed to be talking about. Rehearse it plenty of times beforehand, and test whatever equipment you'll be using.

If you have to give a talk to an outside organization or be on a panel, be absolutely sure of what they're looking for and how long they want your remarks to be. Don't just rely on the initial e-mail. I always arrange to speak (far in advance) to one of the key people involved. It's amazing how often what I learn from that person differs from what appeared in the initial e-mail.

If you are receiving an award, find out if the presenters want you just to accept or to make a small speech. And always figure out how long the speech should be. Once when I was receiving an award, I discovered that one of the other honorees had not realized that he was supposed to give an acceptance speech. I could see him hurriedly scrawling down his comments on his program. When he got up to speak, he described the event and the award completely wrong.

You should prep even for events that are slightly less formal, such as business luncheons and dinners. Tell the person who sent you the invitation that you'd like to know who will be joining the table. That information is almost always given out if you ask. Then check out your tablemates on Facebook, LinkedIn, and Google. When you meet them, don't start reeling off facts about them—you'll sound like a freaky fan—but steer the conversation to areas you know they're interested in.

Watch your body language. When you walk into a room or you're standing up giving a talk, do your best not to touch your face or fool with your hair. Those kinds of gestures may feel calming, but they translate as insecurity. If you are sitting down with people, drape one arm over the back of the chair (the other should be on the armrest). A Northwestern University study found that when a person used this position around her boss, she seemed more influential. Other studies have shown that sitting in an expansive dominant pose (one that takes up space) not only makes you feel more powerful but also decreases stress.

Take a public speaking class—and refresher courses whenever you can. I took my first public speaking class when I was in my mid-twenties. It was a four-week course offered through one of those adult ed programs you see advertised on the street in Manhattan, and though it was dirt cheap, it was incredibly valuable. Later, when I could afford it, I worked one-on-one with a fantastic woman named Pam Zarit. No tips you receive from me or anyone else will compare to actually being in a course and having to get up and speak—and then be critiqued.

Take advantage of any opportunity you can to speak publicly. It's true: the more you speak, the less freaked you will be. I'm convinced that everyone has a certain threshold in terms of the number of speeches they must give before they don't feel like dry heaving. It may be five for you or twenty-five. Keep going, and one day you will get there. And you will be so glad you did. Panels are good to start with because you don't feel so front and center.

If you're giving a speech, take the time to make sure it's a damn good one. Two things I learned from Zarit: know the needs of the people whom you are talking to, and let them know you know those needs as soon as you start. One of your early comments could be something like "I know you're here today to learn how we can help our students feel more engaged, and I have some terrific answers from a pilot program we did." And tell the truth. "Even if you don't love everything you're saying," says Zarit, "find the seed that's authentic—the truth/benefit you can really relate to."

Work hard to make your lead compelling (with a story, for instance, or a provocative stat). One way to structure a talk or speech—especially when you're new at the game—is to promise the audience that you are going to give them three things to take away—and then do just that. That structure will give you a sense of security. Plus, people like to know where a talk is headed, and they seem to like things in threes, partly because it's an easy number to remember. Check out Facebook COO Sheryl Sandberg's excellent TED speech on YouTube as proof.

Write and edit your remarks, and then let them sit for a day so you can come back to them with a fresh eye. The better your speech, and the more you believe in it, the more confident you will feel.

Steal a few moments before you go on to get centered. Step briefly away from people—or even go into another room—and let yourself relax and be still for a moment. Repeat a positive mantra to yourself (i.e., "I have great information to share today"). One of *Cosmo*'s cover photographers told me that when he was watching Beyoncé shoot a video, he noticed that she seemed to be in a "meditative state" in the seconds before they began. "And then, in one instant," he added, "she suddenly had all this energy surging through her."

Before you start to talk, take about five or ten seconds and roam the room with your eyes, making contact with people in the audience. I know—it sounds TERRIFYING. But I learned this trick in my first public speaking class, and it works fabulously. People will look back expectantly (and some even warmly) and you will feel far more relaxed.

Pause before you state key points. That's another Zarit tip. People find it very compelling.

When you make eye contact with individuals in the audience—and you must—hold it for at least a few seconds. People love that, too.

Always end with a great kicker.

Videotape yourself giving a speech and have the guts to watch it. Note your strengths (to be leveraged the next time) and your weaknesses. Did you use lots of fillers, such as "um," or were you lacking in energy? It may be painful, but this is how you will blossom.

{ 9 Ways to Look and Sound Powerful }

You know a powerful woman when you see her, don't you? She generally has a certain aura around her. Over the years, through my work, I've been able to meet a number of women who have a lot of power in their jobs—Hollywood studio presidents, for instance, and U.S. senators. I once even had the privilege of hosting a luncheon at the White House with then First Lady Hillary Rodham Clinton. Talk about a woman with an aura.

But I've also met women with power who seem a little wussy. A few years ago, I was asked to join a meeting with several people from an outside company who were going to be doing business with us. I was in a rush and hadn't reviewed the list of names and titles that had been e-mailed earlier, but it didn't matter. As soon as I sat down, I was able to determine who was the woman running the show. She talked in a strong, deep voice and seemed to own the table.

But I was wrong. That woman turned out to be the PR director. The head of the company was the woman next to her—whom

I'd barely noticed. Her body language and voice paled next to her subordinate's. Though I now knew whom to direct most of my questions to, the top woman had lost ground with me. I could never rid myself of the notion that she wasn't as strong as she should be—and that made me wonder about the quality of work I could expect from her.

"In order to be a powerful woman, you have to present yourself powerfully," says body language and communication expert Dr. Lillian Glass.

When you radiate power through your physical actions, such as your body language and your voice, you immediately signal to those around you that you are the person in charge and you deserve respect.

There's another reason you need to develop a powerful aura: it can act like a force field that repels anyone around you who is prone to backstabbing, idea stealing, or other kinds of nasty behavior.

As you gain confidence over time, you'll naturally begin to come across with more authority. But you may still need to work on your aura, as many powerful women have. For instance, before Margaret Thatcher entered politics, she submitted to a substantial makeover of not only her style but also her voice, and she felt no need to apologize about it. "It may sound grittily honorable to refuse to make any concessions," she once said, "but such an attitude in a public figure is most likely to betray a lack of seriousness about winning power."

Here are some aura-creating strategies:

1. Watch your posture. Sit up straight, and stand up straight. "Slouching, whether you're sitting or standing, gives the impression that you're weak and insecure," says Glass.

2. When you're having a conversation with someone, point your toes directly at the other person. It shows that you aren't intimidated.

3. When you're talking to someone, hold the other person's gaze. Glass points out that most powerful people make you feel as though you are the only person in the room.

4. Go deep with your voice. "Deeper voices just seem more powerful," says Dr. Glass. "Squeeze down on your abs when you speak to assure your pitch is low." Thatcher's voice was considered too shrill, and it got worse when her vocal cords were overused. She took voice and elocution lessons to lower her pitch and even drank hot water with lemon and honey to help.

Glass recommends that you modulate your voice so that it's not too soft (you'll seem weak) or too loud (you'll seem desperate for attention). You don't want to speak in a mono-tone, though. Also stress adjectives or descriptive words so that there's plenty of life and enthusiasm when you're speaking.

5. Lose the uptalk. That's where your pitch goes up at the end of sentences. The inflection pattern of powerful people goes down at the end so it sounds like they are making an emphatic statement. If it goes up, you sound uncertain of what you're saying. Also avoid fillers such as "um" and "you know." Tape yourself in conversation and note how many fillers you use.

6. Smile less, nod less. These are ways we connect with others and display attentiveness to a speaker. Both sexes smile and nod to people more powerful than them, but studies show that women tend to smile and nod more to peers. It's nice that we connect so well to others, but smiling or nodding too much can make you seem needy to please.

7. Don't touch your hair or your face. Watch powerful women on YouTube. They rarely play with their hair or touch their face out of nervousness.

8. Never let them see you sweat. No matter how rattled you feel in a particular situation, do your best to keep your cool around your subordinates. Let's say one of your big projects has gone bust. Or you've just been chewed out by *your* boss. Instead of venting to a subordinate, take a walk around the block or meditate for fifteen minutes with your door closed. Sympathy from a subordinate may feel good at the moment, but what he's probably thinking is "What does this mean for me?" or "How soon can I tell someone about this?" Sharing only encourages worry and gossip. Also, be careful of what you share with peers.

9. Go against the grain. Have you ever noticed how people who are very powerful sometimes operate differently from the rest of us in social situations? According to the "approach/inhibition theory of power," the powerful experience fewer social constraints than others, and it shows in their behavior. Individuals who feel powerful are more likely to act in "goal-congruent" ways—by switching off an annoying fan in a meeting, for instance. In a 2011 study called "Breaking the Rules to Rise to Power," the authors say that "given that power is associated with lack of constraint, individuals whose behavior appears unconstrained by normative pressures may be perceived as powerful."

I saw a fabulous example of this once. A company I worked for had invited representatives of a major food company to chat with editors about their business. The organizers of the meeting laid out food from the company for people to snack on. At one point when the person in charge was speaking, she got up, walked over to the table, picked up a cookie, returned to her seat, and then ate the cookie as she spoke. Trust me, no one else in the room would have dared to do that.

Another example, one of my favorites: When I had lunch with Helen Gurley Brown after I received the *Cosmo* job, I noticed she ate her salad with her hands. She told me she always did that because she thought it just looked sexier!

{ Drain the Swamp as You Slay the Alligators, or Possibly the Best Work Advice I Have Ever Been Given }

Take a sec to think about what that phrase means. The first time I heard it—from a management guru whom we interviewed when I was running *Working Woman* magazine—I was momentarily confused, but after a minute I got it. The advice was simple and brilliant; yet I also could see how tough it might be to adhere to it.

The phrase is a derivation from what's supposedly an old southern expression: "When you're up to your ass in gnats and alligators, it's easy to forget that the initial objective was to drain the swamp." It means that when you're working toward a long-term goal (draining the swamp), your time and energy can be eaten up by urgent, daily tasks (slaying alligators) that don't necessarily aid you in achieving more important future objectives.

If you're in sales, for instance, your daily, slaying-the-alligator tasks would include meeting with prospective clients and drumming up business. Draining the swamp, however, might include doing major research on emerging opportunities or creating a totally new presentation to use while pitching.

Unfortunately, draining-the-swamp stuff often gets sidelined when you're forced to slay a whole lot of alligators. The guru's point was that somehow, no matter how insane things are, you have to *learn to do both*.

I started trying to follow this advice as soon as I heard it. But I didn't go to town with the strategy until I started running *Cosmopolitan*. From the moment I arrived, I saw that *Cosmo* was a wonderful but crazy place to work at. It ran far more editorial pages than most other magazines, had a bigger staff, supported lots of international editions, had just launched a website, and was actively creating brand extensions. My books editor at the time, John Searles, told me a story that seemed to sum it all up. After he'd edited one of the sexy thrillers *Cosmo* often excerpts, his assistant brought the copy back in and pointed out a mistake. He'd written, "With one hand Jack sipped his wine. And with the other hand, he stroked her thigh. And with the other hand he dimmed the lights." That seemed to sum up *Cosmo*: three hands required at all times.

I quickly realized how easy it would be to become mired in all the day-to-day duties and drama of running the magazine and never get around to focusing on what was necessary to *evolve* it. So I systematically set up an hour or so every single week to drain the swamp. At that time, no matter how much I needed to be looking at photos, editing articles, or trying to convince Hollywood publicists to let their clients be on the cover in a particular month, I stepped away and brainstormed about the future.

Sometimes I'd spend the time digesting e-mails from readers

about what they were looking for in the magazine; sometimes I'd have editors present an analysis of ratings to acquire a sense of which features were working and which weren't. And sometimes—oh, and this is the part I loved the most—I'd sit at a restaurant counter with a glass of wine and a notepad and dream up ideas.

No matter how nutty your job gets, you have to drain the swamp. *Book* the time. Because if you don't, the big-picture stuff will slip away from you. And in the end you will be swallowed up by alligators.

{ 11 Things I've Learned About Choices, Decisions, and Risk }

As your career takes off, you'll have to make lots of decisions—some easy, others, perhaps, enough to make your stomach churn and bring on sleepless nights. No matter how talented and skilled you are, not all of your decisions are going to be correct, and let me forgive you for that right now. You can't always make the perfect call. But you need to figure out how to increase the number of smart decisions you make and reduce the number of duds. Should you hire that person? Should you go with that deal? Should you send that e-mail? Should you take that job? Here are a few pointers I've picked up.

1. Having too many things to choose from is not a good thing. I learned this from Barry Schwartz, a professor of social theory and social action at Swarthmore College and the author of the fascinating book *The Paradox of Choice*. Schwartz believes that because of the excessive number of choices available today, you can end up with "choice overload." This can make you agonize over decisions and even lead to decision-making paralysis. So do your best to limit your choices. Dr. Schwartz's strategy: "Identify one or two aspects of the decision that are most important to you and use them to filter out all the options that are not good enough with respect to those aspects. You can then use less significant aspects of the decision to choose among the much smaller set of options remaining that survive your first screening."

2. Good enough is almost always good enough. That's what Dr. Schwartz told me when I asked him for the single most important advice he could give people on making decisions. "If people can accept this," he said, "then having to choose from large sets of possibilities becomes much easier."

3. If you are making a choice based on the success or failure of a previous decision, be as sure as you can be why the other choice worked. In August 2002, I ran Keira Knightley on the cover of *Cosmo*. She was wearing a pink-and-black top, posed against a pink background, and her hair was long, shiny, and gorgeous. The issue ended up selling more than 2 million copies on the newsstand. So of course I wanted another Keira Knightley cover.

But when I did focus groups on covers a few months later, a fascinating fact emerged: It appeared that only a small percentage of women who'd bought the issue had realized who the cover girl was that month (it was still early in Keira's career). They had just loved the luscious look of the cover. I'd made a decision to try to do Keira again based on the wrong info. What I really needed was another *pink* cover!

4. Review your decision-making guidelines.

I believe it's beneficial to develop certain principles that direct your decision making. Some of mine: never hire an assistant candidate who shows up late for the interview; never share a confidence with someone who blabs about other people; never use green as a background color on a cover. But periodically you have to examine these principles and ask if they still (or really) make sense. When I recently met Nicole Lapin, the feisty personal finance expert who created the website Recessionista.com, we talked about bad money decisions. I mentioned the fact that many young women spend at least three bucks every day on a morning latte and that financial experts often point out what a stupid choice this is. A smarter one would be to make coffee at home. "Maybe not," Lapin said, shaking her head. "What if buying the latte gets you revved up about your work and going in every morning, and because of that energy you get promoted and then you're making far more than the thousand dollars you spent on the lattes? Sometimes you need to challenge the cliché."

5. Use the phrase "I'll get back to you" as seldom as possible.
Employees hate these five words. To them it's often code for "It may be days or weeks—or even never—before I get around to telling you what you want to know." When someone uses this expression, he isn't generally buying time to mull something over; rather, he's putting off

having to make the decision—because he's unsure of what to do. Even if your intentions are good when you make this "promise," it ends up translating as indecisiveness. So learn to make instant decisions on things that aren't major issues. Let your gut guide you to an answer, and then spit it out. "I'll go with the red one" or "How about the fifteenth, then?" or "Unfortunately, I have to say no."

6. When you can't decide, it may simply be because you don't have enough information. So get *more* information. Trendera founder Jane Buckingham reinforced this concept for me. When I was once torn between two job candidates from the outside, I heeded Jane's advice and gave them each an additional project to do. The results told me what I needed to know.

7. Unfortunately, it's easy to talk yourself into a bad decision. Let's say you're right out of school and a friend of your parents has offered you an entry-level job in her special events company. What you're really interested in is being a journalist, so you graciously turn down the offer—though the friend tells you the door will be kept open. A month passes. Then several more weeks. You don't receive any other offers. You begin to wonder if you should take the job after all. The job even starts to sound better to you. There's even some writing involved.

Try to always strip away what might be coloring a decision—like a desperate feeling or a need to do something quickly. When deciding to go with a choice you initially didn't like, ask yourself: has anything really changed?

Over the years, I did covers on more than a couple of

actresses whom I'd originally decided weren't the right fit. The only times it paid off were when something suddenly changed about the actress's profile—she'd done a new movie that people were buzzing about. It never worked when I simply "came around" to the idea.

8. Practice decision making. When I won a Woman of Excellence Award from the radio station Magic 106.7, WMJX, in Boston several years ago, I discovered that one of the other awardees, the Los Angeles cardiac surgeon Kathy Magliato, had graduated from my college. It was fascinating to learn about her awesome career—which has included doing heart transplants—and I asked her to write an essay about determining the right decisions when the heat is on. Dr. Magliato said that in order to learn to be better at trusting her gut and making smart, split-second decisions, she repeatedly threw herself into tough situations so that thinking under pressure would become second nature. "As a resident, I'd run to get there first when the hospital called a code blue," she said. "I deliberately put myself in those crazy moments to learn how to think on my feet and be sure I knew what I was doing."

Making instant decisions on routine matters is great practice for not being intimidated by bigger decisions. If your job doesn't require much decision making, do committee or volunteer work that gives you more opportunity.

9. If you are making a risky decision, you need to calculate the worst-case scenario. I'm often amazed when I hear people talk about risks they've taken without ever considering the downside. Do the math.

How bad could the ramifications be? My brother Jim, a hedge fund professional, says that in finance they call this evaluating "the risk of ruin." Let's say you want to ask your boss for more money or for the chance to take on a new project. He's been testy lately, and you worry he'll get ticked off. Is it worth the risk? When you do the math you realize that nothing bad is really going to happen. There's surely about a zero chance your boss is going to want to fire you. And though there may be a 60 percent chance he'll be irritated, that's bound to blow over. Jim told me that in his business you put guardrails or hedges around any risk to protect yourself. In the above instance, the guardrail might be not letting yourself become all bent out of shape visibly if your boss adamantly says no—which could work his last nerve.

10. Read *10-10-10* by Suzy Welch. This concise book outlines a really cool concept for making decisions.

11. Then let it go. Don't allow yourself to agonize or second-guess. Many decisions can be course-corrected if they turn out not to be perfect. Try literally washing your hands. A University of Michigan study found that when people did so after making a decision, they were less likely to second-guess.

{ It Pays to Be a Little Paranoid }

Over my many years in the magazine business, I've had to fire dozens and dozens of people—some for cause, others as part of downsizing during rough economic times. And regardless of the reason for the termination, I *always* feel lousy. I know that the dismissal will turn the person's entire world topsy-turvy for at least a while.

But I've often walked away from these situations with something more than an awful feeling. I've been struck by how utterly clueless many of the people were about what was going to transpire. Their eyes widened, their jaws dropped, and frequently the first words out of their mouths were "Omigod, I never saw this coming."

Yet in so many of the situations, they *should* have seen it coming. The people I've let go for cause had always had several warning conversations and follow-up memos. And in cases of downsizing, employees might not have been provided with direct clues internally, but they should certainly have picked up—via company and/or industry buzz and possibly even from news headlines—that times were tough and that if layoffs were required, their names might very well be on the list.

No one enjoys living in a state of constant worry, but I think it's smart to be a *little* bit paranoid—and I feel my own career paranoia has served me well. I have never thought my phones were tapped or someone had put a transmitter under my skin. But (maybe because I'm always at work on a murder mystery) I tend to be on the alert for danger, spot it early, and, when possible, act on it before things turn ugly. I recommend that you do the same.

I'm not saying you should make mountains out of molehills. Sometimes random things happen that appear worrisome but aren't. I once accepted a terrific job that unfortunately involved reporting to a hyper, mercurial editor in chief. When I asked a friend who'd worked in the company for advice, she offered this guidance: "If she looks at you weirdly one day, give it twenty-four hours. She might just be having a bad-hair day." In other words, sometimes a weird look is just that and nothing to get agitated about.

What's key is to do what I suggested in "Develop a Golden Gut": play connect the dots. One situation may not matter, but when something similar or related occurs, allow it to pique your curiosity. Let me give you an example from my own career. After connecting the dots, I learned what I needed to know about handling a hairy situation, and then took a few steps that saved my butt.

I was in the final year of my contract as the editor of a magazine (December would be my last month), and though I felt there was a decent chance my contract would be renewed, I was also conscious that the magazine was in a tough field and there was a fair amount of turmoil going on.

In June, my boss—let's call this person B for boss—called to invite me to lunch. Though I'd heard through the grapevine that B was renewing contracts only late in the year, I wondered if an exception was going to be made in my case. But all B wanted to do at lunch was chat. Hmmmm. It was a dot that I made note of, but since there were no other dots to connect it to, I chilled for a while.

Two months later B asked me to lunch again, in a super nice restaurant this time, and I figured, okay, today the talk would turn to the future. But not a word was said that day either. Two lunches within six months of my contract ending, and no mention of my staying. Two dots to connect. And that aroused a little paranoia. The next day I began reviewing my financial situation, just to be sure I knew where I stood—and reassured myself that fortunately I would be fine if things unraveled. I also met with a couple of headhunters to discuss what was happening out in the world. And I set up some tentative freelance gigs.

In late October, still not having heard anything, I e-mailed B and suggested we get together to discuss the situation since my contract was up in less than two months. "I've been meaning to talk to you" was the response. B arranged for us to meet in a week and a half for breakfast. No fancy restaurant this time. Another dot to connect.

I'll spare you the gory details of what happened over tasteless quiche and coffee that morning. The bottom line was that B wanted to renew my contract but under really shabby terms. Because it was now so terribly late in the game, B must have thought I was stuck, that I'd have no choice but to accept the deal, and even told me, "Of course, you can take your severance package instead, but I suspect you'll want to renew." I smiled and said I'd like a few days to think everything over.

What B didn't know was that my paranoia had helped me prepare for that moment. All my ducks were in a row. I wrote a letter to B a few days later saying thank you for the great time together but I was resigning and taking the severance package. Immediately after receiving the resignation letter, B asked to meet with me, begged me to ignore the previous conversation, asked me what I wanted, and then gave it to me.

Okay, I was particularly lucky in that situation—I'd had months to ready things. Sometimes you spot a sign of trouble but you don't have the time to deal with it as adequately as you'd like, or there's no easy Plan B. But still, in most cases, paranoia allows you to jump-start your thinking and begin to put a plan into play. Don't ignore odd little moments that make your tummy queasy. And don't tell yourself, "Oh, it's just a rumor." When I was a young writer, I interviewed a PhD candidate who was studying rumors, and he told me something I've never forgotten: *rumors are both sloppy and precise.* They may not be a hundred percent accurate, but there's often a grain of truth in them. You need to investigate further to get to the bottom of them.

14 Things to Be Paranoid About

- Being called in by your boss and reprimanded more than once about the same issue

- Being called in by your boss and reprimanded with someone else from the department in the same room (this person is known as a witness)

- Being called in by your boss and reprimanded with someone from HR (eek!) in the room

- A written follow-up from your boss after a reprimand

- Suddenly being excluded from important meetings

- Being given the cold shoulder by your boss

- A large decrease in praise from your boss

- Coworkers avoiding eye contact or conversation with you (or whispering after you've walked by)

- One of your subordinates suddenly being included by your boss in meetings you should be attending on your own

- A recession

- An economic downturn

- Any news or rumors that your field is in trouble

- Any news that your company or organization is in trouble

- Consultants in suits suddenly appearing in your workplace (they have more than likely been hired to find ways to cut costs and encourage your company to work with a trimmed-down staff)

{ Go Big or Go Home, 2: You're Going to Have to Break the Rules }

During the summer when I was seventeen and working as a counter waitress at a Howard Johnson's restaurant in upstate New York, I learned one of the best work lessons of my life.

Waitressing at HoJo's wasn't what you'd call a fun job, except for the drop-dead gorgeous short-order cook, a college senior, and the fact that employees were entitled to all the ice cream they wanted during their meals there. There was a hitch, however, attached to the ice cream bonus: You weren't allowed to indulge in any of the sundae toppings—no hot fudge, for instance, or butterscotch or whipped cream. Not even a few nuts and cherries! I was complaining about this one day to another counter waitress, a cute, devilish girl named Tracy who loved to regale me with tales of driving her parents' car really fast down backcountry roads and dating brazen bad boys. Tracy and I happened to have our lunch break at the same time that day, and as we carried our trays down to the employee dining room, I noticed that, like me, she'd helped herself to a few scoops of vanilla ice cream.

"Isn't it mean of them not to let us have any toppings?" I said.

Tracy smiled mischievously. "Oh, I can fix that," she whispered.

A few minutes later, after we'd gobbled down our grilled cheese sandwiches, Tracy slid a spoon through her scoops of ice cream, all the way to the bottom of the dish. An interesting cross section appeared: at the bottom of the bowl was a layer of nuts and cherries, topped by whipped cream, then hot fudge, and then finally the ice cream.

"It's an *upside-down* sundae," she said, smirking.

Brilliant, I remember thinking. I had an upside-down sundae nearly every day for the rest of the summer.

It took a little while, though, for me to see that the upside-down sundae lesson I learned that day could be applied to many other areas of life. If you want the cherry in life, to say nothing of the hot fudge and whipped cream, you have to be brave enough to break the rules sometimes. You have to take what you've been told to do and twist it, toss it, or turn it upside down so that you end up with something brilliant and delicious.

Maybe you're a natural rule breaker and it's served you well so far. Congratulations. But there's also a decent chance that you've managed to get pretty far in your career by being sort of a Goody Two-shoes. You've listened to your boss, worked hard, and been promoted for it. The problem is that being a good girl, as I wrote in my first career book, *Why Good Girls Don't Get Ahead . . . but Gutsy Girls Do*, gets you only so far. If you want to supersize your career, you need to bend and break some rules and even make a few new ones of your own.

By breaking the rules, I don't mean calling in fake sick on Friday or dancing drunk on the bar at the office Christmas party. I mean implementing things in a fresh and daring way. Here's how to think about it.

Breaking the rules means ignoring the phrase "That's the way we've always done it here" and instead trying a brand-new, possibly mind-blowing approach. There are plenty of rules that are out of date or never made sense to begin with and deserve to be challenged. Kate Spade once told me that the night before she was going to take her first handbags to a trade show, she sat with them in her living room and realized that there was a problem. The bags were black nylon, simple, clean, and fresh-looking (her goal had been to create a product in which fashion met function), but she suddenly felt there was no place for the eye to go to when you looked at them. So she grabbed a pair of nail scissors, clipped out the label from inside the bag (the one that said KATE SPADE NEW YORK), and sewed it onto the front of the bag. Then she did the same thing to the rest of the bags. By ignoring the rule at the time that said that labels are supposed to go on the inside of handbags, Kate Spade created her phenomenally successful signature look.

Breaking the rules means doing what has been deemed impossible by simply tackling it in a whole different manner. Shortly after I became the editor in chief of *Child* magazine, I decided to conduct a series of focus groups of mothers with young kids. If I was going to be successful at my job, I needed to understand the main concerns of my audience. But the general manager informed me that there was no money in the budget for focus groups. How frustrating, I thought, because the company that owned *Child* seemed to be doing well. There were even two executive dining rooms in the building that top management, including the editors in chief, were allowed to use and simply charge the cost back to the company. With no ding to my magazine budget, I could entertain writers, experts, whomever. And then it hit me: why not bring in *mothers* for lunches and let them talk to my executive editor and me directly about their issues? So I started doing that on a regular basis—without, of course, telling anyone that the "guests" were readers. These were probably the only focus groups in the world whose participants were served gourmet food and glasses of Pinot Grigio.

Breaking the rules means knowing it's better to ask forgiveness than permission. During my first year at *Cosmo* we scheduled a fashion story that would feature clothes with Native American touches, and we decided that the perfect place to shoot it would be South Dakota. One day I stopped by the photo director's desk to see how the plans were going. He told me we had a fabulous location, with lots of big sky and impressive buttes. "Maybe if we're lucky," I said, "some buffalo will stroll by when the photographer's shooting." The photo director looked at me almost indignantly. "Well, I've rented a herd," he said. Wow, I remember thinking, he rented a freaking herd of buffalo. Impressive. Before I could say anything, he added, "They're the same buffalo Kevin Costner used in *Dances with Wolves*." Okay, even more amazing. Those buffalo were members of the Screen Actors Guild. I realized later that if the photo director had asked me if he could rent a herd of buffalo, I probably would have said no—an unnecessary extravagance. But since he'd just done it and the result would be fantastic, I was delighted.

When you ask permission to do something bold and different, you may very well get a knee-jerk "no" from the person you're asking. But if you just go ahead and do it, she may love it.

If you haven't been a rule breaker up until now, you're going to have to take a deep breath and do it. Start small. Initially you may want to give yourself a little safety net. Let's say your boss asks you to come up with ideas for an off-site retreat guaranteed to improve everyone's energy and motivation. She mentions places where these retreats have been held in the past, implying that you should find something similar. But you come up with an idea that's incredibly unusual (holding it at a clown-arts college!), one that you're convinced will get people totally psyched. Present a few standard ideas to your boss, but then say you have a wildcard idea you'd love her to consider, as well. That way she sees you as someone who can think both inside and outside of the box—and it will make it easier for her to entertain the wildcard concept.

Here's a bit of good news about rule breaking: it becomes easier the more you do it. I won't lie; sometimes you may find yourself in hot water for having done something daring, but mostly you will discover that the right kind of rule breaking reaps big rewards, which will encourage you to do it again and again.

Two final pointers. First, you need to consider whether your gutsy move is the best way to accomplish what you want or just you being gutsy for gutsy's sake. When I give speeches in different parts of the country, women sometimes come up to me at the cocktail party beforehand or at the book signing afterward and hand me something they want me to take a look at; it might be an article they've written or a product they've created. And invariably they say something such as "I know you think it's important to break the rules, so that's what I'm doing. I'm handing this to you directly rather than mailing it to you."

Here's the problem with that approach: when I'm giving a speech, I always travel with just a carry-on suitcase (which most people would realize if they thought about it), so why would I want to have something else to lug home with me?

So think it through. Does your rule breaking make sense for what your goal is? Or are you just being a show-off?

Second, you need to make rule breaking part of your regular

repertoire, not something you do on a sporadic basis when the mood strikes. When I arrived at *Cosmo*, I quickly saw that as the editor of an edgy magazine, I'd better be a rule breaker 24/7. I developed the habit of starting every day with the question "What am I going to do to break the law today?"

{ Advanced Networking (Never Say You're Too Busy to Do It) }

I don't have to tell you that's it's important to network. Every career book and article recommends it, and you probably did your fair share of it when you were first breaking into your field. Networking also happens regularly among supersuccessful people—to some degree because it's an almost organic part of their work lives. They're invited to lots of occasions because of their jobs, plus they've got expense accounts, which allow them to take people out to meals and go to events and conferences. Their companies may even cover membership in social clubs.

What I've noticed, however, is that when you're at a midlevel of success, it can be easy to let the networking trail off unless you start looking for a new job. You may become so busy that you hate leaving your desk at lunch or skipping out early for a cocktail party. You may also feel you're beyond those gigunda industry meet and greets. As for dining with new contacts, you probably don't have a huge expense account that allows you to do much of it.

But you need to keep your networking going at full throttle. The chance to meet, talk to, and get to know new people not only provides you with a ton of great info but also many of them can become valuable resources—if not today, at some point. When I was selling my second nonfiction book, the editor who bought it said that a big advocate for the book in her company was a woman who'd once sat next to me at an industry luncheon.

First and foremost, be sure to join any important professional associations in your field. Your company may even pay for membership if you request it. If you have to pay the dues yourself, they're at least tax-deductible. If you feel that some of the events or cocktail parties those organizations hold are for people on a more junior level, volunteer to be on a committee with more senior players. Check your calendar each month, and make sure you always have events like this booked.

Take advantage of invitations you receive to professional events, even if you may not know a soul. Once you're there, spend a few minutes scoping out the scene. Say hello to anyone you know, even vaguely, just to warm up. Don't be afraid to introduce yourself to individuals you recognize and would like to meet or anyone who simply looks interesting. It's a networking event, so no one should be weirded out about your sidling up to them and saying hello.

Of course, breaking into a group can be intimidating and potentially awkward. "One way to ease into a group conversation," says Hilary Gumbel, a consultant for the U.S. Fund for UNICEF (and wife of TV journalist Bryant Gumbel), "is to be interested in what is being discussed without any particular motive. Curiosity is a healthy and natural icebreaker. By indicating interest in the subject of the conversation, you are then interacting with people and can eventually focus your attention toward the particular person you want to meet. The opportunity to be introduced will present itself."

When you shake hands with someone you've just met, hold the person's gaze for as long as you can. Years ago, when I was writing an article on the power of eye contact, one of the experts I interviewed, who'd studied eye contact in baboons, told me that if you look away first, it can be read as a sign of submissiveness. Many people (and this holds particularly true for women) always look away first, sometimes just out of habit. When you hold a person's gaze, it fosters a connection, and outlasting the other person can make you seem intriguing to him or her on a subconscious level. When I sat next to former president Bill Clinton at dinner (I know, *president-name-dropper*), I discovered that he's as legendary as people say for making you feel as if you're the only one in the room. Holding your gaze is part of how he does it.

Now it's time for you to make chitchat. If you feel at all awkward dealing with strangers, there's only one secret you need to know to make it easier: *people love to talk about themselves*, especially to a receptive audience. If you ask lots of questions and give people your ear, they will find it intoxicating. After I first spent a little time with Helen Gurley Brown, I discovered that she was a master at asking questions of people and listening intently to the answers. Sometimes she wouldn't respond right away but instead would seem to consider the answer in her mind, as if she really wanted to understand it. That kind of pregnant pause almost guaranteed you would tell her even more.

So ask and listen. It's fine to start with basic questions such as "How long have you worked at such and such?" When the person responds, don't just nod or jump in with a statement about how what she just said relates to you somehow; instead, probe further about what she revealed. "Dig deeper," says Gumbel. "Connect to their interests, passions, and experiences. Humor also helps. Find something ironic or funny to build your commonality—a movie, book, or personal experience."

As long as you are taking the time to go to something, show up at the right moment and make it count. A few months ago a former work colleague and I realized that we'd both be attending a conference in Massachusetts and decided to drive up together. A couple of days beforehand, the woman announced that she needed to support a friend by attending a talk the friend was giving, meaning that she would miss the afternoon session of the conference. Then, the night before, she called me to say that she had to run a personal errand in the morning and would meet me at the conference. In the end, she attended only the lunch. I realized that she'd paid for the conference and spent hours traveling there and returning, but reaped little from it beyond the rubbery chicken served at the meal.

If an event seems worth your time, don't just do a drive-by. Arrive when a critical mass of people will be there (a friend of mine calls this "the swell") and in time to hear any remarks. An event planner I know says that for a two-hour business cocktail party, the best time to catch the swell is about twenty minutes after the start. And if you leave thirty minutes before the end time, she says, you won't miss anything.

It's nice to exit with a few good business cards in hand. If you meet someone you like or who seems key to know, follow up with an e-mail saying you enjoyed meeting the person. If it seems appropriate, suggest getting together for lunch, or breakfast (cheaper!). And it's essential to have a few restaurants that you return to again and again. The maître d' will look out for you when you're with an important guest (don't forget to sometimes tip him as well as the waiter).

In addition to meeting people, I like to come back from every event and speech with *one* good idea. Telling myself in advance that I'm going to do that nudges me to ask the kind of questions that help an idea to form.

Everyone you meet should go into a people file (organized by categories) that you keep on your computer or phone. Include a few details about the person. Selected names should be placed on your "big-mouth" e-mail list. People on your big-mouth list then get sent an e-mail notification when you have important career news—for instance, you've switched jobs, been promoted, or started your own business (*not* when you have a Funny or Die video to share).

If you suspect that one day you may want to ask a person you've met for a professional favor, do what Marisa Ollins, the PR director of Henri Bendel, calls "the pre-ask": contact the person at some point without needing anything. Offer congratulations on news you've read about him or her, or share a link to a story that relates to a topic you discussed when you met. If you've already had some exchanges with the person, it's easier to ask for his help later. But don't become a stalker. A few young women I've met casually have sent me way too many e-mails applauding what I do. I'm waiting for the one that says, "Congratulations! I hear your Pap test was normal."

When you do ask for a professional favor, be polite but direct. "Unlike men, women tend to beat around the bush too much," says Julie Kampf, the president of JBK Associates. "You need to come right out and ask rather than warm up with chitchat." Say something such as "You once said you'd be glad to introduce me to so and so, and I'd love to take you up on that offer now. Can you make an e-mail introduction?"

And then thank the person, for God's sake. Not just by e-mail. When someone does a professional favor for you, send a handwritten note. Or even a bottle of wine if it was a big enough favor. I cannot tell you the number of times people have networked with me and been all gushy gushy when they asked for a favor, and once I *did* the favor, I never heard a peep from them again. If you're one of those people and are reading this, please lose my number.

{ When Bad Things Happen }

No matter how terrific your job is and how good you are at it, sometimes things go wrong. Sometimes, in fact, they can go horribly wrong. I cringe when I think of the big goofs I've made over the years.

One crisis can be very different from another, and so they have to be handled on a case-by-case basis. But here's some basic wisdom on staying cool in different types of crises and coming out relatively unscathed afterward.

Something big just blew up in your face, and you have to act on it _now_. It's never fun when the sh*t hits the fan. Let's say you've organized a big business dinner and that night the speaker just doesn't show. Not only will your guests be pissed off, but the next day your boss will blame _you_. In this kind of crisis you need to salvage the situation as best you can at the moment, and you also have to salvage your reputation.

A year or so ago I had the chance to interview Teresa Irvin, a detective supervisor with the Los Angeles Police Department's Mental Evaluation Unit. I'd read about her work dealing with people having mental breakdowns and threatening to commit suicide, and I wanted to ask her how she handled such terrifying experiences. She told me something that's stuck with me ever since—that in a crisis we often have a little more time than we realize. And you should use that time to make a smart, rational decision. "Count to ten," she told me, "and give yourself a chance to think. Ask yourself questions: What could happen in the next twenty minutes? What should I do right now?" And tell yourself to breathe, she says. That can make a big difference.

Your speaker didn't show? Is there a possible substitution? As an alternative, could you do a Q-and-A session with someone dynamic in the audience?

Sh*t-hits-the-fan moments often occur when you're doing something publicly, such as making a presentation. The moment you throw a lot of people into the mix, the greater the chance for disaster, to say nothing of humiliation. One thing that's important to realize is that the more frenzied you make the situation, the worse it will be. Grace under pressure can save the day. Let me tell you two stories.

When I was younger, I signed up to see a presentation by a legendary fashion editor. PowerPoint presentations didn't exist yet, so her talk involved slides and a carousel, the standard method back then. As expected, the editor drew a big crowd and everyone was all abuzz as she strode to the front of the room. After she'd given a brief intro and gotten through about two slides, the carousel jammed. A young AV guy was eventually called in, but despite sweating bullets for several minutes, he couldn't fix the machine (I'm sure, by the way, that he never worked in this town again!). Rather than talking off the cuff, the editor announced haughtily and with great irritation that she couldn't do the presentation and sat down. How lame is that?

Fast-forward to a recent charity event in the ballroom of the Waldorf-Astoria hotel. The entertainment was the fabulous Sheryl Crow, and I was lucky enough to be sitting at one of the front tables.

She started to perform, but horror of horrors, neither the mike nor the amps were working. Sound guys swarmed the stage trying to fix the mess, but they couldn't get things to work right away. Sheryl looked totally unfazed. Finally she strode over to the podium at the side of the stage and started singing into the mike on the podium. Awesome.

If things are blowing up in public, don't look frazzled or share the trauma or your anxiety with the audience or other people (just think of some of those bad Oscar-presenter moments). Breathe, smile, and say something like, "Please bear with us while we sort out a few technical problems."

After any kind of mess-up, do a postmortem with yourself and/or your team and figure out if there was any way you could have prevented the problem or reduced the chances of it happening. Your speaker didn't show? Well, did you confirm and reconfirm? Did you fail to acknowledge a flakey vibe from him? Did you send a car for the speaker so that you could monitor his whereabouts?

Also—and this is important—was there a moment where you should have trusted your gut and immediately initiated Plan B? Lili Root, the executive director of events marketing at Hearst, told me she had once put together a charity event at which all the wine was being donated. "I looked at the amount of wine that night," she said, "and knew that it wouldn't be enough for the number of confirmed attendees—even though the 'wine expert' was insisting it would be sufficient. We found the nearest liquor store, and in the middle of the event, someone went out to buy more—running up Fifth Avenue with a hand truck full of cases of wine."

Stepping in early with Plan B can be how you end up with a glitch rather than a fiasco.

Something you were sure would be a success bombs. It's a double whammy when a project goes wrong. Not only must you contend with the bad results, but at the same time you have to face the fact that your judgment might have sucked, and it's hard not to lose confidence in yourself. You want to fix the problem, yet you wonder if you've got what it takes to see things clearly enough to do that.

The best step to take after any kind of screwup—big or small—is to obtain as much information as you possibly can. I talk about this a lot in "The Secret Weapon That Will Make You a Winner (and Save Your Butt)," but it's especially critical to do when a project goes off the rails. That is a moment when you might love to stick your head into the sand, but don't! Ask people who worked with you—directly or indirectly—to put their thoughts about it in writing. They're often far more honest this way.

I learned early on as an editor in chief that the smartest move to make during any kind of newsstand slump is to "go to the rug." I throw a year's worth of issues onto the rug in my office and stare at them, looking for patterns and reasons for the slump. Often I *do* see what was wrong. I've pulled myself out of more than one slump that way.

You make a big fat mistake. If you know how to fix it, go ahead. If you don't, get direction from people you trust who can help you.

Equally important is how you discuss matters with your boss. If it's critical that she know about the mistake, don't let anyone beat you to the punch. You have to be the first to tell her so you can present the info as accurately and unhysterically as possible. Tell her that you have an issue and in the same sentence tell her that you also have a plan to fix it.

In some situations you may wonder if it's best to stay mum. I do think that a let-sleeping-dogs-lie tactic works in certain cases. If you have a handle on the problem and there's unlikely to be any serious damage or repercussions, it might be best not to draw un-necessary (and unwanted!) attention to it. The litmus test is to ask yourself this question: "If I don't tell my boss and she finds out after the fact, would she be seriously pissed that I didn't inform her?" If the answer is yes, buck up and confess. But again, have the solution in hand.

You are called onto the carpet by your boss. Being called into your boss's office for a reprimand (or worse, a reaming out) can make you feel as though you are in fourth grade again. In that kind of situation, I have three words of advice for you: hear him out. Do not interrupt. Do not bristle. Just listen. If you start to cry, glance at a bright light (it's been shown to squelch tears). If that doesn't work, say something such as "I'm sorry, I want to hear what you have to say, but I'm reacting a bit strongly right now. Can I schedule a time to talk to you in a little while?"

Once you have fully heard your boss's complaints, replay his words back to him as best as you can. That not only lets him know you heard them, it also guarantees that you haven't missed anything in the heat and awkwardness of the moment. Use positive words rather than negative ones. Instead of "What you're saying is that you don't feel I do my work fast enough," say something such as "So what you'd like is for me to turn around my work more quickly." Ask for clarification on any points if necessary. You need specifics. Not as a challenge, but so you know exactly what he wants you to do differently. Don't leave in a huff or with your tail between your legs. Thank him for sharing his thoughts and let him know you take his concerns seriously.

Afterward, follow up with an e-mail restating the points you discussed and assuring him that you will definitely be making the changes he's asked for.

Here's the most important point about dealing with a "talk"

from your boss: be sure you have really heard what he said. Let go of your natural defensiveness and ask yourself: are his complaints legit? I read a study once that said that over time, male bosses sometimes stop critiquing female employees because they get prickly or teary-eyed; the end result is that some female employees never gain valuable insights. If you sense that the criticism is legit, you need to address it.

But what if you sense a perception problem? Maybe your boss has said you're not spending enough time meeting with clients. You know you *are*, but now you must take steps to alter his perception. Send him updates after you meet with clients, keep him abreast of your plans.

You are fired. I've never been fired, but publishing can be a precarious business, so from the beginning of my career I thought a lot about how I would handle that kind of blow (and as far as I know, it might have been close to happening at any number of points). I drew much of my inspiration from friends and colleagues who'd been there and not only survived but thrived afterward, often having the last laugh. Here are the four things they all seemed to do.

1. They gave themselves a short period to wallow in their misery. Then they got busy—with networking, with exploratory interviews, with putting their name out there.

2. They sought out the best professional guidance possible. It helps, I think, to see a career counselor and/or take full advantage of any outplacement services provided with a severance package, which may include job counseling and access to an office. If you aren't offered outplacement services, ask for them. If you are, try to obtain even more than your company normally gives—for instance,

six months' worth instead of three. Those who used out-placement services benefited not only from the advice they received but also from being able to go to an office every day.

3. They asked themselves what had gone wrong. Instead of blaming their former employer, they examined what they might have dealt with poorly or miscalculated, such as not noticing that the company was in trouble or recognizing that the job wasn't a good fit to begin with. Recently I found a letter from a young editor I'd had to let go at *Working Woman*. Several months after she left, she wrote me, saying that it had been good for her in the end because she saw that she was better suited to other things. About five years ago she sold the Internet company she'd started for $20 million.

4. They didn't burn any bridges. No matter how angry they were, they were gracious and never bad-mouthed their former company or boss.

{ Why You Must Manage Your Career as Well as Your Job }

Throughout this section, I've talked about all the steps you must take to be successful in your job—everything from scheduling time each week to focus on the big picture to managing your subordinates effectively to breaking the rules. But there's something else you have to pay attention to as well: while you brilliantly do your job, you must also brilliantly "do" your career. You need to take steps to make certain you're poised and ready for the next exciting move up.

It's not simply a matter of keeping your résumé polished. By managing your career, I mean growing your skills, making new contacts, religiously watching for opportunities, and going after opportunities in a totally gutsy way.

I know, it sounds like doing two jobs at once, and you've already got plenty on your plate. But if you don't manage your success, it can slip away from you. You receive a promotion you crave, put your nose to the grindstone, and the next thing you know, five years have passed. One day you hear an announcement that someone down the hall, someone lower on the ladder than you, has accepted an incredible job. And you feel almost weak in the knees about the news.

Just contemplating this scenario can make you hyperventilate. But try not to think of it as one more huge task you have to tackle but rather as an exhilarating challenge. This isn't about doing something that will pay dividends for your company or organization. It's about doing something just for *you*.

Begin right where you are. The first step to taking charge of your success is to make sure you're performing in a way that allows your boss (and people above him) to view you as a person who should continue to move up in the organization. That means doing your job incredibly well. But as the career expert Adele Scheele points out, you have to also be taking steps in your job that prep you for the next level or levels. And those steps are different.

"In managing your job," she says, "you have to define the goals that your organization wants, build a team to deliver them, and spend time in building relationships with your superiors and clients within your organization. In managing your *success*, you need to expand that focus to taking on more or other duties—leaning toward or creating the next opportunity—while learning to take credit for your team's work (a tricky balance) and building a reputation, including one among your peers."

Try to imagine how your boss might describe you to someone right now. A dynamo? A star? How long has it been since you made your boss say, "Wow!" If not, ask yourself why. Have you been working on automatic pilot lately or, worse, slacking off as you deal with crazy personal demands? Have you been so busy focusing on the day-to-day that you haven't been doing *more* or generating any dazzling ideas for the future? Have you failed to toot your own horn? Then it's time to get your mojo back. Block out time to generate ideas. Suggest and take on projects that will produce strong results. Keep your boss abreast of your accomplishments.

I may be wrong, but I've always thought that a presentation I made at a management conference when I was still the editor of *Redbook* helped me land the *Cosmo* job. I was assigned to a committee that had been asked to generate magazine ideas and then present the best one at the conference. I volunteered, to the other committee members, to take on the job of fleshing out our idea, putting the PowerPoint slides together, and then doing the presentation. It was a big extra chore, but I kept telling myself that something good might come from it. When I'd finished my presentation, my boss gave me a thumbs-up from her seat in the audience. I sensed that she saw a side of me that day that she hadn't witnessed before. It wasn't much longer before I was named editor of *Cosmopolitan.*

Of course, if you have a *particular* job in the company in sight, you want to prove that you would be ready for it by taking on responsibilities and projects that will be required in that position. And *looking* the part.

Plus, let them know you want it. "Women don't make their wishes known as much as men do," says MetricStream CEO Shellye Archambeau.

Have a flex plan. To me, it's pointless to have a five-year career plan. There's just so much potential for change in our lives and our career fields—why get locked into a rigid plan? In 2005, I gave a young writer the chance to create a blog for Cosmopolitan.com called—well, what else, The Bedroom Blog. Blogs had just emerged, and I felt we should have one on our site. The writer did a terrific job, and she soon had a huge following and a new "career." But think about it: if a few years earlier the writer had made a five-year career plan for herself, "writing a popular blog" would never have been on it.

Better, I think, is to have a more relaxed plan that has several *possible* targets but also allows for serendipity, changes in the landscape, and your own evolution. Aim high, but be flexible and open. If someone tells you about an exciting opportunity that you feel is the wrong fit for you, step back and ask, "Why not?"

Make sure you're ready. If you don't have all the right skills—whether it's public speaking, Web design, app development, whatever—for the next big job, get them. If you can't learn them on the job, take classes.

Sharpen your specialty. At several points, I've talked about how important it is to develop a special expertise that helps set you apart from the pack. If you haven't yet, start. Think about what keenly interests you, your expertise, and also what's missing in your job or field. When Archambeau, joined IBM early in her career, she found that the big emphasis there was on sales. She looked for any chance to develop an expertise in marketing—"there were small pockets where you could do that"—and when the company shifted its focus under new leadership, she had an edge.

Do at least one thing a week that's totally career focused. It's the draining-of-the-swamp concept, applied to your career rather than your job. Attend a speech or lecture, take a class, go on YouTube to hear a motivational speech by someone really successful, such as Susan Taylor, a former editor in chief of *Essence*, or an interview with a high-earning businesswoman such as Safra Catz, president and CFO of Oracle. The TED Conference videos are also good to check out, especially the powerful speech by Facebook's Sheryl Sandberg. I always feel jazzed after hearing a successful woman speak.

Check in regularly with your Personal Board of Directors (PBOD) (see "What You Need Even More Than a Mentor"). As your career advances, you're going to want to garner their wisdom, insight, and objective take on matters involving your goals.

Do the math. Have you stayed where you are too long? Look at the careers of women above you, and consider how much time they invested in each phase of their career. One way to tell if you've overstayed is by noting how you feel when someone in your company leaves to go elsewhere. If you're still growing in your job, you will probably not be bothered by their departure. But if you've been where you are too long, it may bug you or you may find yourself making excuses about the person, such as "Why would she want to go *there*?" or "I wouldn't want to make a change now—not in *this* economy." That kind of defensiveness should be your wake-up call. So should any flagging of your energy and enthusiasm for your work. That can be a big clue that it's time for a new challenge.

Here's an interesting thought to consider: sometimes the best time to leave a job is when you feel happiest. That's because it could mean you've worked your way into a nice comfort zone. And you've stopped stretching!

Kathleen Rice, the dynamic DA of Nassau County, Long Island, told me that her career has always been about going after projects and jobs even if being in them would make her feel initially vulnerable.

Take your pulse. Before you prepare to make your next move, take time to think about how engaged you are in your field. Do you still love what you're doing and feel excited about the logical next step? Or are there rumblings of discontent in your tummy? Whose career have you been envying lately? What responsibilities light your fire? When do you feel most in the zone at work? You might be ready for a real change or just a shift to the left or right.

Several years ago, as Dr. Holly Phillips, the medical contributor for *CBS This Morning*, began making more and more TV appearances on medical issues, she realized how much it appealed to her. "I didn't want to be a TV *personality*," she says. "What I wanted was to be a *doctor on* TV. People rely on TV. This is a way to educate them. I also like the narrative it opens up in the medical community." She set out to find a career in TV that would allow her to still work as a physician one day a week.

Review the chapters "Advanced Networking (Never Say You're Too Busy to Do It)" and "12 Ways to Get Buzzed About." You want to be meeting people who can help you and making sure people hear the right things about you.

With each job opportunity that comes up, ask, "What will it do for me?" Will it advance your career? Will it give you a whole new set of skills? Is it as good as it looks on paper? Would you be choosing it just to make a change or because it's a smart choice? When you tell the story of your career one day, will this move make sense? At *Family Weekly* I was promoted from senior editor to executive editor, the number two spot, and then left to run the articles department at *Mademoiselle* for just a small increase in pay. But I was going to a much classier magazine and one far more in the public eye. Plus, I'd be back in a field (women's magazines) where I'd probably be able to rise faster.

Then go big or go home. When the right job comes up, you mustn't wait for them to come after you. You must go after that job ferociously. Use whatever contacts and sponsors you have to get in the door. Tell your prospective employers you want it and what you will do for them. I know of a talented magazine executive editor who heard about an editor in chief job when the company was in the final round of interviews. She called the contact person and was told that the company president was leaving that day for an overseas trip and would be unable to squeeze in an interview with her. The editor said she would be willing to accompany the president to the airport in the limo and make her pitch on the drive. She did—and she won the job.

If the right job doesn't exist, consider creating it. I approached a company once and suggested a job I thought would be great for them and that I'd like to have. They actually said yes to my idea. Though in the end I decided not to do it, experience made me see how open people can be to the right idea. Sometimes they don't know what they're missing.

If you are offered a job that's almost perfect but is lacking something you need, ask if the employer will work with you to make it closer to what you want. Sometimes all it takes is a little crafting. One thing that bugged me about the *Mademoiselle* job I was being offered was that the title was articles editor, not nearly as nice as my current title, executive editor. I asked the editor in chief to consider changing the title to "executive editor, articles," and she did.

{ What to Do When Things Change (and They Will!) }

One day not long ago when I was riding the elevator at work, I overheard a comment by a woman that was so naive, it startled me that it was coming out of the mouth of someone who was clearly in her thirties. She was complaining to a colleague that a photo shoot that was supposed to happen in two weeks had been moved up to the following Tuesday.

"I can't believe they changed it," she said. "I was counting on next week being a slow week."

I guess she hadn't gotten the message: things today are in a near-constant state of change, and there probably won't be any slow weeks anymore. A *Fast Company* article pointed out that we are in the middle of a "next-two-hour era," meaning that things are changing so quickly, we don't even know what the next two hours will bring.

All this change can be disconcerting. Not only must we deal with the alteration in schedules and procedures and work habits, but there's the ripple effect that so often follows. Change often leads to not only more work but a whole different kind of work. Over the course of my time in magazines, I have seen editors in chief shift from producing magazines to becoming brand managers and even TV personalities.

Though change can be scary, it's essential to learn to deal with it well. To succeed, you must not only handle change effectively but also be a change *agent*, someone who both acts as a catalyst for change and then manages the process successfully.

I first started thinking a lot about handling change when I was the editor of *Working Woman*. We'd interviewed a management guru who'd told us that the work world was being transformed and we'd no longer have down periods when we'd be able to grab a breath, the way people had done in previous years when, for instance, a budget was finally completed or a project put to bed. We had entered, the guru said, a period where work was always going to be like white-water rafting.

That statement caused me to gulp when I read it. I had a demanding job and young kids, and the idea that things were going to become even more chaotic had zero appeal. But as I thought about the analogy, I began to find it relaxing. Up until then, I'd been resistant to the notion of rapid change. Accepting change rather than fighting it made it easier.

Acceptance, though, can take you only so far. You then have to learn to navigate the rapids.

See the sexy side of change. When Dr. Helen Fisher, a biological anthropologist whose specialty is romantic love, spoke at a *Cosmo* salon, she told us something that I've never forgotten. According to Dr. Fisher, one of the ways to help keep feelings of infatuation alive in a relationship is to always do new things together. That's because novelty drives up the levels in the brain of dopamine and norepinephrine, neurotransmitters that are associated with energy, elation, focused attention, and motivation—the central traits of love.

Consider how Dr. Fisher's theory might relate to change. Change is novelty, after all. It can be an opportunity to feel excited, energized, and elated—*if* you allow it to happen. When you think about it, haven't many of the initially scary changes you've faced in life turned out in time to be thrilling?

So alter your view. Vivien Jennings, the founder and president of Rainy Day Books in Fairway, Kansas, a woman who could have been rocked by the enormous changes in the book business but wasn't, put it this way: "Embrace change as an ally and an opportunity."

And if you have people working for you, make sure you share that view with them, because they're probably more nervous than you are. Don't complain or appear panic-stricken in front of them. **Instead of asking "Why is this happening?" ask "What can I take control of?"** Put yourself in charge as soon as possible. For instance, if you unexpectedly end up with a new boss, you can control, to some degree, her perception of you by being open and offering to take her up to speed, rather than hiding out in your office.

And consider this: though we sometimes worry that change is going to knock us off our feet, it doesn't always involve as much of a disruption as we fear, and taking control won't be as hard as it looks. Says Trendera CEO Jane Buckingham: "One of the things I hear the start-ups in Silicon Valley talk about is how key it is to know how to pivot. Not reinvent, *pivot*. You look at where you are going and adjust slightly. I've always liked that quote of Bill Gates, where he says we tend to overestimate the change that will occur in the next two years and underestimate the change that will occur in the next ten."

So relax and consider how you will pivot, not overhaul. The definition of "pivot" is to step with one foot while keeping the other on the ground. Think of the ground as the things you already know and the skills you already have. Your other foot needs to reach for new information.

Pivoting is what Vivien Jennings has done—and done well. One of the ways she'd been building her book business was with author events. I've been lucky enough to participate in a few, and they're terrific. The events had become an important way to drive book sales, but the store wasn't big enough to accommodate a large audience. "If people can't sit during an author event, the experience isn't going to be optimum," she says. "So we decided to go off-site. We began holding events in a variety of places—from restaurants to businesses to churches." Books were sold, of course, at these events. Lots of books, and many events had an entry fee. Creating all these special events was a great new revenue source. "And it did something else," she adds. "It took us into the community rather than made the community have to come to us." That helped create even greater customer loyalty.

Be a just-in-time change agent. A just-in-time system usually refers to handling inventory, where you store only the right materials at the right time and at the right place because more than that involves waste. You can use that approach with change. One of the aspects of change that can make your heart pound is how much knowledge you are suddenly going to have to acquire in order to stay in control. But in so many cases, all you really need to learn is what you will require at the present moment and in the right-ahead-of-you future. Remember: It's a little like handling white water. Concentrate on the rapids you need to deal with now, and don't worry about what's far around the bend.

Take something for yourself. Don't be so busy thinking of how you will cope with change in your job that you neglect to determine what might be in it for *you*. In one of my editor in chief jobs, I had to enlist a group of staffers to work on an exciting brand extension. They complained about all the extra work and wondered why they weren't being compensated. Yet to me it was clear that the skills they were learning could enable them to start their own businesses one day. Figure out how to leverage change for yourself—with new contacts or skills to be acquired if you play your cards right.

{ Bravo! You Landed the BIG JOB. Now What? }

There will be good jobs in your life, jobs that you've worked hard to attain and signal that you're seriously on your way. Then there's the BIG JOB, the one that puts you on top, that makes you a boldface name in your field. If you've been reading this book, that's probably what you're aiming for. And if you've used the strategies that I've discussed so far—developing game-changing ideas, being a dynamic boss, managing your *career* along with your job—there's every chance that you'll get there.

My first BIG JOB was running *Child* magazine. All the editorial-side decisions of the magazine—regarding covers, content, PR, etc.—rested with me. I walked into work that first day feeling nervous but exhilarated.

After you've landed a BIG JOB, it would be nice if you could (after uncorking a bottle of champagne to share with those close to you) simply settle down to the work at hand. But you can't. People are watching you now. They are expecting results. And some of them are expecting you to fail. Love the BIG JOB, delight in the power and prestige it offers, but, as you roll up your sleeves, know that you must also navigate the situation intelligently and carefully.

Do not—I repeat, *do not* go in acting like a hard-ass. In an attempt to look invulnerable, some women start a BIG JOB with a take-no-prisoners approach. Though that kind of toughness may work in certain cases, it has the potential to backfire big-time, especially when employed in the first days and weeks of a new job. At first people almost wet their pants when you walk into a room. But then they start gathering and whispering together and begin to feel strength in numbers. They start bad-mouthing you behind your back and both consciously and unconsciously begin to do things to undermine you and your mission.

The far more effective approach, I think, is to present a picture of someone who is sure of herself, ready to make a difference, open to discussion, inclusive, and willing to make stars out of the people who perform well as the new mission is tackled.

"The worst thing you can do is be prescriptive," says Michele James, a cofounder of the executive recruiting firm James & Co. "You need to listen, be available. It's in this period, too, that the soft data will start to bubble up."

Nail down your vision—and share it. I talked earlier about how it's important to have your mission in mind. In a BIG JOB you need more than a mission, you need a *vision*. It's the difference between having a few goals you wish to execute and creating a winning, enticing, and perhaps totally new direction for the future. A vision not only gives *you* a road map to follow but also helps the people who work for you feel energized and engaged. Boil it down to a compelling sound bite and share it.

Many of the visions drummed up by leaders are too fuzzy to provide much help to anyone. Others are so earnest that you wonder if people feel kind of creepy being associated with them. One way to make a vision both clear and exciting is to make it *visual*.

That's what Ann Edelberg did when she took over the job of producing MSNBC's *Morning Joe*. "I decided to treat the show like an incredible cocktail party," she says. "Every day I wanted the show to feature the next big thing, the thing with street cred, and nothing that said 'has been.' I always erred on the side of edgy and cool. If the show was a restaurant, I saw it as Nobu—cool and sexy and hip, even though not everyone would want to eat there. The guests we invited had to fit within those parameters. And I told the guests to view being on the show not as an interview but as a conversation."

Unless your job is to salvage some huge disaster, it's not necessary to trash what was done before you arrived. I'm always surprised by new editors in chief who come into a magazine and use their first letter from the editor to explain how they're overhauling a product that really sucked before they got there. That kind of letter must make both the staff and the readers feel like bozos. Focus on the future, not the past.

As soon as you can, meet with your direct reports one by one. No matter how crazy busy you are, find the time to do this in the first week or two. People get offended if you don't. Tell them in advance that you'd like an update from them regarding what they're working on. This is a good chance to start to learn what's really going on and begin to *sense* where the land mines are. You may be tempted to try to probe for a little dirt, but at this point people are in defense mode, so they're probably not going to tell you where the bodies are buried. And you don't want to look too eager for dirt.

This is also a time to share your vision individually with your top people. There's no need to go into tons of detail. That's because you're still figuring it out, and also it helps to be a bit of a mystery now. Tell them you will share more as the weeks unfold. It's good to keep them guessing a little, make them feel intrigued. And besides, anything you say is likely to be repeated.

Divide and conquer. Though some people will respond to your presence graciously and embrace your vision, others will make you feel as though you're an interloper who has disrupted their perfect ecosystem. A few may even bare their teeth like wolves whose territory has been threatened.

I've taken over five different magazines, and I've always been stunned by the way some people respond to a new boss. When I started at *McCall's*, one senior editor strolled by my office, popped her head in the door, and announced that there were certain ways things were done there and she'd be glad to show me. Sometimes even the good ones become victims of a pack mentality.

What they don't seem to realize is that you may have been given carte blanche to fire anyone you desire. But don't be rash. Take a few weeks to get the lay of the land, determine who's worth keeping and who isn't, and begin to engender loyalty.

In the beginning, avoid big group meetings if at all possible. Let your gut tell you who the best people are and spend as much one-on-one time with them as possible. Tell them you'd like their impressions of something fairly neutral—like on an article about the field or a report that was done just before you arrived. That will help you (1) gauge their strengths and weaknesses and (2) begin to form a bond with them.

Once you sense you can trust someone—and the person's judgment—pick his or her brain to learn as much as you can about the operation. You want to figure out the history, the real obstacles, the festering problems—all of which will enable you to hone your vision and the strategies you need to implement to pull it off. You don't want to look desperate. But you can say things such as "I'd like to hear what *you* think about the way this plan was implemented" and "You were here when the study was done. What, in your opinion, are the key findings?" Because you're new, you won't have all the answers, so let people guide you to a certain degree—without looking needy for the info.

When I arrived at *Working Woman*, the three senior editors seemed to greet me with—dare I say it?—disdain. I was seven months pregnant the day I started and had no experience in business reporting, and they clearly thought I'd duped the owner of the company. (One of them later wrote an article admitting that she'd been too much of a good girl to throw her hat in the ring for the big job, but I clearly hadn't been, even with a belly the size of a beach ball.) But there was an associate editor named Louise who I quickly realized was incredibly well informed about business and business writers and also eager to embrace a new boss. I started working with her as much as possible.

A few weeks after I started, I asked Louise for insight into a move I wanted to make. "I think it's time to introduce a couple of new columns in the magazine," I told her. "I'd love to hear your recommendations for columnists." She gave me two names, and as I looked into them, I realized they were perfect. We signed both of them within a month. Today, I almost can't believe who those two columnists were. One was Gail Collins, who now is the marvelous *New York Times* op-ed columnist, and the other was Andy Grove of Intel, who a decade later was named *Time*'s Man of the Year. Louise, wherever you are today, thank you!

Know as you go. When you land a BIG JOB, you may be past the point of requiring a course in Web design or public speaking, but there's still stuff you must know to succeed. And you probably have to put your hands on it fast. Instead of freaking about it, consider what you need to know *this minute*.

After Alexa Hirschfeld started Paperless Post (that's the incredible company that allows you to send fun and gorgeous e-vites) with her brother, she said she read about fifty books—by everyone from Peter Drucker to Seth Godin—but only when the info was required. "I would pull in as much information as I needed to know at that time about the thing I was trying to solve," she says. "Sometimes I would feel that if I didn't end up finishing a book that night, I might not be able to do my job the next day."

When I became the editor in chief of *McCall's*, it was the first time I was editing a magazine that had to sell big-time on the newsstand, and I didn't feel my cover line writing skill was particularly strong. I'd always admired direct response copywriting (have you ever received an enticing pitch in the mail to buy something or subscribe to a magazine? That's direct response writing) and bought several books on the subject. Then I went a step further: I paid one of the top writers in the field to come in and teach me as much as she could in a morning. It was one of the smartest things I ever did. (Come on, you didn't think I came up with cover lines such as "Never Lose an Orgasm Again" without any training, did you?)

And the day I started at *Cosmo*, I hired Jane Buckingham as a contributing editor. Jane is an expert on Gen Y and Gen X, and I knew, as a baby boomer, that I needed her insights if I was going to run *Cosmo* successfully.

Do one big thing and thereby buy yourself some time. When I was at *Working Woman*, a top female executive we interviewed shared that tip for starting a BIG JOB. It's such wise advice. Yes, you need to get the lay of the land and gather info, but people are waiting for you to *do something*. So do something smart and splashy but relatively low risk. It will manage expectations and allow you time to really get your game on.

But once you've acquired the knowledge you need, don't sit tight, take action. Sooner is almost always better than later. One of my favorite quotes is from Shakespeare's *Julius Caesar*: "There is a tide in the affairs of men / Which, taken at the flood, leads on to fortune." Take it "at the flood."

Beware of haters. Subordinates who had wanted your position (or some of the duties of the position) will attempt to sneak responsibility or power away from you. Let them know (without losing your cool) that it's not acceptable, or they will keep trying until they are successful.

Fire the dissenters. Because you must. Give people a chance to come on board, and if they don't, get rid of them. Otherwise, they will drag you down, I swear.

Be a little bit scary. It's not bad, as I said, to keep people guessing, and it's not bad to keep them on their toes. You don't have to be bitchy or mean. Don't talk too much; make them wonder what you're thinking. It will guarantee that they're less complacent and more focused during your first days and months in your new job.

Part III

{ Success: How to Savor It }

One of the events that partly shaped my sense of how I hoped to live my life as a career woman happened when I was still in college and long before I was even certain what I wanted to do professionally. It was my junior year, and the school had invited a professor from a neighboring women's college to come and talk about feminism. My college had only recently gone coed after 175 years of being an all-male institution, so we had hardly any female professors of our own. Almost all the girls on my floor decided to attend the lecture. The women's movement was in full bloom then, and we were eager to hear someone discuss how it might impact our lives.

I was curious, too, about what the woman would look and sound like. Back in the early and mid-seventies, there weren't many female role models in the career world. I wondered if she would wear a snappy pantsuit, which was popular then for working women, or if she'd be all jean-jacketed out, like many of the feminists I saw in the media.

The lecture turned out to be amazingly inspiring. The woman lit a fire in many of us about all the emerging possibilities for women in the world. Here's the funny thing, though. I don't recall anything specific she said that night, but I do remember in vivid detail what she wore. She was dressed in a gorgeous black cocktail dress—and that was the thing that helped shape how I wanted to live my life.

Why was that dress so important to me? At the time there was a lot of the emphasis in the media about the struggle ahead for women. And it *was* tough in so many respects. But what that dress said to me was this: you may have to struggle at moments and you will have to work your butt off, but you can be a success, and you can have a fabulous, delicious time while you're at it.

So that was always my vow to myself: to make certain that any success I achieved enhanced my enjoyment of life rather than undermined it. I never wanted to be a workaholic or someone who found herself buried under mounds of work on the weekend or preoccupied with the office while I was on vacation.

Did I manage to accomplish that? I think I've done a decent job of honoring my vow. I live in Manhattan, a city I adore and take advantage of. I love to travel, and I have done my fair share of it with my husband and kids—we've even been to Antarctica. On weekends I walk, read, and often entertain friends at dinner parties. And I've also managed to pursue my crazy back-pocket dream of writing murder mysteries.

Yet I'll be honest: it took me a while to figure out how to work things to my advantage, especially when my kids were small. Sometimes there was just too much to do. Other times I made it worse by failing to get a handle on a situation or biting off more than I could chew. One night when my kids were small, I gave an outdoor dinner party for twelve at our weekend home in Pennsylvania. I was a fool for organizing such a big dinner when I already had so much on my plate, but I hated not taking advantage of the summer.

It turned out to be a gorgeous night, and because I had a woman helping me in the kitchen, I felt in control. But during one trip to the bathroom, I became overwhelmed with fatigue. I lay my head on the sink to take a very short catnap, hoping that it would revitalize me. It worked perfectly. I returned to the table, feeling completely refreshed. But when I picked up the conversation exactly where I'd left off, one of the guests leaned in and whispered in my ear, "You've been gone forty-five minutes!"

Let's just say I've been on a learning curve. And today I'm much better at keeping the craziness at bay and savoring the success that's come my way. Because it *can* be done—maybe not always, but lots of the time, partly by using some of the great skills you employ at work. In this part I'll offer some of the strategies I've learned—everything from bringing more bliss into your life to wrestling down an insane day to managing your time ingeniously. I even offer a few thoughts on making time for your own back-pocket dream.

{ The Bliss Quiz: Is Your Success Making You Happy? }

When you're really, really busy juggling work and life, it can be hard at times to assess how well you're handling everything. To me it's a little like riding a bike fast because you need to get someplace in a hurry. You're pumping and pumping and making the best time you possibly can, but you don't really consider how you're peddling or even the ground you're covering.

Sometimes a wake-up call is forced on you. You leave your wallet on the counter of the pharmacy or your kid's teacher tells you he failed to hand in a project you didn't even realize he'd been assigned, and you come face-to-face with the fact that things have slipped out of your control a little—or a helluva lot.

I've never forgotten one moment of awakening for me. My husband and I had gone away with our young kids for a family beach vacation (which, when your kids are little, really shouldn't be defined as a vacation). We'd arrived at the airport and were headed by van on a dusty, hour-long ride to the resort. It had been a tough time for me at work. My company was in the process of being sold, and though we didn't know it officially yet, there was a lot of weirdness in the air.

All of a sudden my husband, clearly empathizing with what I'd been experiencing, reached over and gave my shoulders a quick massage. It wasn't until his hands touched my rock-hard shoulders that I realized how rattled and bummed out I'd been feeling. I knew I needed to use the vacation not only to enjoy my family but also to try to find my way back mentally to a less frazzled place.

Many women feel under enormous stress today, even women who don't have young kids in the mix. In early 2012, I did a website poll at *Cosmo* asking women if they felt they were headed for a burnout. Among women eighteen to twenty-four years old, an absolutely shocking 84 percent said yes, and among those twenty-five to thirty-four, 86.5 percent said yes. And in all age groups, around 90 percent said they often felt stressed and overwhelmed. Those numbers aren't a surprise when you think how much pressure we're all under these days as workplaces demand an ever-expanding amount of our time and energy.

So I doubt I'm being presumptuous in saying you want less stress and more pleasure in your life as a working girl. The first step is to assess what your stress-to-bliss ratio is. Take this quiz for a quick evaluation.

1. A long weekend is coming up, the kind where you get Monday off as well. What will you use the extra day for?

a. To take a long bike ride I haven't had time for lately.

b. To get a jump start on an upcoming work project—dressed in my PJs

c. To catch up on laundry and finally repaint my bedroom.

2. What's the most recent piece of advice a friend gave you?

a. "You ought to write self-help books—your advice is that good."

b. "I think you'd enjoy our nights out more if you weren't always checking your e-mails."

c. "Try to get more sleep. The bags under your eyes are big enough to pack for a weekend trip."

3. When you have a ton on your plate during a certain period, what word or phrase would your romantic partner, use to describe you?

a. Crazy busy

b. Crazed

c. Crazy

4. If you have kids, how do they generally grab your attention when they need it on a busy night?

a. They just say, "Hey, Mom?"

b. They start nagging or whining.

c. They give the cat a bubble bath.

5. Look down at your nails—how are they holding up these days?

a. I make sure to keep on top of them because it's an instant confidence boost.

b. The polish is a little chipped, but they're not *hideous*.

c. The manicurist would need a weed whacker to deal with my cuticles.

6. What's the last part of your bedtime routine?

a. Slathering on some rich body butter before slipping between the nice new sheets I treated myself to

b. Catching up on reading in the tub

c. Checking e-mail, Facebook, and Twitter one last time

7. **Everything is going wrong at work today. How do you calm down and regroup to make it through the day?**

    a. I step out for a short walk.

    b. I take a deep breath and remind myself that in a few hours the day will be over. Till then, I just keep trying to fix anything that goes wrong as fast as possible.

    c. I drain a double cappuccino, run damage control for the rest of the day, and apologize the next day to anyone I snapped at.

8. **When was the last time you called your best friend or sister to catch up?**

    a. Yesterday. We try to swap stories at least once a week even with our hectic schedules.

    b. Does texting count as an actual conversation?

    c. When I wished her happy birthday—three months ago.

9. **Your partner whisked you away for a BlackBerry/iPhone-free weekend at a country inn. How many times did you secretly check your messages?**

    a. None. The only electronics used were the toys in the bedroom.

    b. None while we were *there*. But I used the whole drive home to catch up. That wasn't part of the agreement.

    c. Whenever he went to the bathroom or stepped out of the room—just to make sure my in-box wasn't blowing up.

10. **Your favorite thing to do alone is:**

    a. Read a fabulous novel

    b. Check out all my saved-up Pottery Barn catalogues

    c. *Alone?*

If you answered mostly a's, can I please meet you? It's clear that you've brilliantly managed to find a way to savor your success and not let craziness from work bleed over into your personal life. You are excellent at fully engaging in what you're doing without mentally being dragged elsewhere. (And your friends and family appreciate it.) Plus, it seems that not only do you make time for yourself, you also know how to find the bliss in everyday moments. You're helping to keep the body butter industry in business, but hey, you deserve it.

If you answered mostly c's, I'm probably not telling you anything you don't already know: work and stress are getting the better of you. You must be working tough hours, or maybe you're under an extreme amount of pressure right now, or you may have more on your to-do list than seems humanly possible to manage. There's a good chance you also have kids under five years old! You may know you need to do something about your situation, but you feel so under the gun that you don't even try. You arrive home from work feeling crazed, and that sensation has barely subsided by bedtime (and checking your messages before bed doesn't help).

If you answered a lot of b's (with a few a's and c's thrown in), I can relate. I was a "b girl" for many years. B's mean that despite how busy your life is, you make an *effort* at least to keep things balanced—even programming in some "me" time. The trouble is, your approach is kind of catch as catch can, so you end up never allowing yourself to fully savor and enjoy. Skimming the Pottery Barn catalogue is good, but it's never going to bring you lasting pleasure.

In the next chapters you'll find some strategies for preventing work pressures from infringing on your personal life and increasing the amount of blissful moments. If you answered mostly a's, I bet you'll still find inspiration. If you answered mostly c's, I hope the advice will help you begin the process of taking back your personal life. You're going to need more than a few scented candles to make it happen, but once you start, you'll have momentum.

If you answered mostly b's, you may need the advice more than you realize. I suspect that most women fall into the b category. We think we are doing okay, but our efforts are only skin deep. It's great to have a wake-up call. Mine was when my husband gave me that massage. Maybe this quiz will work like that for you.

{ Why You Must Absolutely Be the Boss of Your Personal Life, Too }

As successful working women, we're good at managing people and projects and making things run as we want them to. We know how to delegate, ask for help, close out a project, and set aside time for what matters. But we don't always bring those great bossy skills to our personal lives. Thus we sometimes find ourselves stuck doing tasks we can't stand, dogged by unfinished projects (such as the overstuffed hall closet or the unopened Rosetta Stone), and with not nearly enough time for the activities that give us pleasure. Lately a professional friend and I were trying to arrange a lunch, and she sent me the following e-mail: "The twenty-sixth isn't good. How about the thirty-seventh?" It was as if her subconscious was telling her that she needed many more days in a month to fit everything in.

Did you take the quiz in the previous chapter? If you did and the score made you see that you're not savoring your success, it's time to make an adjustment. Because the opposite of not savoring is often mega stress and misery, and that not only keeps the pleasure away, it also hurts your health. Here are the best solutions I've learned.

8 Ways to Reduce Craziness and Stress

1. Stop using the phrase "I'm so busy." This is a tip from my longtime friend Judsen Culbreth, former editor in chief of *Working Mother* magazine and now an editor of *Mobile Bay* magazine in Alabama. As she points out, "words have this tricky way of becoming our feelings." Meaning that if you say you're busy, you will certainly feel busy. If you say you're crazed, you will feel crazed.

2. Regularly pose the question to yourself, "Why am I doing this?" Followed by "Does it have to be done at all?" If the answer to the second question is yes, ask, "Could anyone else do it?" These questions help you see that there is much you can actually let go of, allowing you to focus instead on your priorities. For instance, asking myself the first question forced me to realize that I was sending out Christmas cards because I thought I should rather than because I wanted to. How great it felt to let that task fall by the wayside.

3. Nail down your "no" phrase. It's so darn hard to say no. Therefore women end up saying yes when they don't want to simply because they can't spit the word out. Figure out a phrase that's going to work for you whenever you need to decline graciously, and rely on it every time. It should be concise (so you get it out quickly), polite (you don't want to be rude), slightly vague (you don't want the other person to offer an alternative for you to say yes to), and unequivocal (you want to sound sure of the decision).

One phrase that works well is "Thanks for thinking of me, but unfortunately I won't be able to at this time." Do *not* elaborate.

And say no right away. Don't tell the person you'll get back to her because then not only will you agonize about the decision, you'll disappoint or annoy her because she thought it was a possibility.

4. Be open to reengineering. I'm sure you've developed some terrific routines for accomplishing personal stuff. But it's good to step back from time to time and question them—even the ones you have down to a science. Ask yourself: (1) does this work as well as it should? and (2) is there possibly another, *better* way to do it?

Judsen Culbreth's husband taught her about reengineering after she'd had her second child and was balancing being a mother and wife with a demanding job. "I asked my husband what more he could do to help now that we had a new baby," she says. "One of the things he picked was shopping for my older child's clothes. But instead of taking her to the store with him—always stressful—he took out a tape measure and measured her arms, inseams, etc. He wrote the information on a two-by-five card and took *that* to Macy's instead. He'd reengineered a task and made it far less crazy. I learned from watching that."

5. Don't be dogged by a long personal to-do list. Is there really no one to delegate a task to? Then deal with it as soon as possible. One of my biggest mistakes after my kids were born was that I allowed a monster to-do list to stalk me like the hound of Hell. The smartest thing I could have done was to occasionally take a personal half day and wipe everything off my list, but I never wanted to use my personal days that way. I would have been so much better off doing so and preventing that hound from relentlessly nipping at my heels every day.

6. Don't always see stress as a demon. Mika Brzezinski points out that stress isn't going away, so we should "embrace it, learn how to harness it, and make it work for us." Tell yourself you're going to convert stress into energy to power through a project so you get it out of the way.

7. Ask yourself if you need to be working as late as you do. Have you ever noticed how people love to brag about how many hours they work each week? There's the sixty-hour week and the eighty-hour week and even worse. Yes, many of us have ended up in downsized conditions and have no choice but to work longer. But are you doing it simply because it's become a habit or because other people in your office are doing it and you feel you have to follow suit? Test the waters and leave earlier. Watch the sunset at home.

8. Resist multitasking. Many studies have shown that when you multitask, neither activity is done well or with true satisfaction. (I once tried to do a radio interview at my desk while reading e-mails and lost my train of thought!)

8 Ways to Bring on the Bliss

1. Figure out the things that give you great pleasure (or could give you great pleasure if you were already doing them), and find a way to include them in your life. When I was the editor of *Redbook*, my life was particularly zany. My kids were young then, and I dashed home from work each day just after five, fixed dinner, supervised homework, read to the kids, and then, after they went to bed, worked for several more hours. My husband and I had just bought an old town house in Manhattan, and I was also trying to contend with renovations that had left parts of the house in shambles. My idea of "me" time back then was watching *Law & Order* reruns at 11 p.m. I felt frazzled most days.

One afternoon, my eighty-something next-door neighbor asked me to attend a lecture with her at the Explorers Club. Because I admired her fiercely and knew she lived alone, I could not bring myself to use the "no" phrase I advocated earlier. The talk turned out to be on Turkey, and as the lecturer's slides flashed on the screen, I had an epiphany. With all the demands of my life, I'd let one of my great pleasures—travel—slip away. I made a pledge to myself to bring it back with at least one trip a year.

The key thing is to build good stuff into your schedule. Dr. Holly Phillips says that one of the activities that affords her the most pleasure is seeing her girlfriends, so without fail she has drinks with her friends on a certain night of the week.

2. Be in the moment. When your life is packed, it's easy to get caught up in thinking about what you need to do next or what happened just before. My yoga instructor, Angela Attia, who is also an extremely talented aerialist (and Stanford grad!), taught me something life-changing from the Tantric philosophy, the type of yoga she practices.

"We need to learn to be more present in every moment and fully enjoy whatever is there at that moment," she says. "It's all about bringing your mind to what your body is actually experiencing right now." So, for example, if you eat a piece of chocolate, you want to savor every morsel of it. If you walk down the street, you want to take a moment to notice some interesting piece of architecture or simply how warm your toes feel in your new socks. "We have to keep giving ourselves reminders to come back to enjoying all that our senses have to offer us," Attia says. "Because in between will be moments when life's mundaneness or hectic pace takes us away from that."

3. Ask for what you want. I talked a lot in part I about the importance of asking for what you want on the job. But you must also ask for what matters in your personal life.

Sometimes what you need involves an intersection of your work and your personal life, such as the ability to work at home on Fridays because you have a young child. Bite the bullet and ask your boss. One of the most outrageous things I did in my early thirties, before I was an editor in chief, was ask my boss for permission to take a three-week vacation. Newly divorced, I was overwhelmed with a desire to escape from it all, and when I heard about a chance to tag penguins in Patagonia with a World Wildlife Association–sponsored program, I knew it was the trip for me. Yes, I had a pit in my stomach when I asked her if I could go, but I also presented a plan for how things would work in my absence. To my utter thrill, she consented. The next year I summoned my nerve to ask again—and that time I worked with Earthwatch restoring an archaeological site on Rarotonga, a magical island a few hours southwest of Tahiti.

Here's the one thing to keep in mind: though the old expression is "It never hurts to ask," it *does* if you leave your boss with the wrong impression. You don't want him to suspect that you aren't fully invested. It can all be in how you phrase the ask. For instance, instead of saying, "I want to be with my baby more," say, "Having one day a week when I'm not commuting will give me extra time to focus on the big picture." Instead of "I just love how cute penguins look in those little tuxedos," say, "I've found that travel really charges me up and makes me even more creative. I know I'll come back full of ideas."

4. Instead of multitasking, try maximizing your time. Sometimes it's okay to kill two birds with one stone if one activity actually enhances the other rather than distracts from it. Book clubs are the perfect example— they're a way to connect with friends and also be mentally stimulated. When my son was small, I noticed that he enjoyed spotting and mentally cataloguing things he saw in nature. It nudged me into thinking about myself and nature, how I had loved fishing when I was younger, and how I missed having time for outdoor hobbies. Then suddenly I had a brainstorm: I decided to see if I could interest my son in bird-watching and make that my hobby, too. It turned out he loved it, and we've spent many, many hours sharing this hobby.

5. Savor your job. Sometimes you can get so caught up in complaining about how nutty your job is that you lose sight of its awesomeness. Think about how you look to others. Strut your stuff. Accept an exploratory interview with someone who wants to pick your brain, and enjoy talking about your job and what makes it so good.

6. Have a pretty bedroom. With no stacked laundry piles anywhere. Having a beautiful sanctuary you can retreat to each night is one of the most blissful things in the world.

7. Discover half-hour power. No matter how packed your day is, try to leave thirty minutes each day—block it out—to recharge your batteries somehow. If you don't have kids, it could be a half hour before work when you meditate. If you have kids, read and only read before turning out the lights.

8. Go big or go home. Bring the same zest to your personal life as you do to your job. Don't postpone the fun—even if you have to schedule it in.

{ Terrific Time-Management Tricks }

When I was in my mid-twenties, I suffered from a really annoying problem: I was a terrible procrastinator. Though I was a hard worker, I couldn't seem to get on top of my assignments. I was always turning things in at the very last moment, and sometimes I even pulled all-nighters to finish articles. I hated the anxiety my procrastination caused in me. So one day I vowed to tackle it.

Here's what I did: I began reading books on time management. And I even wrote articles about it so I could speak directly to authorities on the subject. Two of my favorite experts were Alan Lakein, the author of *How to Get Control of Your Time and Your Life*, and Edwin Bliss, the author of *Getting Things Done: The ABCs of Time Management*. Over the years I've even come up with a few tricks of my own.

If you want to get organized and use your time brilliantly, I suggest you read one of the books by those experts. There are also workshops on the subject, some of them offered online. But to tide you over, here are the strategies that have worked for me. Follow them, and I can practically guarantee that you will feel you have more hours in your day and use them more productively.

Find the time of day when you're most "in the zone." I've always been a night owl and spent years skulking around the house when my family was in bed, reading, working, and watching a cable TV show about a vampire cop. But when I started to write my first mystery, opening my laptop at ten each night, the words came out in terrible fits and starts. After a few weeks of experimenting, I discovered that I was far more creative in the early morning. (Studies show that many people are actually at the top of their game in the morning.) So I rose early to write, and my novel began to come together. Having had that eureka moment, I also began focusing on my creative magazine projects early in the day, and saved the more routine stuff for afternoons. It made me far more efficient.

To determine when *you're* in the zone, think about when you're most productive and most engaged, when your thoughts begin to flow.

Assign a value to the things you do. Lakein talks in his book about ranking tasks as A, B, or C, and that's one way to do it. (In his autobiography former president Bill Clinton said he read Lakein's book as a young man and still has the "A list" he jotted down then.)

Another way to do it is to ask yourself, "How freaking important is this, *really*?" In other words, will it really pay off for you at work or home? I once called a pal of mine, an editor in chief with two young kids, on a Sunday morning and was told by a babysitter that she was doing a cable TV show in New Jersey. As I set down the phone, I couldn't help but wonder how important an appearance on a little cable show could have been for her professionally, especially since it meant sacrificing part of a Sunday with her family.

She already had plenty of TV experience, so this wasn't adding to it, and she would hardly be reaching many readers at that hour. And yet I could also see how she might have been talked into it by her PR person or said yes as a knee-jerk response.

I started thinking about how often I automatically said yes to things that were just plain stupid—because they sounded good or had once been good or someone had led me to believe they were good.

Throw overboard anything that doesn't matter— and don't look back. Now that you've assigned a value to activities in your life, eliminate those that don't count. You can either delegate them to someone else or just plain dump them.

Regularly review your "delegated" list and add to it. I learned this from a successful woman I interviewed for a book years ago. She said that women know they need to delegate, but they make their list once and don't update it. Her point: you should constantly be thinking about fresh ways to delegate or let go of something—because new options are always emerging.

Never handle a piece of paper more than once. I think I first heard this from Lakein. Such a fabulous tip. Every time you pick something up from your in-box (or look at it on your computer) and then put it back down (or close it), promising yourself you'll deal with it later, you use up seconds that eventually add up to minutes. Vow to take action the first time you glance at something. If it's a letter, answer it. If it needs to be filed, file it. If it requires your opinion, give it. What this means is that you must go through your in-box and e-mail only during parts of the day when you've allotted yourself enough time to deal with each item effectively.

Do the math. Periodically it's good to figure out how much time certain activities suck up. Add up the minutes or hours. When you see the results, you may want to delegate or eliminate some stuff.

Surfing the Web, for instance: 30 minutes a day equals 3½ hours a week equals 182 hours a year, which is 7½ days a year! When we polled *Cosmo* readers about their social media habits, 40 percent of those who used it were engaged for more than two hours a day. Great if it makes you happy. But could you use some of that time for other, even more valuable activities?

Slice the salami. Okay, if I had to thank one person for the fact that I've been able to write mysteries and thrillers while I had a full-time job, it would probably be Edwin Bliss. In his book he recommends a tip he calls "slice the salami," and that technique made all the difference for me. Bliss points out that we often fail to tackle important tasks not because we aren't capable of doing them but because they seem too big and unappealing—like a huge hunk of salami.

That was the problem for me. Writing a book seemed so daunting. In my twenties I'd tell myself I was going to spend an entire Saturday morning writing, but then I'd find any reason to avoid sitting in front of my laptop—sometimes because the rug pad needed trimming! Bliss's advice is that you must slice a big project into thin, appetizing amounts so that you won't be put off. That's what I finally did; rather than vowing to write for a full morning, I told myself I would work on my mystery for fifteen minutes each morning. It seemed easy enough to pull off, and I sat down religiously each Saturday and Sunday morning. Even with just fifteen minutes of writing, the pages began to accumulate. Before long I was staying at my desk longer. My new goal became thirty minutes, then an hour, then two hours, and so on.

This principle works in so many areas: projects, hobbies you hope to start, even exercise. My yoga teacher, who also teaches Pilates and aerobics, told me that in her years of experience she has found that following the Christmas holidays, people who sign up for one session a week are far more likely to stick with it than those who sign up for two or more sessions a week.

Start before you're ready. One of my weaknesses in terms of time management is that I need to get "all ready" for a task. Before I write in the morning, for instance, I like to have my tea prepared, my desk nicely organized, and even a few news stories skimmed. There's nothing wrong with morning rituals or feeling organized before you begin, but this kind of fluffing can suck away both time and even mental energy. The next thing you know, it's nine o'clock, not eight, when you planned to start, and you're less raring to go than you were an hour ago. Here's a trick someone taught me: jump into the task for a few minutes, and then take care of getting organized. Before I even sit down with my tea, I turn on my laptop and reread the last page I've written. That way I'm already engaged and excited, and it's easier to come back and officially begin.

Pick a number. When I tackle fiction on weekend mornings, I have a specific goal: five pages. Having a set goal in mind—no matter what your task—helps drive you to the finish line and prevents you from becoming distracted by another project.

{ How to Handle an Insane Day }

'm sure you've had more than a few insane workdays. Me, too. One of the worst for me may have been when I had to moderate a panel at a management conference several days after my father died. No one in my company would have minded if I'd bailed, but I didn't feel comfortable leaving the organizers and panelists hanging. So I sucked it up—but I felt as though I were in some horrible altered state.

Though I haven't seen the last of insane days, they have at least decreased in number over the years. That's partly due to the fact that I don't have young children right now. When your kids are little, you not only have more demands on your time and energy, but you're less resilient because you're so freaking tired. But I also have grown better at managing stress and general craziness.

Step one: I do my best to spot when an insane day is headed my way and then, if possible, shift what I can. Former *Working Mother* editor in chief Judsen Culbreth likes to point out that stress is caused not by doing too many things but by doing too many things you don't like. For me, at least, insane days definitely involve an overload of unpleasant activities. So if I see that there are lots of ugly meetings on the same day I'm supposed to go to the dentist and call my accountant, I try to rearrange some. If a potentially insane day is looming for you, move things around if possible. If it means canceling on someone, don't go into a long explanation. Describing how badly your day is going to be will only make you feel more worked up. And the other person won't have any sympathy anyway.

If, despite your best efforts, your day begins to turn into a nightmare—your sitter was late, making *you* late, you spilled coffee all over your new pants, and the job candidate you just hired backed out—try to grab a few minutes by yourself in a quiet space (away from the craziness if possible) and then just breathe. And relax. I'll never forget something Dr. Ruth Westheimer did when I brought her in to speak to a group of editors and advertisers at *Mademoiselle*. She asked if she could spend a couple of minutes in my office beforehand, and then she sat quietly by herself, eating a sandwich. It made me see the value of a few key moments alone to center yourself— away from the hurly-burly.

This is especially true if your insane day involves giving any kind of presentation or speech. People, I've found, love to try to grab your attention right before you have to speak publicly. Don't hesitate to say nicely that you need a few moments to yourself.

Once you've chilled a little, consider what's still on your plate and how you're going to tackle it. This is a time for triage. What seriously needs your attention right now and can't be ignored? What can be put off? What could someone else help you with, including on the home front? When I was first married with young kids, I stupidly didn't ask for help on many occasions when my husband would have been happy to give it. When you ask for assistance, there's no need to sound freaked or frantic so that you guarantee the other person will *get* it. In fact, this can be off-putting. Just say something such as "I need to sort out a problem here at work, and I'm going to be an hour late. Can you stick the pork chops in the freezer and order takeout instead? Get whatever sounds good to you." Then *let go* of any aspect of what you've delegated.

When you're feeling superstressed, pick your food and drink wisely. This is not the moment for a king-size pack of peanut butter cups or a bag of potato chips from the office vending machine. Sugars and starches (which turn into sugar) will only heighten your manic feeling. Instead go for cheese, nuts, or a piece of chicken or turkey. These all contain tryptophan, an amino acid that helps your brain produce serotonin, a feel-good chemical known to reduce anxiety. And be careful about your caffeine intake. It can add to your jitters.

When you're having a bad day, you may yearn to reach home and vent to your partner or your friends. Here's a crazy strategy that's going to go against what you've probably heard but I firmly believe in: resist the urge to vent. We're encouraged, especially as women, to share all that's bothering us, to let it out, unload. From my first days at *Cosmo*, I began to learn how different men and women were in this regard. You practically have to use the Jaws of Life to extract anything from a man. Over time at *Cosmo* I became intrigued by the guy approach and wondered if there was any merit to it. And then I began hearing research that stressed the value of *not* getting it all off your chest.

One study, from the University of Toronto Scarborough, found that people who avoided thinking about their work problems at home and distracted themselves with something else—books or music, for instance—experienced less conflict overall than those who tried to find solutions or vented to pals.

When a workday is tumultuous or ugly, try leaving it at the door when you come home. Some studies don't support this, but I think it works. Instead of talking and possibly churning everything up, read, watch a movie you've been dying to download, play Scrabble, or take a walk after dinner. When you're feeling calmer, you may want to ask for advice on how to handle a specific issue, but chances are you will arrive there on your own.

{ Setting Boundaries }

Ordinarily I wouldn't think I had anything in common with a rich European banker, but recently, for just a moment, I did. It was reported that the chief executive of Lloyds bank in London had returned from a leave of absence he'd taken to deal with exhaustion. According to his boss, the banker had been suffering from "a failure to switch off," and the situation became so bad that during one stretch he wasn't able to fall asleep for five nights in a row. The irony: I was reading the story online as I periodically glanced at incoming texts and flipped through *House Beautiful*. Suddenly I paused and wondered: Did *I* have a problem switching off? Was I too tethered to work and to all things digital and no longer good about giving myself time to chill and enjoy? In other words, had my BlackBerry made me its bitch?

Maybe. According to the productivity expert Julie Morgenstern, many women are suffering from a failure to switch off. And in some instances, she says, we have become addicted to our handheld devices. Sure, iPhones and BlackBerrys are fantastic in many ways. They provide tons of information and make life easier, but they can also create problems if we're not careful.

For one thing, Morgenstern says, any kind of digital devices can interfere with sleep. That's because they tend to energize us, and you don't really want that at 11 P.M.—unless you're planning on going clubbing. "It's a little like drinking a can of Diet Pepsi just as you're getting ready for bed," she says.

We also need screen breaks to help us think. "In order to synthesize and retain info, you have to give your brain a chance to disconnect for a while," Morgenstern notes. "Otherwise, your brain can't learn." Try sometimes banishing your smartphone to the zippered compartment of your purse, and use the time to fully engage in the book you're reading, the art show you're seeing, or the conversation you're having.

Not only is it relaxing and restorative when you do that but also interesting thoughts come and ideas flow. Paperless Post cofounder Alexa Hirschfeld says she disconnects not because she feels frazzled by the barrage of e-mails and texts but because a break— for instance, leaving her phone off while she's going through an art gallery—makes her more creative. "Diversity of experience contributes to a fertilized mind," she says. "I don't want to be a successful career person; I want to be a successful *person.*"

Last, constantly checking e-mail and texts can be a giant time suck. Each time you glance away from what you're doing to check and then go back to your activity, you're using up seconds—and those seconds add up to minutes and hours.

You can't ignore messages, especially where work is concerned, so what do you do? Morgenstern recommends getting into the habit of looking at your e-mail only about five times a day, for around twenty to thirty minutes each time. This not only allows you to switch off but makes your e-mailing much more efficient. You're not glancing away from other activities, and since you've arranged a solid block of time to address your e-mails one by one, you won't have to come back to some later.

Morgenstern also recommends not checking e-mail around the "edges of the day." Reserve that time for bubble baths, chick lit, and the cute person sharing your bed.

"But, but, *but*," you may be saying, "I can't." "My boss won't let me." "Other people won't let me." To some degree that may be true, depending on your work and your field. Yet you may have become an enabler, allowing and even encouraging people to reach you—by phone or e-mail—because you always respond immediately. Experiment by not replying at certain times and see what happens. Your coworkers will begin to know your boundaries. Even some bosses can be trained.

{ Drain the Swamp as You Slay the Alligators, 2 }

Earlier I talked about the importance of building time into your work schedule each week to step away from your usual day-to-day tasks and focus on the big picture for a while. During that hour or so, you need to ask yourself: What should I be paying more attention to? Have I let any important goals slip between the cracks? What should I be focusing on most while going forward? Then you must create pockets of time each week to implement your plans. From the moment I arrived at *Cosmo*, I initiated this strategy, and it played a key role in my success.

But over time I came to see how important this strategy can be for your personal life, as well. When you're chugging away like crazy at your job and trying to handle a personal to-do list that might include caring for kids, it can be easy to lose sight of big-picture personal goals that are important but not urgent. All of a sudden a few months or even years have zipped by and you haven't made a dent toward accomplishing what really matters to you.

That's why you need to plan time every week to think about draining the swamp in terms of your personal life. You can do this at your kitchen table, at a sidewalk café, or sitting on the grass in the park. Experiment with different places until you find a spot that encourages you to get into the zone. And take notes. You can use the Notepad app on your iPhone or iPad, or a regular legal pad, which I tend to do because writing with a number two pencil helps my thoughts form better for some nutty reason.

Start, just as you would at work, with questions: What should I be paying more attention to? Have I let any important goals slip through the cracks? What should I be focusing on going forward? Am I happy right now? Is something missing? What could make my life easier, more rewarding? Then devise an action plan.

Why is it necessary to book the time to do this? Because no matter how well intentioned you are, you may find that it doesn't happen automatically, especially when you are in a demanding career. I have a friend who worked for years as an agent in Hollywood and calls her thirties "the lost decade" because they went by so fast without her realizing that she hadn't achieved what she wanted on the personal front. "I just woke up one day and saw that I didn't have a husband and didn't have kids—things I wanted—and it probably was too late to make that happen. I'd been so busy, I hadn't really noticed that the time was slipping away."

Even when I knew I had to think about the big picture in terms of my personal life, I found it hard to do when my kids were young. I barely had time to roll on deodorant each day, let alone drain the damn swamp. When my first child was born, my husband was anchoring three newscasts each night, so I was on my own after 5 P.M. I'd rush home from work, take care of my son, and then, after he went to bed, I'd cook dinner for myself, handle household stuff, and tackle the work I'd brought home.

My husband still laughs when he recalls how one night he called to see how everything was going and I told him, "Good, good. Hudson and I went out for a walk and then we played for a while and then I read him a few books before his bath." There was a long pause. "Is something the matter?" I asked. "Well, his name is *Hunter*," he replied. At least I knew it started with an H!

But once my two kids were older and began sleeping longer on Saturday mornings, I set up a time each week for swamp draining. I'd take a mug of coffee and a notebook up to my little office in the barn at our weekend home and start jotting down questions: Could I be handling tasks better? Am I connecting with my kids after work as well as I can? Are there any changes I need to make? Is there something I still long to do? Whenever I found my way to the last question, one thing kept popping up: I wanted to write a murder mystery. It had been a dream of mine since I was twelve. At one of those Saturday-morning coffee klatches with myself, I started to toy with the idea of an editor in chief whose nanny dies, and I wrote down the following sentence: "Cat Jones was the kind of woman who not only got everything in the world that she wanted—in her case a fabulous job as editor in chief of one of the biggest women's magazines, a gorgeous town house in Manhattan, a hot-looking husband with a big career of his own—but over the years also managed to get plenty of what other women wanted: like *their* fabulous jobs and *their* hot-looking husbands."

That's where it began for me. I told myself I needed to find a way to write mysteries (see "Terrific Time-Management Tricks" and "Make Your Back-Pocket Dream a Reality [While You've Still Got a Day Job]"). Two-and-a-half years later, my first mystery *If Looks Could Kill* was published. And it still had the same first sentence.

But draining the swamp isn't just about tapping into an old dream. It's also a chance to think about how your life is running and what could be changed or reengineered to make you happier or more fulfilled on a personal level. Think about even the good stuff—

such as how you spend your time in the evenings after work—and ask yourself if it could be even richer or more productive.

You may feel you do this anyway on a fairly regular basis, yet I think it's best to block out the time. This may sound horribly corny, but it doesn't hurt to ask yourself, "It's 8 A.M. Saturday. Do I know where my mug and notebook are?"

{ Men, Love, and Success }

Okay, you've got this wonderful career going and you've also happened to find a really good guy, someone to spend this chunk of your life—or maybe your whole life—with. Nice. But as blissful as it can be to have both a wonderful career and a wonderful guy, sometimes those two things don't mesh perfectly. Your crazy schedule and his crazy schedule may mean you don't spend as much time together as you'd like or that the time you *do* spend together feels fragmented. Or maybe you sense that he doesn't recognize how demanding your job really is and isn't the sympathetic ear you long for. Or maybe he doesn't help out nearly as much as you need him to, particularly if there are kids in the mix.

I'm not a relationship expert (despite the fact that I've sometimes played one on TV!), but I've discovered a ton about men, love, relationships, and sex from working at *Cosmo*. I admit it: I've used a lot of what I learned in my own marriage, and I think my marriage is better for it. First and foremost, men are really different from us and they respond to the world differently. That's the starting point of the wisdom I've gained.

Men really want to please us. From the moment I arrived at *Cosmo*, I was struck by how many e-mails were sent by guys admitting that they read the magazine regularly. Sure, they were looking for ways to make women fall for them and get them into bed. But the most often cited reason a guy gave for why he read the magazine was that he wanted clues about how to please the woman in his life.

Though men may want to please us, they often don't know how. Guys, I've learned, find women incredibly baffling, far more than we realize. After I started the column "Sh*t My Guy Says," one woman e-mailed us to say that one day when she was in her bathroom using a blow dryer with a diffuser, her boyfriend walked in and asked, "Is that a ray gun?" A *ray gun*? I love that story because it shows how alien we seem to men at times. Because they don't always understand us, they can fail to see what matters to us or what's going to tick us off. For instance, if your boyfriend or husband neglects your anniversary, it's not because he doesn't care about you; it's because anniversaries don't matter to many guys.

One of the most important ways to enable a guy to please you is to tell him how to do it. Don't make the poor dude guess. If you love earrings but never wear necklaces, let him know so he doesn't buy the wrong gifts (trust me, he probably hasn't noticed that you never wear necklaces). If you need him to make the plane reservations because you're in the middle of a huge work project, tell him.

Men sometimes can find their partner's success hard to deal with. The number of women outearning their husbands has been steadily rising, and that number will continue to grow. According to recent census statistics, in all but three of the biggest cities in the United States, young women aged thirty and above are making more than young men in the same age group. And in many instances, those numbers reflect the fact that women are experiencing more career success than men.

Now, some guys will not only not mind your success and the fact that you bring home a bigger paycheck, they'll be delighted. Others, however, will feel awkward about it, particularly if their career is in a slump or not on the same trajectory as yours.

So what should you do if this is you? Alon Gratch, a New York–based psychologist, the author of *If Men Could Talk: Translating the Secret Language of Men*, and one of the best experts on marriage I know, offers this advice: "Don't neglect your relationship in pursuit of your career. Work very hard to relate to your spouse in the same way you always did, even as your relationships with others around you change, as you become more assertive, successful, powerful, or visible."

If the disparity becomes a nagging issue, you will need to get it out into the open, and you may even want to seek couples counseling to help you address the situation.

Men can seem like terrible listeners, but it's sometimes because of the way we talk. Is there a woman alive who hasn't sat across a table talking to the guy in her life and realized that he was starting to fidget like crazy or glance down at his smartphone? It's monumentally frustrating, especially because we pride ourselves on being good listeners.

Michael Gurian, a social philosopher and therapist and the author of *What Could He Be Thinking?*, told me that one of the reasons men don't listen well is that women can overwhelm them with more words than they can handle. Guys don't communicate the same way we do, and sometimes the trick for getting a better response is to edit yourself more. "Men are good listeners when people cut to the chase," he says. "They are bad listeners when people are very tangential and link gobs of sensory and emotional details together." Think about what you're going to say before you say it, and focus on only the most important stuff. Save rambling conversations for girlfriends.

In a conversation, men need to know what we want from them, especially when we're talking about work matters. This is especially important because men tend to quickly offer solutions, even when we aren't looking for any. Gurian points out that a guy will do better listening to you when you're clear about not only what the topic is but also how you would like him to respond. Let's say you just found out that twenty people are being laid off in your department, and though your job seems safe for the time being, you're concerned about the future. You don't want his advice right now—you're too worked up at the moment—you just want to convey the info. Tell him, "I want to share some news from work. Maybe later we can brainstorm about how I should handle it, but right now I just want to fill you in."

When you want a man to help at home, you need to be very clear. If you are going to be able to savor your life as a successful working woman who has a husband or live-in partner (and possibly kids), you need that guy to play at least a fifty-fifty role in the household. The way you ask can make a big difference. Men are not going to volunteer to do stuff, and it's not necessarily because they're lazy. They often don't know what's a priority in your mind, and they don't respond well to general comments. You have to make very specific requests. Don't say, "I need you to help more" or "Why can't you give me a hand in the mornings?" Say, "It would really help me if you were in charge of making breakfast for everyone in the morning."

Men don't like to open up, but it's possible to get them to. If you're trying to manage both a relationship and a career, you're going to need your guy to tell you what's on his mind. Is work okay for him? Is he anxious about a certain matter? Does he need something from you that you're not providing at the moment? One of the best things I learned about relationships came from

Dr. Gratch. He says that men can feel vulnerable when they open up, so they often resist doing it. To encourage your guy to be more forthcoming, you need to be both casual and concrete.

Casual: Meaning, don't pounce or make a big issue of it. If you sense there's a work issue for him, don't ask, "What's *wrong*?" Wait for a casual moment and say, "Work must be crazy right now, huh?"

Concrete: Meaning, don't be vague. And leave the emo at the door. Instead of "Are you really worried about your big presentation tomorrow?" ask, "What are the key points you hope people take away from your presentation?"

The best time to talk to a guy is often when you're side by side. Studies have shown that guys engage better when they're not experiencing sensory overload. So a good opportunity for a conversation isn't necessarily when you're face-to-face but rather when you're driving in the car or cooking dinner together.

Men need to be babied sometimes. *Please*, you may be thinking, we all want and need to be babied. Women, though, tend to be better than men at babying themselves—we indulge in, for example, massages and manicures. Guys don't do that as much. And besides, your guy really wants to be babied by *you*.

You don't have to go to any elaborate efforts to baby him. But if you're watching TV with him, give him a ten-minute foot rub. When you're shopping for groceries, pick up the kind of cookies you know he loves. When you're ordering something online, add a little item that will be a surprise for him. Such gestures can fall by the wayside when we're in overdrive at work, but they don't take much time— and they inspire devotion and reciprocity.

Men are rarely going to be the ones who make sure there's a lot of good stuff planned in your life together. When you're both busy in your careers, the fun, romantic stuff you did during courtship may become lost in the shuffle.

Unfortunately, if you want those times back—and I'm sure you do—you're probably going to have to be the one to make sure they happen. Don't take it personally. Most guys just don't seem hardwired to be this type of organizer.

By the way, there's nothing wrong with *scheduling* fun, romantic activities weeks in advance rather than simply hoping things happen spontaneously. And there's nothing wrong with scheduling sex either.

Men hate nightgowns. In a poll we did once at *Cosmo*, men said that the most lust-busting outfit a woman can wear to bed is one of those T-shirt-style nightgowns. A guy generally won't come right out and admit it to you, but he doesn't like it when you fall into too much of a comfort zone with your appearance. He wants to see you wear something sexy to bed, not that T-shirt nightgown. He also doesn't like granny panties and mom jeans. Men, after all, are visual creatures. And as the psychologist Stan Katz says, "The way you look and dress will always be a driving force in a man's attraction to you."

Your guy wants you to look, dress, smell, and feel nice. Those things fuel his arousal. I know, you have only so many damn hours in your day. But know that if you want him to be entranced with you, you need to make your appearance at home as big a priority as your appearance at work.

Men love sex. You know that, of course. But many women aren't aware of how *much* sex guys want or how much they mind when the frequency declines. If you keep turning him down because you're busy or tired, it's not okay with him even if he doesn't say as much.

Men love novelty. And so do women. The anthropologist Helen Fisher has found that having novel experiences releases dopamine in the brain, the same chemical that floods it when you're in the throes of infatuation. So do things as a couple that you've never done before.

Men love mystery. And so do women. That's something else Dr. Fisher has spoken a lot about—that being slightly unknown to our partner fuels his desire. A new study also shows that telling a man less makes him curious. Yes, it's great to keep him abreast of what's happening in your work world, but don't tell him everything. Intrigue him.

{ How to Be Smart About Maternity Leave }

Maternity leave can be a tricky business. You are over the moon with joy, and you want the time with your newborn to be as glorious—and as unintruded upon—as possible. But you also don't want your absence to have a negative impact on your job and your career. You can't afford to fall behind, for instance, or lose clout or create too many problems for the people picking up the slack while you're gone. In many instances, a company must hold your job for you until you return, but still, some women have come back from a maternity leave to find that the ground has shifted in subtle ways, that their standing isn't what it was before. That means you have to play things wisely.

How you should handle your leave depends a whole lot on your position and your work environment. How much can be delegated in your absence? How much do you still need to be in the mix? Is your team supportive? Are there any jackals in the midst who might start circling the minute you're gone?

Your strategy will also need to factor in the type of boss you have. It's important to realize that your pregnancy will most likely be viewed by your boss—despite the smile plastered on her face—as a pain in the ass. She is going to worry about how much your department or area will suffer during your departure, how much extra work it means for her personally, and whether you'll even come back after your maternity leave. Bosses can get weird about the whole thing. Some get weirder than others.

My two maternity leaves—and how I handled them—couldn't have been more different. When I had my first child, I was the number two at a magazine, not running the show; the number two in my own department filled in for me. She was extremely competent and totally up to the task, and I ended up having practically no contact with the office during that three-month period. When I had my second child, I was running *Working Woman* and barely had a leave. I worked from home for six weeks, spending plenty of time on the phone every day and having packages of articles and layouts messengered to my apartment, sometimes more than one delivery a day. I spent the next six weeks working half days at the office. I didn't love it, but I felt I had no choice.

In hindsight I realized I'd made mistakes with each. But I learned something from those mistakes. I've also gained wisdom from watching colleagues and subordinates handle their own leaves—successfully or not.

My first piece of advice: before you even tell your boss your news, determine in your own mind how things should be handled in your absence. If you have a plan in place, one that you can quickly bring up after you've broken the news, it will diminish that internal "Oh, no" response that your boss is bound to have as you speak.

When should you tell your boss? Before you begin to show! Though all women are different, you generally start to show around the twelve-week mark. Your coworkers are on the lookout for baby bumps in the workplace almost as much as the paparazzi are at celebrity events, and trust me, someone will spot the change in your waistline if you wait too long. That will lead to gossip, and if your boss learns the news via the office grapevine rather than from you directly, she will feel totally blindsided. And don't tell anyone else at work before you tell your boss. As I learned the hard way, you can't count on people to keep the secret.

If you do need to wait until after you're showing to tell your boss, there are ways to disguise your bump. The celebrity stylist Samantha McMillen says you should buy tops one size up so they won't be tight on the bump but then make sure your pants are fitted or wear leggings. "Loose on top of loose just makes you look big all over," she says. She thinks that in general dresses are best—especially ones with a tie at the waist to camouflage the protrusion. Also, a "fun big necklace or scarf draws the eyes up."

When you feel the moment is right, grab private time with your boss—not when she's super busy—and tell her the news. Express your happiness with the situation but quickly emphasize how committed you are to your job and that you have a solid plan for how things will run in your absence.

Many women choose to wait to break the news until they hear the results of the amniocentesis. The procedure can't be done until you're fifteen weeks pregnant, and then you must wait two weeks for results, which means you won't be announcing your condition until you are more than four months pregnant. When you tell your boss you're pregnant, you may want to explain that you didn't want to break the news until you were sure everything was okay with the baby.

Whenever you announce, provide key details about your pregnancy: the due date, as well as anything else that's critical. Women sometimes fail to offer important info (or else leak it out in dribs and drabs), partly, I think because they're nervous about how a boss will respond. Sometimes, too, they assume that a boss should know the ins and outs of pregnancy when he or she simply does not. If you fail to divulge information in a timely way, it will make your boss feel even more hyper about the whole thing.

At one magazine, a key editor of mine who was expecting twins mentioned in passing that her last day in the office was just a few weeks away. "Wait, what do you mean?" I asked, totally baffled and panic-stricken. As far as I knew, she wasn't due for three more months. She went on to explain that with twins, women often have to go on bed rest as early as five months. But I'd had no idea. Suddenly I was scrambling.

Once you go on leave, it's important to try to maintain regular contact with your workplace, especially, of course, if you are in a major position. I think I made a stupid mistake by going cold turkey with my first leave. My boss, I could tell, was uncomfortable with my pregnancy and even made remarks such as "Oh, you'll be so bored at home you may want to come back in a month." I decided to disabuse her of this idea by having as little contact with the office as possible. But it would have been better for me to touch base with her and my department during my leave. I could have kept it to brief calls, and that would have reassured her.

But don't get sucked into more contact than you should have. Set guidelines about the type of e-mails and calls you want to receive so you don't have too many and they occur at times that are best for you. And if you pick up a hint that a nasty coworker is trying to poach your territory, remember what I said in part II about nipping bad behavior in the bud. Call the person on it. Say something such as "I hear you've been asking a lot of questions about the Stanton business. You may not be aware of it, but I'm overseeing that business on my leave. If you have any questions, please e-mail me." The very fact that you've gotten wind of that person's actions all the way from Babyville should give him or her pause.

Don't be a martyr and do more work than necessary. Yes, people will have a bigger load in your absence, but there's nothing wrong with having a baby and you shouldn't be penalized. When I took the job as editor of *Working Woman*, the owner knew I was pregnant and told me that there was a "big enough orchestra to handle things" when I was gone. Since he'd reassured me, I should have asked for backup freelance help to make my leave more manageable.

Speaking of asking, don't hesitate to try to do some negotiating for what's best for you. Do you want four months off instead of three? If you think your workplace can handle it, go for it. Also, let me tell you a little secret. Though many companies have policies guaranteeing to cover your salary for only six weeks, some bosses manage to cut under-the-table deals for female staffers. If you have a good boss, there's nothing wrong with hinting a little. ("Is that the best that can be done, do you think?")

The best time to negotiate is early on, when your boss is worrying that you might not come back, not two weeks before you burst.

What if you decide during the leave that you prefer to be a stay-at-home mom for a while? That will make your boss pissed as hell because, in some cases, he will assume that you knew and didn't say anything because you needed the health insurance coverage and workman's comp. But it can be hard to know for sure what you want until you're in the thick of it.

If you find you can't bear to leave your baby, arrange to go in and talk to your boss as soon as you've made your decision, and don't beat around the bush. An executive editor once called me a week before she was coming back from her maternity leave and asked if I'd ever consider making the (hugely demanding) job part-time. Huh? I wished she'd raised the issue much earlier. So cut to the chase. Explain how much you appreciate everything your boss did, but you didn't know until it was time to return that it wasn't going to work for you.

And you know what? I'd send a gift with a nice note thanking your boss for being understanding. That way you've done your best not to burn any bridges.

{ My Kids Aren't Serial Killers—Yet }

'm not going to lie: If you decide to combine motherhood with a successful career, there will be times when you are more bone tired and stressed than you have ever been in your life and there may even be moments when you wonder if you should toss in the towel and just take care of your kids. Or scale back. Trust me, I've been there. But due to the fact that my husband worked in a precarious business—TV news—I decided I couldn't even consider an option such as becoming a freelance writer. I will be eternally grateful for the fact that I stayed on my career track, because it would have been tough to maneuver my way back on. Plus, now that my kids are young adults, I see how much they benefited from the fact that I worked.

We've gone through various stages as a culture in terms of how we view working mothers. In the 1970s and '80s, the media often glamorized the concept; magazines did cover stories with titles such as "Having It All." Then the media became fascinated with the supposed underbelly of the concept. Working mothers were pictured looking harried and wailing things such as "My baby likes our nanny more than me!"

Things have finally settled down a bit. So many mothers have no choice but to work these days and research has shown that children of working moms not only do okay they *thrive*. We're more realistic, however, about the challenges and sacrifices. Most new mothers who plan to continue working have enough advance info to know that life with both kids and a job can be nutty at times.

One of our favorite family stories involves my son and the dentist. When he was about twelve, he started going to his cleanings alone and I was always delighted to learn from him that he had no cavities. When he was about eighteen, we discovered that he had never actually gone for all those cleanings (my husband and I had been too busy to notice that the charge had always been for a no-show). I nearly blew a gasket. I told Hunter he *had* to go in for a cleaning—I think I might have also threatened to not pay for his college education—and quickly made an appointment for him. When he returned home that night and recounted the experience, he made my husband and me howl with laughter. He explained how a wide-eyed dental assistant had guided him into a child-size examining chair, placed a small bib around him, and then asked if he wanted blueberry- or strawberry-flavored mouthwash. Without thinking, I had booked him with the same pediatric dentist he'd used as a child.

Laughing that hard helped me forgive myself for not being totally on top of his dental care. You will make mistakes. You will feel guilty. But you will get over it. Here are some strategies, most of which I learned from other working moms.

On the Job

If you want the work-family equation to make sense, you need to love your job. According to former *Working Mother* editor in chief Judsen Culbreth, study after study shows that the working mothers who are happiest are the ones who feel passionate about what they do.

You must also work (1) for a boss who doesn't bust your chops about your need to balance and (2) in an overall work environment where the idea of bearing and taking care of offspring isn't viewed as weird or annoying. A professional friend of mine told me recently that when she was employed by a very forward-thinking nonprofit company (you would recognize the name!), some of the moms who worked there in high-powered jobs always left their coats on another floor so that when they departed for the day, it wouldn't be obvious. It can be draining to have to function that way or to work for a boss who doesn't respect your situation. My advice, if that's your situation, is to do what you can to find a more hospitable, mommy-friendly environment that lets you flourish professionally.

A week after I returned from my first maternity leave, my boss called me into her office and told me she didn't want me leaving at five every day. Her attitude really worried me—she hadn't even allowed me a week of adjustment—so I found a new job three months later. My new boss, a father of two, had no concern about when I left as long as my job was done right.

But sometimes even the most seemingly sympathetic bosses have only so much sympathy to spare. People you work for (or with) may secretly assume that you have less to give because you are doing the balancing act. You know that isn't true, but avoid behavior that might inadvertently reinforce that view. Keep kid talk, kid pictures, and kid videos to a minimum at work. And I'm a firm believer in using statements such as "I have a doctor's appointment" or "I need to leave at four thirty today," rather than "I have to run my daughter to the pediatrician." Be vague. Also, I forgive you here and now for any white lies you tell in the name of motherhood, okay?

Though you don't have less to give in terms of talent and effort, you probably will have less to give in terms of time. If you have a baby or young child, you are going to want to arrive home at a reasonable hour most evenings. The one thing I will tell you with ab-solute surety is that no one will ever announce to you in a meeting, "Oh, my gosh, it's five thirty. Don't you have to get out of here?" So you have to take a deep breath and dare to set your own schedule. Yes, be cognizant of your boss but also of your *own* needs. Remind yourself that some of the people who clock long hours are there not because they have work to do but simply because everyone else is. Try to figure out the plan that will suit you best, and don't feel bul-lied by offhanded comments or looks from coworkers.

How can you get your job done brilliantly and still manage to leave at a reasonable hour? Letena Lindsay, the head of L2 Pub-lic Relations, a mother of young twin boys, and one of the most fabulously pulled-together women I've ever worked with, says she learned her main survival strategy from a baby nurse who helped her for a few weeks after the boys were born. "My life was suddenly split into all these different facets," she says, "and I wondered how I could handle everything. The baby nurse told me, 'You have to work smart and not hard.' That just stayed with me from the moment I heard it."

So many working moms have told me that they became far more efficient when they had kids—and turned ruthless about their time. Take a look at what's on your plate, and figure out what can be elim-inated, delegated, or shortened time-wise. Lindsay says that in the

PR world, clients are often given regular reports that list every voice mail message left on their behalf. That was something she unloaded. "I tell a new client that I appreciate the fact that other agencies do these kind of reports, but I don't think it's a good use of my time. I'd rather spend time focusing on getting coverage."

And *do* work late sometimes. A colleague of mine told me that the best advice she acquired about going back to work after her child was born was not to become caught up in a rigid new schedule. "I worked a bit late one night a week," she said. "And not always the same night. So there was never this sense of 'Oh, she's always out the door by six.' "

Of course, if you work for a business where it's essential to put in maximum hours (i.e., a law firm), you have some deciding to do. Will you be okay with seeing your child a minimum amount of time on weekdays? Could you arrange to do your job part-time?

When you first return to work after maternity leave, your brain may feel a little fuzzy, but that will clear up soon enough. Try not to coast. Look fully engaged, even if you have to kind of fake it. Review the tips in "Beware of Sudden Promotion Syndrome."

When your kids are small, you also have to be realistic. Before you go after a new job or a promotion, consider what support systems you have. Ask yourself whether the timing is really right for you. When I became editor in chief of *Working Woman* magazine, I was seven months pregnant with my second child. During the interview with the company CEO, a little voice in my head had whispered that I might be taking on more than I should, especially considering that my husband worked nights as a TV newscaster. A month after I started, I came down with pneumonia and pleurisy, in part, I think, from exhaustion. In hindsight, I wish I hadn't taken that job. I was still young, and other opportunities would have emerged if I'd stayed put for a while.

In other words, don't bite off more than you can chew.

What about the notion of dropping out temporarily when your kids are small? Certainly many moms toy with this idea, if only briefly. It depends on your needs, your child's needs, how many kids you have, and the kind of business you're in. If you're considering it, but wish you didn't have to go there, ask yourself if there's an alternative to dropping out altogether? Part of the reason Letena Lindsay started her own agency was to create a job that would allow her more time with her kids than a corporate job would.

And here's an interesting insight I heard from Marisa Thalberg, the founder of ExecutiveMoms.com: "Sometimes women tell me that they don't think it's worth it for them to continue working because they barely break even once they pay the sitter and their commuting costs. But if you love your job and you're still even a little bit ahead financially, I believe it's worth it. Because when you try to return to the workforce years later, you may not regain the ground you lost."

On the Home Front

One of the smartest things I did as a working mom was to be a sponge around other moms and learn everything I could from them. With the exception of the names of Saturday-night babysitters, they will share all sorts of good info with you and also the strategies that have worked for them. Even consider doing a weekly or biweekly coffee session with other moms where you just swap ideas.

A great piece of advice I heard from a mother pal of mine involved how late to keep up my new baby. I hated the fact that I had so little time with him in the evenings. "Babies don't have to go to bed at seven or eight o'clock, you know," she said. "*You* choose the bedtime." So I did. Until my kids were in school, I kept them up to nine thirty most nights and they took the longest naps in recorded history.

It goes without saying that a good partner can play a vital role in how you pull it all off. Sometimes guys don't do as much as we need them to because we don't ask the right way (see "Men, Love, and Success") or we inadvertently box them out. When I was the editor of *Child*, I learned about a phenomenon women engage in called "gatekeeping." We're so overwhelmed with baby love and wanting everything done just right for our newborn that we don't let our partner in or we constantly critique the way he does things. Then, when we're finally ready to ask for his help, the damage has been done. Let him in. Then bite your lip if you don't like how he does things. I remember the first time I went out to run errands on a Saturday afternoon and left my husband with our baby, who was about six months old at the time. "Do *not*," I told my husband, "let him fall asleep—or he won't take his regular nap later." When I returned later, I found the baby sitting up in his high chair, wide-eyed and happy. But his face was crusted with hardened cereal. My husband explained that while Hunter was finishing his cereal, he'd started to nod off, so my husband had playfully let the hair dryer blow on him. I clamped my lips together as hard as I could.

One of the most hectic times you have to deal with as a working mom is when you first walk in the door or pick up your child from day care. Your child is clamoring for your attention or for you to just *be* with him. You want to give that attention, but you probably feel you'd be better able to if you could quickly brush your teeth, leaf through the mail, and throw something into the microwave. But kids don't get the concept. "At moments like this, I think it pays to be a 'just-in-time' mother," says former *Working Mother* editor in chief Judsen Culbreth. "Put your agenda temporarily aside. Be mindful and in the moment with your child. Those ten minutes on the swing set *now* can save you hours of whining repair later."

Two other things that help during busy workweeks: systems and rituals.

By systems I mean certain procedures or routines that solve problems. Years ago a friend of mine worked as a nanny for two Oxford dons who were rarely home in the evenings. The kids—a young boy and a girl—had a big lunch each day and then teatime treats, so for supper my friend was instructed to take a wide selection of leftovers from the fridge and put them on the table for the kids to pick from. That meant a lot of taking out and putting back, so my friend told the kids that from now on, three things would be "featured" for supper each night. One night the mother happened to dash through the kitchen and noticed the pared-down fare on the table. "My goodness!" she exclaimed. "I'm sure we have leftover ham. And deviled eggs, as well." "But, Mummy," the little boy told her, "they're not being featured tonight."

I love that story because it highlights how much kids not only adapt to systems but also find them reassuring (as long as they're not horribly rigid). Systems can be everything from "Stories are read after teeth are brushed" to "Mittens always go in the wicker box by the door."

Rituals are kind of like systems, but they're far more fun. Around the time I had my first child, I read a profile of a woman who had been one of the first female powerhouses on Wall Street. The reporter had interviewed her adult children, who said that despite their mother's demanding job, they'd been very happy growing up. They had always had dinner together as a family, and weekends had been sacred. That made me think about my own working parents and how much regular rituals had played a wonderful part in our life.

Kim Kardashian told me that when she was little, her family followed a nightly ritual called "peak and pit." At dinnertime, they'd go around the table with each person describing the peak moment of his or her day and then the one moment at which the person felt in the pits. I wish I'd known that one years ago. Rituals are an absolutely delicious part of family life.

Speaking of parents, there's one other thing my mom did that totally influenced me. She was the school librarian, and she sometimes had me come in and decorate the display windows of the library. I loved doing that so much. So from the time my kids were small, I tried to engage them in my work. For instance, I had them make lists of what celebrities should be on the cover of whatever magazine I was editing. I showed them cover shots and had them pick their favorite ones.

And here's the funny thing: not only did they like doing these tasks but their judgment was also really good, because as kids, they relied totally on their gut instincts!

One last point. Despite how helpful other mommies often are, you're bound to come across a few who aren't. Sometimes, for instance, they can be horribly braggy not only about their kids but also about the perfect life they have set up. Unsolicited comments that begin with the words "We always . . ." or "In our house . . ." should be ignored.

They can also be judgmental, particularly if you work and they don't. A terrific Hollywood agent I know told me that the parents' group at her child's private school recently gave out awards and the one she received was for "World's Fastest Drop-off." Pretty damn bitchy, right? But remember, you can't worry about being liked on this front either.

{ Discover Rotisserie Chicken and Other Ways to Keep Life Simple }

When I decided to introduce a food column in *Cosmo*, Katie Lee, the author of the terrific cookbook *The Comfort Table*, seemed to me to be the perfect person to do it, and she agreed. Instantly it became clear that she was a dream to work with, and I loved the recipes she created. They were always delicious but also incredibly easy.

As I got to know Katie, I would sometimes ask her advice about food to serve my family. I know that fast food—pizzas, Subway sandwiches, Chinese food, whatever—can be a real lifesaver for a working mom, but I was never a huge fan of takeout. Sitting down to a good meal was one of the few rituals I could squeeze into my life, and I thought, as long as I'm doing it, I want to do it well. The only problem: I sometimes made myself a little nuts pulling it all together.

One of the best tips Katie Lee gave me was to make rotisserie chicken a part of my repertoire. Have you ever had one of those things? They're the chickens you see roasting on spits in furnace-size ovens behind the deli counter of most supermarkets. (Try to get beyond the fact that the chickens appear to be in a medieval torture chamber or the ninth circle of Hell.) Once I tried one, I realized that they were flavorful and moist and all you have to do is add a green salad and a baguette to make a simple but hearty weeknight meal. If you want fancier fare, you can roast carrots, potatoes, and onions in a pan in the oven with a little olive oil, salt, and pepper and scatter the roasted veggies around the chicken on a platter.

I started having rotisserie chicken regularly. It made dinner *soooo* easy. The chickens also forced me to think about the whole notion of simplicity and how I probably needed more of it in my cooking and home life. I realized that in my quest to serve good food and make entertaining friends and family a priority, I probably guaranteed that things were more complicated than they had to be. When I had friends for dinner, I'd always find myself adding another dish late in the game or coming up with something *extra* to do.

One night in particular jumps out in my memory. I was having friends over for an August barbecue, and I'd planned to serve grilled chicken with corn on the cob and a plate of tomatoes from the farmers' market. But that afternoon I started thinking I needed more. I'd seen a recipe in the *New York Times* for a salad made of tomatoes and peaches, so I decided to go for it. I spent at least a half hour peeling peaches, and when I served them with the tomatoes it was a big soupy mess. The tomatoes alone, with some great olive oil and basil leaves scattered on top, would have been so much better.

Around the time Katie introduced me to the pluses of rotisserie chicken, I took a trip to Greece with my family. One of my favorite experiences on the trip was eating in the wonderful tavernas that were everywhere. We'd sit outside at a wooden table under trees that created patterns of dappled light. The food was simple but wonderful: grilled meat or fish, good bread, and of course Greek salad made with cucumbers, tomatoes, onions, and feta cheese. No complicated sauces or layers.

On the flight back I decided I needed to bring taverna style into my cooking. Rotisserie chicken was one way, but there were others if I kept reminding myself to simplify, to get rid of the peaches layer. The more I thought about it, the more I realized that the taverna approach could be applied to life in general. Say no to "complicated sauces" and extra steps. Ask yourself, "Do I really need it?" "Will anyone notice if I don't do it?"

I really liked this line from one of the blogs of Executive Moms founder Marisa Thalberg (she's also a beauty industry executive): "Relished stolen coffees and many fabulous dinners with fabulous friends. . . . Cooked at almost none of them."

Maybe she and her friends just picked up a few rotisserie chickens!

{ Take Your Own Sweet Time }

When you're in a demanding career, one of the things you are often in search of is time for yourself. You crave the opportunity to disconnect and relax, and if that time includes a spa treatment involving hot stones and scented oil, all the better. This is especially true when you have young kids. Your hours after work and on weekends are pretty much devoted to them, which means there's rarely even a spare moment just for you.

When my kids were young, I felt frayed around the edges from having so little time to myself. I used to fantasize about having a day to do my own thing or even going away for a whole weekend with my husband—but I knew it was impossible. My sitter didn't work weekends, and there were no relatives close by to stay with the kids. Plus because I worked, I believed that weekends needed to remain sacred days just for my kids.

It was only later that I came to see that though big blocks of time to yourself are incredibly satisfying, you don't need that to feel rejuvenated. Small pockets of time here and there can do wonders if you use them correctly. A writer friend of mine pointed this out to me, and as I began to experiment, I saw how right she was. I'd put too much stock into the concept of a whole day or weekend for myself and had failed to see the value in an hour alone.

I talked about this recently over lunch with Maryam Banikarim, the senior vice president and chief marketing officer of Gannett (the media company that publishes *USA Today*), and she said that she not only agreed with the concept but also had a name for it: sweet time. "The reality," she said, "is that you can't just wait for large chunks of time to come your way. Life is busy—really busy—and we're perpetually having to multitask."

So think small. Look for the hour—or even thirty minutes—you can make pleasurable and all yours.

"We talk ourselves out of our restorative moments because we think it has to be a full, weeklong getaway," says Letena Lindsay, the head of L2 Public Relations and one of my favorite former colleagues. "But it could be years before that happens."

Sweet time possibilities: your morning shower (use it to enjoy a fragrant body wash rather than fretting about the day ahead), lunchtime (take a walk rather than eating at your desk), the drive home from work (listen to an audiobook), the moment your kids go down for a nap on the weekends (read a book and *then* focus on chores). Banikarim finds airplanes to be one of those rare places where she can still have uninterrupted alone time. "I love to use the trip to read or to watch a movie," she says.

One catch: you need to carve out sweet time for yourself because no one will carve it out on your behalf. Lindsay, the mother of twins, goes for a thirty-minute manicure and hand massage every week. And every Wednesday morning she has her "*Sex and the City* coffee hour" with a friend—after they drop their kids off at school.

That's not to say you don't deserve a weekend away with your partner or a girlfriend or even alone. But if you schedule plenty of sweet time into your life, you won't feel in desperate need of it.

{ Make Your Back-Pocket

Dream a Reality (While You've

Still Got a Day Job) }

Despite your professional success, is there something you've secretly yearned to do but haven't tried yet? Perhaps it's a dream you've never breathed a word about to anyone. I can relate, because for years I had a crazy back-pocket dream myself. As a young girl I liked reading books, but when I stumbled on a copy of *Nancy Drew and the Secret of Red Gate Farm*—with its spooky cover and eerily provocative title—I suddenly became a ravenous reader rather than simply an avid one. I devoured that mystery and then proceeded to read dozens of others in the series. My passion for the "Titian-haired" sleuth made me long to become a private detective (I used to walk around my hometown in a little trench coat with a rubber pistol in my pocket). Later, as I came to realize what a terrible wimp I was, I vowed instead to one day satisfy my fascination with corpses and perplexing puzzles by *writing* murder mysteries rather than actually solving them.

That desire got tucked away for years as I pursued another

aspiration—to be a magazine editor—which also happened to offer more financial security. But as I mentioned earlier, I pulled that old dream out of the back pocket one Saturday morning when my kids were sleeping in. With the encouragement of my awesome agent Sandy Dijkstra (who'd represented me for nonfiction books), I wrote several chapters and sketched out an outline for *If Looks Could Kill*. It was the story of an irreverent true-crime journalist named Bailey Weggins who discovers the dead body of her boss's beautiful young nanny. She'd been poisoned—and there were plenty of suspects. I *loved* working on it.

I was also motivated, I must admit, by a desire to create a professional Plan B. I knew of so many magazine editors in chief who had been unceremoniously dumped by their companies when they were in their fifties, and I decided that if that happened to me one day, I wanted to have a backup way to earn money. I gave myself eighteen months to complete the book.

But then *Cosmo* Sunday happened. That's when I was called out of the blue on a Sunday morning, asked to come in to work, and handed the job of a lifetime. As I accepted the position, trying to conceal my angst about it, one of the thoughts racing through my head was "Well, now I'm never going to be able to write my mystery." I felt heartsick about letting that old dream go.

Five months passed, and the Christmas holidays rolled around. Since I had a few days off, I decided one afternoon to read over the pages I'd tucked away back in August. One of the lines caught me totally by surprise. I'd written that Bailey had found the dead nanny lying on a copy of *Cosmopolitan*. I had no memory of adding that detail—but I instantly took it as a sign from the gods. Maybe I was *meant* to finish the mystery while editing *Cosmo*. So I did it. Since then I've written five more Bailey Weggins mysteries and two standalone thrillers, *Hush* and *The Sixes*.

Whenever I'm invited to give a speech to a woman's group, there's generally a Q-and-A session built in at the end. Almost without fail the first question anyone asks is "How do you manage to do both?" What the questioner means is "How can you manage having a demanding full-time job and still write books?" Some women, I think, are simply interested in hearing a few time-management tricks that they can apply in various areas of their lives. But many, I suspect, have a back-pocket dream of their own and really want to have it see the light of day.

If you've got a dream like that, pull it out and take a fresh look at it. Does it still excite you? Could you leverage it financially? Your girlhood dream may have been put aside—or, worse, trampled upon—but that doesn't mean it's not valid.

There may be a certain time in your life when it's better to tackle that dream than others. I never wanted my mystery writing to infringe on my kids, so the best period to start was when they were sleeping later on weekend mornings. I dragged myself out of bed at six and wrote for a few hours before they came padding downstairs, hunting for French toast. You don't have to do everything at once. Think of yourself as a *serial achiever*, someone who will probably live a long life and can take on different goals when the timing is right.

But one day you're going to have to take a breath and *plunge in*. Begin with a very simple task, such as writing the first sentence (I did that) or prepping the canvas. See how it makes you feel.

It will help if right from the start you realize that some stuff in your life is going to have to go and then decide what that stuff will be. I used a lot of time-management tricks to help me build writing into my day (see "Terrific Time-Management Tricks"), but I still had to jettison certain routines and activities. I gave up my plan to become a decent tennis player. I never again spent a Saturday afternoon prowling around Saks or Bloomingdale's in search of booty. Instead I started shopping online at night and began to use a personal shopper for major fashion purchases (they're available free at major department stores). And when Facebook took off, I decided I would have to postpone using it, except for my author page, to another time in my life. Last, I read far fewer books than I would have liked. But the pleasure I've experienced from being an author has outweighed the losses.

You might also have to shape-shift your dream a little to make it more doable. I did. I'd always wanted the lead character in my mysteries to be a private eye, but that would have meant a ton of research, and because of my full-time job, I didn't have time for research. So I made my character a magazine writer. It meant I would still have to research all the forensic and crime-scene material for each mystery—which I enjoy—but I didn't have to spend ages learning what it was like to be a private eye. I could even paste snippets from my job right into the book.

It also helped for me to integrate my mystery writing with my family. I introduced my kids to many of my favorite mystery movies, including the four fantastic Miss Marple films of the 1960s with Dame Margaret Rutherford. I once even had my daughter, Hayley, follow me through the woods so that I could hear the sound of someone tracking me. Needless to say, today they both have a love for the macabre.

So as I said, plunge in. You will be tired at times, even cranky, and at some moments you will wonder if you are nuts for doing it. But I bet you won't regret it.

{ Reinvention: A Brief Course }

You may have read, as I have, that the average person will have at least five careers during his or her lifetime. But guess what? That statistic turns out to be completely untrue. Or rather, it *could be* true, but nobody knows for sure. There is actually no data on the subject of how many careers the average person will have in a lifetime. Someone just threw out that number at one point, and it stuck.

Yet, despite the lack of research, I'd say there's a more-than-decent chance that many of us will end up changing careers at *least* once. Even if you love your work and your field, there may come a time when you're no longer being challenged or excited and you start to grow restless, eager for something new. And you don't have to be plugging away for twenty-five years to feel that way. The Atlanta-based psychiatrist Dr. Ish Major says that he's had plenty of thirty-something patients who find themselves at a crossroads. "Maybe you blazed through ten or fifteen years of your career, and then you find yourself asking, 'Is this *it*? There's got to be more.' "

And of course sometimes the need for reinvention isn't a choice: it's thrust on you because your field runs out of steam or suffers a setback.

So let's start with the idea of you in charge of the situation. You used to love what you are doing, but now you're feeling bored or discontented by the area you're in, and you're ready for a switch. Yet you're not sure what your shiny new career should be. It would be nice if you had a eureka moment—and those do sometimes occur. But since you may not have time to wait for it, why not hurry it along?

That's sort of what my friend Amy Archer did. Amy and I were writers together at *Glamour* magazine when we were both in our twenties. In her late twenties, Amy took off to see the world for a while and then ended up teaching, at Brown University and at several prestigious prep schools. One day, sitting at her desk at a school in Portland, Oregon, she had a startling epiphany.

"It was three days before the first faculty meeting," she says. "I was thinking about school projects, and I realized—I can't do this. I was almost shaking. I knew then that what I wanted to do was become a photographer. I went to the head of the school and told him I had to leave."

Archer had actually been nudging herself toward that moment for a while. She loved photography and always had her camera out. The summer before the new school year began, she'd taken a pretty serious photography course in Aspen. So the idea of finally doing it full-time had begun to crystallize long before that shaky moment at her desk. Her reinvention, like many, was really an evolution. If you see a thread of something beginning to run through your thoughts, follow it. Take a class, explore on the Internet, have lunch with someone who's already doing it.

Shock Reinvention

What if a need for reinvention isn't a choice but something that's been thrust on you—because, for instance, you're downsized out of your job and you realize that opportunities in your field are drying up. You come to sense that it's time for a whole new ball game.

The first step, says Dr. Major, is to begin to let go of your former self. "You have to deal with the finality of who you used to be. It can be like grief. What I hear a lot is 'I don't know who I am without that.' But what I tell patients is that whatever it was, it wasn't the biggest part of them. They need to get in touch with their essential self." How do you do that? Dr. Major suggests asking five friends and five family members to describe you in one word. "In most cases," he says, "seven out of ten people come out with the same word. And that word will say far more about you—your essential self rather than your social self."

It may not be necessary to totally shift gears. The executive coach Terri Wein suggests meeting with people who "value your skill set" and who can brainstorm with you about how to take it in another direction. A friend of mine who was let go after running a big special-events department found great happiness as a freelance consultant who specializes in generating concepts for events.

What if it *is* time for something brand new? How do you begin to figure out what that is? The "threads" probably are there, but you're going to have to tease them out. Note the everyday moments when you are "in the zone"—when you have total focus and single-mindedness of purpose. Maybe it's when you're doing something with your hands. Also, think about what captivated you as a girl, what captured your fancy then. "If you have to reach outside of you, you've gone too far," says Dr. Major.

Another good strategy is the "taking the bus to Cairo" approach I talked about in "What Are You *Really* Lusting For?" in part I. You're looking on the outside but letting it connect with your internal longings and needs.

Your First Foray

Now to begin. Archer's advice: "Find something easy and minuscule to get you over the hump of 'Where do I start?' " Instead of going out and just shooting pictures, Archer dug out old notebooks of hers in which she'd made notes about photography and also found the negatives of pictures she'd taken years before, including a series of candid shots of the singer Tom Waits. Her first step was to make prints of those photos. She was working with something familiar, and that made plunging in easier.

She also found it helpful to place herself in an environment where people were doing what she now wanted to do. "There was a wonderful darkroom in Portland run by a group of women, and I went there to develop my photos," she says. Before long her work began appearing in café shows and then in one of Portland's best art galleries. Recently she shot all the photographs for interior designer Bunny Williams's enchanting book, *Scrapbook for Living*.

Reinvention almost always involves a learning curve, and once you jump in, you'll have to be teaching yourself at the same time. "For me, that was one of the hardest parts of reinvention," says Andrea Kaplan, who started her own PR firm several years ago. "I'd been in corporate jobs in the past and always had assistants. When

I went out on my own, I had to suck it up and go to class to learn Excel. Then I took classes and read books on social media. But now I'm really enjoying the new rhythm of life that comes from not being connected to the same place every day."

Does that sound good? Then go for it!

{ About the Author }

Kate White has been the editor in chief of five magazines, including *Cosmopolitan*, and is the *New York Times* best-selling author of two thrillers, *Hush* and *The Sixes*, and the Bailey Weggins mystery series. White is also the author of popular career books for women, including the bestselling *Why Good Girls Don't Get Ahead . . . but Gutsy Girls Do.*